OF KNOWLEDGE A

OF KNOWLEDGE AND POWER

The Complexities of National Intelligence

ROBERT KENNEDY

PRAEGER SECURITY INTERNATIONAL
Westport, Connecticut • London

Library of Congress Cataloging-in-Publication Data

Kennedy, Robert, 1939–
Of knowledge and power : the complexities of national intelligence / Robert Kennedy.
p. cm.
Includes bibliographical references and index.
ISBN: 978–0–275–99443–3 (alk. paper)
1. Intelligence service—United States. 2. National security—United States. 3. Geopolitics.
I. Title.
JK468.I6K38 2008
327.1273—dc22 2008020107

British Library Cataloguing in Publication Data is available.

Library of Congress Catalog Card Number: 2008020107
ISBN: 978–0–275–99443–3
ISBN: 978–1–4408–3628–2 (pbk.)

First published in 2008

Praeger Security International, 88 Post Road West, Westport, CT 06881
An imprint of Greenwood Publishing Group, Inc.
www.praeger.com

Printed in the United States of America

The paper used in this book complies with the Permanent Paper Standard issued by the National Information Standards Organization (Z39.48–1984).

10 9 8 7 6 5 4 3 2 1

This book is dedicated to the men and women who have faithfully served U.S. intelligence efforts, especially to those who have paid the ultimate price

Contents

Preface

"All thought is art . . . and where judgment starts is the point where art begins."
—Carl von Clausewitz

As the endgame played out it became clear that America and the West had carried the day. By 1991 the world was looking purposefully, if precariously, beyond the Cold War. The conflict, which had extended beyond the Soviet Union, had spanned almost half a century, consumed massive resources, and eventually ended in the demise of the Soviet Union. The "bipolar" world faded away. The great danger of global nuclear conflict seemingly vanished. Visions of a new world order were entertained. Optimists saw the distant possibility of a perpetual peace. Change and momentum were at hand.

America's relief, cautious though it was, would prove premature. The decline of Soviet communism was followed by a disquieting sense of uncertainty. The days of contending superpowers, and the sardonic comfort of an obvious security threat had passed, as had the planning crutch of Mutually Assured Destruction. However, Iraq's invasion of Kuwait and conflicts in such places as Bosnia, Somalia, Rwanda, and Kosovo served notice that the world had yet to reach the "End of History.[1] "What would come next? How should the United States respond to such challenges? What role should the nation play in world affairs? From what corner might new threats arise? How should the United States structure its diplomacy, its security policies, its intelligence efforts, and its military forces to meet the new challenges and threats?

Yet with it all there was an air of complacency. While such post-Cold War conflicts as Bosnia and Kosovo threatened America's broader security interests, they did not directly threaten America. And it would be years before a peer competitor could rise to challenge the United States.

September 11, 2001 jolted the United States from its post-Cold War complacency. The twin failures of the Intelligence Community[2] to anticipate those attacks and to accurately assess Saddam Hussein's nuclear, chemical, and biological weapons programs prior to going to war with Iraq in March 2003 served notice that America's intelligence efforts needed to be restructured to meet the challenges of the twenty-first century. These events, each in their own way, brought the intrinsic issues of security and survival back to the forefront of the American conscience. The tragedy of 9/11 demonstrated that the United States is intimately part of global society, equally subject to its grandest evolutions and its most acute vulnerabilities. And both 9/11 and events leading up to the war with Iraq once again emphasized the undeniable importance of intelligence to America's future security.

During the Cold War America confronted an adversary that could inflict unimaginable destruction on the United States in a matter of minutes. However, that adversary was geographically defined, with a leadership that was relatively conservative, rational, methodical, and reasonably predictable. To obtain critical security information, spies and satellites could zero in on the Soviet Union and its client states. To be sure, there were other threats to U.S. security, but all paled in comparison and many were assumed to be aided and abetted by the USSR. With the end of the Cold War and the continued proliferation of advanced technologies, threats to America's security not only have become more diffuse, but also have become increasingly dangerous. Today's adversaries could be state or non-state entities. Their operations could be directed from within a single state or from many locations around the globe. They may well be led by individuals who are far less predictable and less rational than those who controlled the Kremlin during the nearly forty-five-year-long Cold War. As James Woolsey, former Director of Central Intelligence and Central Intelligence Agency (CIA) director put it, today "it is as if we were struggling with a large dragon for 45 years, killed it, and then found ourselves in a jungle full of poisonous snakes—and the snakes are much harder to keep track of than the dragon ever was."[3] As a result, the demands on intelligence have multiplied significantly.

Of course, neither 9/11 nor the 2003 Iraq War marked the first occasion that intelligence has failed to provide *accurate* information in a *timely* manner. Moreover, intelligence failures have come in a variety of flavors—failures of collection, failures of analysis, failures in timely dissemination, and/or failures in the use of intelligence. In the twentieth century no other incident stands out more than the failure to anticipate Pearl Harbor. But other recent strategic and tactical misadventures, such as the failure to grasp the magnitude of Iraqi efforts to develop chemical, nuclear, and biological weapons prior to the Gulf War of 1991, or the failure to predict such events as the imminent collapse of the Soviet Union, the 1993 attack on the New York World Trade Center, India's nuclear tests, the 1996 attack on a U.S. Air Force barracks in Saudi Arabia, the 1998 attacks on U.S. embassies in

Africa, or the 2000 attack on the *USS Cole* in Yemen, also have added to America's anxieties over the effectiveness of its intelligence system. Nor are intelligence failures peculiar to the United States. Among the more egregious intelligence failures of the mid to late twentieth century were Russia's failure to anticipate the German attack of 1941, despite mounting evidence of a German surprise attack in violation of the Molotov-Ribbentrop nonaggression agreement of 1939.[4] The failure of Israel to anticipate the Arab attack on Yom Kippur in 1973. On the eve of the war Israeli intelligence reported that the possibility of war was "lowest of the low."[5] And the refusal of British intelligence, again despite mounting evidence, to believe that Argentina intended to attack the Falkland/Malvinas Islands in 1982, concluding just four days before the Argentine invasion that an invasion was not imminent.[6]

Past failures, however, should not obscure the U.S. Intelligence Community's many successes. One needs only to consider the vast amount of information garnered from the data gathered by U-2 and SR-71 spy planes, or by satellites collecting photographic data and communication intercepts during the Cold War,[7] to realize that landmark events like the Cuban Missile Crisis might not have been resolved successfully without a last-minute intelligence breakthrough. More recent examples abound as well.[8] Indeed, the Intelligence Community has frequently identified developing threats and, through information obtained, strengthened America's hand in foreign policy and bolstered efforts to preserve and improve America's security. Nevertheless, we should not lose sight of the fact that the intelligence business is a thorny and complex undertaking.

There are, of course, many kinds of intelligence—political, economic, military, social, environmental, health, cultural, etc. There also is intelligence that focuses on internal security issues such as sabotage, espionage, and terrorism. All information gathered provides inputs to analysts and helps shape the options available to policymakers.[9]

Although both the means and ends of intelligence have frequently been criticized,[10] there is nothing inherently sinister about seeking information about the attitudes, beliefs, objectives, capabilities, and intentions of real or potential adversaries. Even allies or friends occasionally are targets of intelligence collection.[11] Put simply, accurate and timely intelligence reduces uncertainties and thus is the critical first line of defense against anyone or anything that could threaten the United States and its allies.[12] It also is the single most important basis for effective diplomacy, successful use of a nation's military power, and the efficacious use of other foreign policy tools. Intelligence is, as Abram Shulsky and Gary Schmitt have put it: ". . . *information* relevant to a government's formulation and implementation of policy to further its national security interests and to deal with threats from actual or potential adversaries."[13] Its "purpose is to gain 'decisional advantages' for political leaders, diplomats, military commanders, and other U.S. government officials in order to secure the country's interests in both peace and war."[14] In a global environment where actors' interests often clash, intelligence represents the crucial education system for our leadership regarding that environment. The information comes from many sources and through a variety of means. It may be gathered covertly through the use of spies. It may be obtained through electronic means, or it may be collected through open sources such as the press, statements by governments, or assessments by academics. However, one thing is certain, knowledge of adversaries, potential opponents, and even friendly states is critical to the power a state can wield in the international system.

On the other hand, intelligence is anything but a perfect science. Of course, science plays a major role in assisting in collecting and processing information. Nevertheless, in many respects intelligence resembles a form of art. Frequently the information gathered is like the nineteenth-century paintings of French neoimpressionist Georges Seurat. It is the eye of the beholder that must bring definition to the dots. Sometimes the available information could better be likened to an abstract painting that is subject to multiple interpretations. More often than not, however, the intelligence collected is incomplete—vast areas of the canvas are blank, have been painted over multiple times, or are cluttered with a confusing array of strokes and colors. Thus the collection of information invariably gives way to its analysis—the application of a skilled eye and well-honed judgment to connect the dots, to unravel the mystery, to bring order and clarity to the frequently obscure and thus provide information that is accurate and useful to policymakers. Here too, science plays an important role. Analysts are called upon to employ scientific methods in evaluating collected information: Predispositions must be exposed, personal assumptions and conventional wisdoms challenged, hypotheses formulated and tested, plausible alternative explanations explored, and conclusions crafted that reflect both the certainties and uncertainties revealed as a result of the analytical process. Nonetheless, more often than not, before a clear picture emerges, it is judgment that must differentiate information from disinformation, hard data from background noise, the relevant from the extraneous. And, of course, the cycle is not complete until the analytical conclusions are communicated to decision makers in such a way that the same picture that emerged for the analyst can be seen and accepted by those who can use it to influence or execute policy. All this requires careful thought and seasoned judgment. Indeed in a very real sense the "Art of Intelligence" begins not with analysis, but with judgments that lead to the selection of the information to be sought, permeates every phase of the intelligence processes, and ends with judgments by key officials on how to use the information received.

It should be noted however, that the Intelligence Community not only is engaged in collecting, analyzing, and disseminating information to the executive and legislative branches of government, and on occasion to foreign governments, but also in counterintelligence activities and covert actions. Indeed, the four principal elements of intelligence are generally understood to be collection, analysis, counterintelligence, and covert action.

Counterintelligence efforts are actions taken to detect and counteract foreign intelligence activity that may adversely affect U.S. foreign policy and national security interests.[15] Covert Action, on the other hand, is not so easily circumscribed.

If the CIA provides financial support to a political party or political movement,[16] this is called "covert action"; if the Agency develops a paid "asset" in the party for the purpose of information gathering, the project is "clandestine intelligence collection."[17] President George W. Bush's commission on weapons of mass destruction defined "covert action" as activity undertaken by the U.S. government that is designed to influence foreign governments, events, organizations, or persons in support of U.S. policy and security interests in a manner that is not attributable to the United States.[18]

This book is about the complexity of the intelligence effort. It is about the multiplicity of internal and external obstacles that confront the Intelligence Community as it undertakes the Herculean tasks of collecting and analyzing data and then disseminating useful information vital to the nation's welfare in a timely manner. As such it includes an examination of the complexities associated with the acquisition of information through open sources as well as clandestine efforts, including intelligence acquired indirectly from the monitoring of spies from foreign entities or directly through their conversion to double agents. It also addresses the complexities of obtaining information through covert operations, such as information obtained from individuals or groups covertly taken captive. It does not, however, examine counterintelligence or covert operations per se, nor does it address the legal issues associated with "extraordinary rendition."[19] The book ends with an examination of the oversight processes, upon which, in large measure, America's security and the protection of the rights of American citizens depends.

Finally, a brief note is warranted about the definition of "intelligence." Some intelligence purists may balk at the frequent synonymous use of the terms "information" and "intelligence"—arguing that only information that has been fully processed and analyzed can rightfully be called intelligence. This debate over definition is not new. Nearly every book on intelligence begins with a discussion of the meaning of the word "intelligence." Commenting on President Truman's preference for a few short paragraphs on large issues to be provided in a "Daily Summary," Secretary of State James Byrnes pointed out that since the summary was purely factual, it wasn't really intelligence.[20] However, Truman decided, according to his Director of Central Intelligence Sidney Souers, that "it was information which he needed and therefore it was intelligence to him."[21] Thus the author's point of departure on the issue of definition is that whether it is simply information or intelligence is in the eye of the beholder. If it is simply factual information but provides the user with useful knowledge in his or her decisional processes, it may well constitute intelligence as far as that individual is concerned.

Robert Kennedy
Atlanta, Georgia

Acknowledgments

I would like to thank Robert Cooper, Richard Houska, George Lotz, and John Weinstein, as well as those who have preferred to remain anonymous, for the many hours they have spent reading drafts and for their valuable insights and thoughtful comments. Thanks also goes to Christopher Chatham for his research assistance early in the project. Finally, I would like to thank my wife Vevonna for her quiet and sometimes not so quiet encouragement, her patience, and for the many hours she has spent reading various drafts. Her editorial and substantive recommendations have been invaluable.

Introduction

> "What enables the wise sovereign to . . . achieve things beyond the reach of ordinary men is foreknowledge."
>
> —Sun Tzu

The National Security Act of 1947 set forth the basic design of America's post-World War II intelligence organization. It established, inter alia, the National Security Council (NSC)—to advise the President on the integration of domestic, foreign, and military policies relating to national security, and the Office of the Director of Central Intelligence (DCI)—to provide the President, heads of departments and agencies of the executive branch, the Chairman of the Joint Chiefs of Staff, and senior military commanders, and the Senate and House of Representatives and their committees with timely, objective, independent of political considerations, all-source intelligence. The Act also established the Central Intelligence Agency. The CIA, a union of the World War II era Office of Strategic Services and other postwar intelligence bodies, was to be completely independent of any policy department or agency, serving as the primary civilian intelligence agency in the government.[1] With just a few key adjustments,[2] this same postwar blueprint for national security has remained intact for nearly six decades.

Following the attacks of September 11, 2001, the Final Report of the National Commission on the Terrorist Attacks Upon the United States (The 9/11 Commission Report) criticized the U.S. Intelligence Community for poor organization and fragmented structure and questioned whether the U.S. government and the Intelligence Community, in particular, were organized adequately to direct resources and build the intelligence capabilities that the United States will need to counter terrorism, and to address the broader range of national security challenges in the decades ahead. As a partial remedy to the state of affairs identified by the 9/11 Commission, Congress passed the Intelligence Reform and Terrorism Prevention Act of 2004 (Public Law108–458), which eliminated the position of Director of Central Intelligence and replaced it with a Director of National Intelligence, who has the principal responsibility previously accorded the Director of Central Intelligence of providing intelligence to the President and other senior officials. To the Director of National Intelligence also falls the responsibility of managing the U.S. Intelligence Community, albeit perhaps with stronger authorities than those held by the former Director of Central Intelligence. Unlike the Director of Central Intelligence, however, the Director of National Intelligence does not oversee the CIA. Rather, the Act established a new position of Director of the Central Intelligence Agency, who reports to the Director of National Intelligence.[3]

Of course, in the final analysis it falls to the Intelligence Community to provide accurate and timely intelligence about the world around us if our civilian and military leaders are to make informed decisions. In the United States the Intelligence Community is a confederation[4] of sometimes competing, sometimes cooperating, sometimes conflicting executive branch agencies and organizations that work both separately—sometimes at cross-purposes and, at times, together to conduct intelligence activities. The very size, plus the fragmented and decentralized nature of the Intelligence Community, with mandates and jurisdictions that at times are overlapping and at times exclusive, contributes significantly to the overall complexities of ensuring efficient, effective, and timely intelligence.

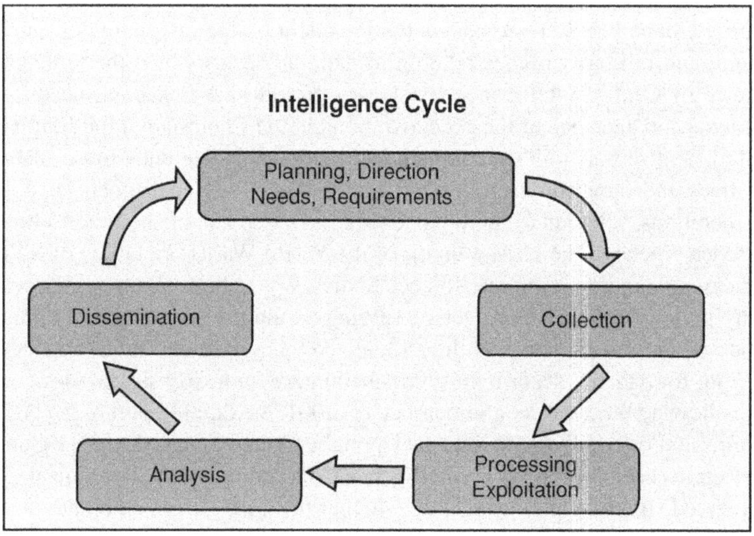

Figure 1. The Intelligence Cycle.[6] (See Appendix A for a brief description of each of these steps in the process.)

The process of planning and direction, collection, processing, all-source analysis[5] and production, and dissemination of intelligence is called the "intelligence cycle" (Figure 1). Collecting, processing, analyzing, and disseminating open-source and classified information gathered through human and technical resources are key responsibilities of the Intelligence Community.

In theory the cycle depends on guidance from public officials. It thus typically begins with the identification of needs by the consumers of intelligence—the President, his aides, the National Security Council, policymakers from agencies of government, military officials, and other senior decision makers who require intelligence to carry out their responsibilities. These requirements, once sorted and prioritized, set the agenda for Intelligence Community collection efforts. Collected intelligence is then processed, initially evaluated and, if warranted based on the initial evaluations, reported to both consumers and the so-called all-source intelligence analysts at the CIA, Defense Intelligence Agency, and the State Department's Bureau of Intelligence and Research. All-source analysts from one or more agencies, as is appropriate to the tasking, then perform a more thorough evaluation and assessment of the collected information by integrating the data obtained from a variety of collection agencies and sources—both classified and unclassified. This assessment takes form as a finished intelligence report and is circulated to the consumers, who provide "feedback" to the Intelligence Community in terms of the degree to which the finished intelligence meets their needs and whether further collection and analysis are required. The cycle is thus repeated until the intelligence requirements have been satisfied.[7]

This book, fashioned in four parts, examines the labyrinth of complexities that confront the Intelligence Community in its efforts to provide accurate and timely intelligence in support of American national security interests. Part I addresses the various factors that affect a nation's ability to plan for intelligence collection, collect the intelligence, and process the information. Part II examines the obstacles confronted by those tasked to analyze gathered information and produce finished intelligence, including their assessments and judgments about the implications of the information for the United States. Part III focuses on issues associated with the distribution and use of intelligence products. Part IV addresses the "quality control" of collection and analysis efforts. Altogether, the four parts provide the reader with a broad understanding of the Intelligence Community and the difficulties it faces as it strives to support U.S. national security objectives through the provision of timely, accurate, and useful information.

Part I

Collection

A nation cannot use intelligence it does not have. The first and arguably the most important task of the Intelligence Community is gathering meaningful information requisite for effective national decision making. The United States collects information by a variety of means such as reconnaissance satellites, aircraft, ships, ground stations, radar, and undersea surveillance, as well as through open and clandestine human sources.[1] In evaluating the performance of the Intelligence Community's efforts to ascertain the nature of Iraqi efforts to develop weapons of mass destruction, the President's Commission on Weapons of Mass Destruction noted that America's efforts were "crippled by its inability to collect meaningful intelligence on Iraq's nuclear, biological, and chemical weapons programs."[2]

Part I examines the planning, collecting, and processing of information and the obstacles to obtaining accurate and meaningful information. Chapter 1 outlines how the Intelligence Community is organized to collect information. It also addresses complexities associated with the first major steps in the intelligence cycle-identifying, prioritizing, communicating, and translating into programs for collection information/intelligence relevant to the foreign policy and security interests of the nation. Chapter 2 addresses the personnel, technological, and budgetary obstacles the Intelligence Community confronts. The intelligence budget, of course, affects all aspects of intelligence. Nonetheless, the issue is addressed here not only because collection and processing efforts represent a substantial portion of the intelligence budget, but also to alert the reader to an issue that has a significant impact on the overall effectiveness of America's intelligence efforts.

1

Planning, Collecting, and Processing

> "Man's flight through life is sustained by the power of his knowledge."
>
> —Austin "Dusty" Miller[1]

ORGANIZATION

Thomas Hobbes' *Leviathan* (1651) conjures up a peculiar yet appropriate image of the state. The head of the giant, symbolizing the government, directs the body in its activity, coordinating the work of disparate parts in order to realize shared goals. To draw crudely from the metaphor, the head, so as to succeed, must be able to well perceive from its surroundings prickly thickets in order to travel safer paths. All the senses play a seminal role in the welfare of the leviathan and without them the lumbering giant would stand blind, deaf, and dumb. Within the context of the state, the Intelligence Community represents these sensory organs; absent their effective functioning, the government would frequently stumble into the unknown. The knowledge it provides yields order and thus strength to the movements of the leviathan.

In the United States the Intelligence Community is the "eyes" and "ears" of the leviathan. It consists of sixteen federal agencies, offices, and elements of organizations within the executive branch that are responsible for collecting, analyzing, and disseminating intelligence. These include one independent agency—the Central Intelligence Agency—and fifteen departmental components—eight in the Department of Defense (DOD), two each in the departments of Homeland Security and Justice, one each in the departments of State, Energy, and Treasury. Each component has a separately identified mission with some unique and some overlapping technical capabilities. In addition to these sixteen entities, there are two important centers operating under the jurisdiction of the Director of National Intelligence: the National Counterterrorism Center and the National Counter Proliferation Center. The members of the Intelligence Community and their missions are listed in appendix B.

The U.S. Intelligence Community gathers information from five primary sources—individuals, communications and other electronically transmitted information not generally open to the public, imagery, technical analysis of events, and a variety of sources open to the public such as print or electronic media.

Human Intelligence (HUMINT), perhaps the oldest form of intelligence, is information obtained from individuals who have access to sensitive foreign information. Human Intelligence includes information gained not only through espionage, but also from a variety of other human sources—foreign service officers, defectors, refugees, scientists, engineers, academics, etc.—who may have or have had access to such information through their contacts with individuals in foreign governments and organizations. Human Intelligence also includes information obtained through "Covert Operations."[2] In the United States the CIA, the Defense Intelligence Agency and, more recently, the Federal Bureau of Investigation are the primary, but not exclusive, collectors of such intelligence.

The National Security Agency has primary responsibility for the collection of Signals Intelligence (SIGINT). Signals Intelligence is obtained from earthbound monitors such as ground stations, aircraft, and ships as well as from satellites. Signal Intelligence has two basic components: Communications Intelligence (COMINT) and Electronics Intelligence (ELINT). Communications Intelligence is information gathered from intercepted communications such as voice, telephone, facsimile, and Internet, whether they be encrypted or communicated openly.

The targets of Communications Intelligence are varied. They span the spectrum from traditional targets such as diplomatic and military communications between national capitals and missions abroad to communications involving economic, scientific, and technical developments, narcotics and human trafficking, money laundering, organized crime, and terrorism.

Electronics Intelligence is information gathered from electronic and data transmissions such as the signals emitted from military and civilian hardware. For example, during the Cold War, information gathered from the electronic emanations of Soviet-built radars and surface-to-air missile systems provided intelligence about their operating characteristics. This enabled the United States to equip its combat aircraft with radar and missile warning systems, which allowed the pilot to identify and avoid and in some cases attack and destroy these systems. Similarly, information obtained from signals sent during the testing of weapons systems, such as those emanating from Soviet ballistic missiles during the Cold War, can provide valuable information about the capabilities of those systems. This kind of intelligence is sometimes called Telemetry Intelligence or TELINT.

Since Signals Intelligence often involves sensitive techniques and sources and therefore can be highly sensitive, it is normally handled in special channels and is available only to specifically designated people.

Intelligence gathered from imagery, usually acquired by satellite, manned aircraft, or unmanned aerial vehicles is known as Imagery Intelligence (IMINT), sometimes referred to as Geospatial Intelligence (GEOINT). Imagery Intelligence is the exploitation and analysis of imagery and other geospatial information to describe, assess, and visually depict physical features and geographically referenced activities on earth. It was Imagery Intelligence that led to the discovery of ballistic missile sites in Cuba in October 1962. During the Cold War Imagery Intelligence also made it possible for the United States to pinpoint the location of such potentially important targets as Soviet ballistic missile sites and military bases. The National Geospatial-Intelligence Agency[3] has the primary responsibility for coordinating the collection and processing of imagery data. Like signals intelligence, some imagery intelligence is available only to specifically designated people.

Measurement and Signature Intelligence (MASINT) is information derived from technical analysis of the distinctive characteristics of a specific event such as a chemical, biological, or nuclear explosion by using sensors to identify particulates in the air or on the ground. Measurement and Signature Intelligence also is used to locate, identify, and describe distinctive characteristics of targets, such as aircraft or submarines through such means as optical, acoustic, or seismic sensors. Intelligence organizations within the Department of Defense—especially Defense Intelligence Agency, the National Geospatial-Intelligence Agency, and the military services—are the primary collectors of such intelligence.

The National Reconnaissance Office designs, builds, operates, and maintains the nation's reconnaissance satellites that support many of the above collection efforts. It also coordinates collection of information from airplane and satellite reconnaissance by the military services and the CIA.[4]

Finally, there is Open Source Intelligence (OSINT) or information publicly available in print or electronic form.[5] Open Source Intelligence includes information gathered from such sources as the internet, newspapers, magazines, books, technical materials, commercially available databases and imagery, scholarly journals, unclassified publications of government and nongovernmental organizations, and radio and television broadcasts.

Collectively these five intelligence sources—HUMINT, SIGINT, IMINT or GEOINT, MASINT, and OSINT—are informally known as the "INTs." While each of the so-called INTs often operates independently, they also can be teamed to operate jointly. For example through human intelligence efforts, the United States might be able to recruit a tribal leader previously loyal to the Taliban in Afghanistan. By comparing his conversations with the Taliban through the use of Signals Intelligence, a higher level of confidence might be achieved concerning his true loyalty. Similarly, Imagery Intelligence might locate a suspected al-Qaeda encampment. Human Intelligence or Signals Intelligence might then be used to verify the identity of those at the encampment.[6]

THE INTELLIGENCE REQUIREMENTS PROCESS

The first major step in the overall collection process is known as the "requirements" or "needs process." This effort includes identifying the information that needs to be collected, assigning collection priorities, communicating those priorities to collection agencies, and the translating of priorities by the collection agencies into programs designed to collect the desired information. Ideally, the "requirements process" should, as a minimum, reflect the policymakers' prioritized intelligence needs and give direction to the Intelligence Community's collection planning. As a nation involved in activities worldwide, the United States has need for a broad spectrum of intelligence—political, economic, technical, scientific, sociological, environmental, and military.

The Intelligence Reform and Terrorism Prevention Act of 2004 assigned the Director of National Intelligence the task of establishing the objectives, priorities, and guidance for the Intelligence Community to ensure the timely and effective collection of intelligence.[7] However, while the Director of National Intelligence is responsible for the overall effort, many agencies and individuals are involved in every step of the process.

Identifying Requirements

At the national strategic level, senior civilian and military leaders, working together with senior members of the Intelligence Community, identify the information about foreign individuals, nations, and events that they will need in order to make informed policy decisions. At the tactical military level field commanders pass their intelligence requirements up the chain of command so that priorities for the collection of intelligence at large unit as well as small unit levels can be identified. Intelligence requirements also are generated from within the Intelligence Community by analysts, based on their expert knowledge and understanding of given situations.[8] The process of identifying requirements is flexible by its nature. The President, Vice President, senior policymakers, the Director of National Intelligence, the National Intelligence Coordination Center,[9] the National Intelligence Collection Board,[10] the National Intelligence Council,[11] Mission Managers,[12] and others regularly inject into the process new requirements based on unfolding events, new intelligence, and a host of other factors.

Assigning Priorities

All intelligence requirements are not equal. During wartime, for example, timely information about enemy troop movements and dispositions is essential to success on the battlefield. Likewise, intelligence that is critical to an eminent policy decision is likely to be of more immediate importance than general information about, say, the underlying beliefs of a newly formed political party in country X. Hence, another major part of the requirements process is assigning priorities for collection. In a rapidly changing and uncertain world, the task of senior U.S. policymakers is to insure that enough intelligence is collected on issues of immediate critical importance while making sure that their guidance to the Intelligence Community isn't so completely circumscribed that it leads to a failure to collect information that is of long-term strategic significance.

Strategic Intelligence Reviews, first published by the National Intelligence Council in May 1994, and Presidential Decision Directive-35 (PDD-35), signed by President Clinton in March 1995 were, at least in part, designed to address this conundrum, providing the baselines for the requirements process in the post-Cold War era.

Strategic Intelligence Reviews were written by the eighteen Issue Coordinators,[13] who met frequently with senior policymakers. These intelligence reviews performed three primary tasks. First they identified core near-term (12–18 months) intelligence issues, priorities, and critical gaps that might exist in policymaker knowledge of various geographic regions and on transnational issues. Second, they assessed the value of current intelligence on those issues. Finally they identified midterm (3–7 years) intelligence needs as a means of assisting program managers in their long-term budgeting.

Presidential Decision Directive-35 (1995) provided collection as well as analysis guidance to the Intelligence Community and outlined a tiered structure of presidential intelligence priorities from Tier 0 (highest) to Tier 4. Highest on the list of priorities was intelligence support to military operations. At a lower level of priority were political, economic, and military intelligence on countries hostile to the United States. Even further down the list was intelligence to protect American citizens from transnational threats such as drug traffickers, organized criminals, weapons of mass destruction, and terrorists, though intelligence support for the war on terrorism was raised to Tier 0 in 1998.[14] The lowest level of priority was reserved for countries that were of little or no interest to the United States[15] In theory the assigned priorities were to settle the issue of resource allocation between potentially competing priorities and bring order and clarity to the collection processes.

In response to the recommendations of the joint House-Senate inquiry into the 9/11 attacks, the PDD-35 system has been altered. Intelligence officials report that Strategic Intelligence Reviews are no longer written and the rigid tier system that had been instituted by the 1995 presidential directive has been abandoned. In early 2003 President George W. Bush signed National Security Presidential Directive 26 aimed at creating a dynamic process for articulating and reviewing intelligence priorities. The Director of Central Intelligence followed suit, issuing Directive 2/3, which established a National Intelligence Priorities Framework. Following passage of the Intelligence Reform and Terrorism Prevention Act of

2004, the task of managing the Framework has fallen to the Director of National Intelligence. The Framework, revised by the Director of National Intelligence, purportedly is designed, among other things, to provide more meaningful guidance on intelligence priorities and allow for increased responsiveness to change—including the ability for intelligence personnel at various levels to alter priorities at their level of responsibility.

Communicating Priorities and Translating Them into Collection Programs

Once requirements have been prioritized, they are assigned to the collection agencies for execution. This process is never tidy. Previous presidents and policymakers have worked with senior members of the Intelligence Community to establish requirements and priorities based on their foreign policy objectives, as well as their perceptions of the threats and challenges facing the nation. In response, collection agencies initiate collection programs. Any changes in intelligence requirements or priorities resulting from a change of presidential administration, senior policymakers, foreign policy objectives, or newly emerging threats and opportunities are difficult to make and thus must be clearly communicated to the Intelligence Community. To accomplish this effectively, senior policymakers must have a thorough understanding of previous requirements and priorities and communicate changes in ways that make clear any subtle differences to those responsible for collection. They must also engage in intensive follow-up efforts to insure that changes in guidance have been well understood and are being faithfully carried out. To meet revised requirements, collection agencies must then translate new priorities into new collection programs and/or reorient existing programs. If additional resources are indicated, agencies of the Intelligence Community must either seek new funding or reduce or eliminate selected collection efforts. Such decisions often involve difficult trade-offs.

For example, following President George H.W. Bush's decision to confront Iraq following its 1990 invasion of Kuwait, intelligence on Iraqi military capabilities and force dispositions was assigned the highest priorities. However, though the Cold War was technically over, uncertainties remained about the future of the USSR and other trouble spots. The critical questions were how much of ongoing intelligence efforts could and should be diverted to support a war with Iraq and the extent to which these changes could be made in a timely manner.

Likewise, as the insurgency spread following the 2003 U.S. invasion of Iraq, President George W. Bush faced similar questions. To what extent could intelligence resources that had been focused since 9/11 on locating Osama bin Laden, or other intelligence resources linguistically and culturally trained to gather information in the Arab world, be redirected to gather intelligence needed in efforts to curb the insurgency in Iraq.

Processing

Once information is collected it must be processed into intelligence that is meaningful and usable by the Intelligence Community analysts and then reported back to the customer or using agency. The vast amount of information received in the form of images, communications, electronic signals, and reports from human sources must be sorted for relevance. Once sorted, pertinent information is passed to the analytical community for detailed analysis relevant to policymaker needs.

PROBLEMS

America's worldwide interests and responsibilities make its requirements massive and drive the size and complexity of its intelligence apparatus. Moreover the secret nature of intelligence collection complicates the entire process. Thus, the process of identifying, prioritizing, communicating, and translating intelligence requirements into effective collection programs and subsequently collecting, processing, and reporting on the information collected is fraught with difficulties. A CIA official concluded: "In fact, the 'requirements system' has few friends. It is untidy, encumbered by process, and generally unaccountable."[16]

Lack of Strategic Vision

Since the end of the Cold War, the Intelligence Community has refocused its collection efforts, deemphasizing monitoring Russian strategic and nonstrategic forces, structures, and dispositions. Greater emphasis has been placed on new concerns, such as ongoing intelligence requirements in Iraq and Afghanistan, terrorism, the proliferation of weapons of mass destruction, cyber warfare, drug and human trafficking, and support for humanitarian and peacekeeping operations. However, the United States still lacks a comprehensive strategic vision defining its role in the world.

- What kind of post-Cold War world would it like to see emerge?
- What role can the United States play in encouraging the emergence of such a world?
- What challenges is the United States likely to confront in attempting to forge such an environment?
- What are the more likely direct threats to America's vision of the future domestic and international order?
- How should the United States relate to the other actors in the international arena?
- What roles might those actors play in support of American goals?

The absence of answers to such questions renders virtually impossible the task of identifying the information American policymakers need in order to structure, prioritize, and support those intelligence programs and intelligence capabilities that are required to advance U.S. foreign policy objectives.

Even today's heavy emphasis on a global war against terrorism, in and of itself, reflects a general failure of strategic vision. The United States is not at war with terrorism per se. Terrorism is only a means used by some adversaries in pursuit of other goals. Answers to weightier questions are needed.

- Who are current and likely future adversaries?
- What are their motivations and objectives?
- What strategies are they pursuing?
- How can the United States best defeat their strategies?
- How can the United States preclude future threats from emerging?
- What other nations and organizations can assist the United States in confronting these challenges?
- What does the United States need to know and do to enlist their support while simultaneously reducing the numbers of those who might pose a threat?[17]

Only by addressing such issues can the United States identify and task the Intelligence Community to acquire the information needed to shape a security environment consistent with U.S. national interests.

New Levels of Complexity

In the last decade and a half, the requirements process also has had to confront increasing complexity. During the Cold War the principal threats to U.S. security were relatively unambiguous. Intelligence efforts could focus on identifying the military and, to a lesser extent, the political activities of the Soviet Union that threatened U.S. security and worldwide interests.

Following the demise of the Soviet Union, there was a general evolution from nation-state based threats to transnational threats. Problems previously viewed as simply challenges increasingly came to be viewed as threats to broader U.S. foreign policy objectives and security interests.[18] Ethnic strife, particularly on the periphery of Europe, threatened the stability of this vital region and ethnic cleansing threatened America's most fundamental ideals. As dependency on information technologies increased, attacks on cyber networks threatened to endanger national political, military, and economic infrastructures, with potential global implications. Drug trafficking threatened to sap America's vitality. Transnational organized crime undermined new democracies and threatened the U.S. economy and the economies of its allies and friends and nations upon whom America depends for scarce resources and/or markets. Trafficking in human beings represented an affront to America's moral values and violated its sense of what the post-Cold War order should represent. Environmental degradation endangered both the health of Americans and others around the world and their future economic progress. All these, not to mention concerns attending the uncertainty of the disposition of Russia's inherited Soviet nuclear stockpile, fissile materials, and technical know-how and their potential use by terrorists or proliferating countries, complicated questions of how much to collect on what, when, where, and how. The Intelligence Community, already reeling from post-9/11 turbulence, was hardly prepared or equipped to address many of these issues.

Focus on the Near-term

The requirements process is further complicated by the natural tendency of policymakers to focus on near-term issues. Each administration sets its own priorities for intelligence based on its experience and understanding of likely challenges to the United States. Unfortunately, all too often policymakers, instead of balancing near-term needs against requirements for sensitive intelligence essential for America's mid- and long-term security, are too focused on the more pressing issues. Of course this problem is not new; Robert Gates, then Deputy Director of Central Intelligence, noted two decades ago:

> One of the CIA's greatest concerns over the years has been the unwillingness or inability of most policymakers to spend much time on longer-range issues—looking ahead several steps—or in helping to guide or direct the agency's long-term efforts. . . . For many years, trying to get senior policy principals to attend meetings to discuss longer-range intelligence requirements has been an exercise in frustration."[19]

With this in mind, one must wonder how far ahead was the policymakers' focus when they moved to increase the role of U.S. military forces in Vietnam, or to end the war in Iraq in 1991, or to ignore the warnings of Chief of Staff of the Army General Eric Shinseki[20] and others, who contended that a significant number of forces would be needed to maintain the peace after the defeat of regular Iraqi military forces in 2003? In each of these cases one puzzles over whether policymakers, before finalizing their decisions, had tasked the Intelligence Community to look forward and assess thoroughly the potential impact of their planned actions on America's broader regional and global objectives. Had they asked the Intelligence Community to assess the impact of planned actions on America's human and material resources and moral authority needed to fashion the kind of world the United States hoped would emerge in the post-World War II and post-Cold War environments? Had they tasked intelligence officials to thoroughly examine the prospects for success in meeting U.S. objectives locally? There seems to be no indication that the Intelligence Community was required by senior policymakers to seek answers to any of these questions. On the other hand, if they had so tasked the Intelligence Community, decisions on methods and means to meet U.S. objectives in each of these cases might have been different.

Some may argue that one or more of the tasks outlined above do not fall within the proper purview of the Intelligence Community. However, precedent has been set by past presidents for the asking of just such questions. Former Director of Central Intelligence Stansfield Turner noted that President Eisenhower, faced with the rapidly deteriorating situation in Vietnam that preceded the French defeat, was confronted with a recommendation, encouraged by Admiral Radford, chairman of Joint Chiefs of Staff, and supported by Vice President Nixon, to drop two or three nuclear weapons to clear out Ho Chi Minh's forces that were besieging Dien Bien Phu. Eisenhower responded by asking the CIA to forecast the likely reaction of the world community too such an attack. In Turner's view: ". . . estimating foreign reaction to moves the United States might make is quite a legitimate part of intelligence."[21] On the other hand, Turner notes that during the administration of President Lyndon Johnson, Director of Central Intelligence John McCone, following up on the President's suggestion that he make policy recommendations, developed a six-point plan for the Vietnam war that was significantly different from that of Secretary of Defense Robert McNamara. Among other things, he called for far more troops and claimed that the "slowly ascending tempo of air strikes" had to be measured against the "increasing pressure to stop the bombing" that "will come from various elements of the American public, from the press, the United Nations, and world opinion."[22] Turner rightly argues that on this McCone was out of line, even foolish to try to advise a master on how to do politics.[23] McCone's error, however, was in making policy recommendations. On the other hand, history proved McCone to be correct on the issue of graduating responses and he was right to provide the President with his view on the likely impact of policy choices on world opinion, both domestic[24] and foreign. To do so is not to make policy. Rather it is to inform policymakers of the potential limitations of selected policies. To not do so is to deny political leaders the intelligence necessary for effective decision making.

Unfortunately, policymakers frequently don't seem to know what information they need until they actually need it.[25] This is at least in part understandable. A nation cannot afford to disregard immediate threats and challenges to its security. Nevertheless, few policymakers are strategists with a historical perspective. Therefore, they are not likely to thoroughly comprehend the notion that steps to solve near-term problems need to be taken only in conjunction with full consideration of their likely impact on mid- and long-term objectives.[26] In the absence of intelligence about future challenges, policymakers will not have the information at hand to make those kinds of strategic choices. One might cite as examples U.S. support for efforts to remove the elected governments of Mohamed Mossadegh in Iran in 1953 or Salvador Allende in Chile in 1973, or U.S. support for dictators like the corrupt and brutal Anastasio Somoza Debayle in Nicaragua, or even U.S. support for al-Qaeda and the Taliban following the Soviet invasion of Afghanistan.

It is almost certain that had policymakers tasked the Intelligence Community to examine the long-term implications of U.S. actions, options more favorable to America's long-term policy goals might well have emerged.

The problem is further exacerbated by the nature of the requirements process itself. In a system that, because of its size, requires that detailed collection requirements be submitted long in advance of their execution, the elephant in the room is the Department of Defense (DOD) and especially the combatant commanders. In the post-Cold War era DOD has been preoccupied with a wide variety of low- to medium-intensity conflicts, the so-called uncomfortable wars.[27] Whether it was such conflicts as the Iraq War of 1991, or U.S. military efforts in Bosnia-Herzegovina, Somalia, or Kosovo in the mid-to-late 1990s, or the post-9/11 wars in Afghanistan and Iraq, DOD's understandable focus has been on the near-term goal of supporting ongoing military operations. With staffs that frequently pale in comparison to the Department of Defense, other intelligence consumers, such as the departments of State, Treasury, or Energy that might have complementary but broader, longer-term, and nonoperational military focus to the intelligence they seek, lack the numbers, diversity of requirements, and "formulaic intensity of the DOD customer."[28] As a result, their effect on orienting a modicum of intelligence collection toward longer-term concerns is minimized. And as one keen observer has noted: "This situation, which tends to focus resources on the here and now to the disadvantage of strategic interests, will only grow more confused with the maturation of the Department of Homeland Security and the inevitable assertion of its national security interests."[29]

Constraints Imposed by the Senior Policymakers

A further barrier to an effective requirements process is the result of constraints imposed on the Intelligence Community by policymakers themselves. Senior decision makers frequently have their own ideas or biases about events that result in constraints on the Intelligence Community's ability to collect valuable information. For example, as the crisis thickened in Iran in 1978 prior to the fall of the Shah, a CIA assessment of events in Iran in August of that same year had concluded that Iran was "not in a revolutionary or even a pre-revolutionary situation." In his briefings to the President, Director of Central Intelligence Admiral Stansfield Turner reinforced this view, telling Carter that the Shah was in complete control of the army, police forces, and intelligence service.[30] According to Turner, the CIA "had not appreciated how shaky the shah's political foundation was; did not know that the shah was terminally ill; [and] did not understand who Khomeini was and the support the movement had . . ."[31] By January 1979 the Shah was overthrown. Why had intelligence failed so miserably?

Christopher Andrew points out that the roots of the intelligence failure lay as much with policymakers as within the Intelligence Community. For more than a decade before the fall of the Shah of Iran, senior policymakers, particularly during the Nixon administration had discouraged the CIA from an in-depth examination of the realities of the Shah's rule. During that time, what Gary Sick called "the unspoken but unanimous view that the shah was Iran and Iran was the shah" had governed American policy. In order not to offend the Shah, upon whom the United States depended for being allowed to monitor Soviet missile testing and development from Iraqi sites, "the CIA had been discouraged from establishing links with opposition figures."[32]

In the absence of such an in-depth look, it is not surprising that their assessment failed to reflect accurately the situation in Iran. Had an in-depth analysis been undertaken at the time, it might have led to policy decisions crafted to avoid what has turned out to be an enduring problem for American foreign policy.

One, of course, must wonder whether the Intelligence Community felt similar constraints in the run-up to the Iraq War of 2003. Failure of the Bush administration to call for a careful reexamination of the intelligence available on the aluminum tubes Iraq was attempting to import, and claimed by some to be for use in centrifuges to enrich uranium, despite the fact that both the Department of Energy and the International Atomic Energy Agency had discredited the claim; continued insistence by senior administration officials that Iraq had tried to import "yellowcake"[33] uranium from Niger, a claim that contradicted prevailing intelligence; the absolute certainty expressed by senior administration officials that Iraq possessed weapons of mass destruction and had developed links to al-Qaeda; oft-voiced Administration concerns that America could not wait for final proof that Iraq had weapons of mass destruction for fear that it might come in the form of a mushroom cloud; and the seeming haste to discredit United Nations inspectors even before their reports were rendered—the sum of such activities might well have served as a constraint on intelligence officials inclined to look more carefully at the evidence at hand, resulting in a kind of self-censorship that limits discussion in deference to favored truths.

Bureaucratic Tensions

The Director of National Intelligence serves as the head of the Intelligence Community. He is principal advisor to the President, heads of departments and agencies of the executive branch, the Chairman of the Joint Chiefs of Staff, and Congress on intelligence matters. He also oversees and directs the implementation of the National Intelligence Program. The National Intelligence Program includes "all programs, projects, and activities of the intelligence community, as well as any other programs of the intelligence community designated jointly by the Director of National Intelligence and the head of a United States department or agency or by the President."[34] It, however, does not include "programs, projects, or activities of the military departments to acquire intelligence solely for the planning and conduct of tactical military operations by United States Armed Forces."[35] These comprise the Military Intelligence Program.

The Secretary of Defense, as the principal defense policy advisor to the President, is responsible for the formulation of general defense policy, and oversees the Department of Defense, which is in turn responsible for the conduct of military operations and is the largest single producer and consumer of intelligence. He also oversees the Military Intelligence Program.

It falls to the Director of National Intelligence to insure that the intelligence needs of all senior policymakers are met, not just those of the Secretary of Defense. However, it is the Department of Defense that garners a lion's share of the budget, provides over 80 percent of the personnel, and manages eight of the fifteen Intelligence Community's federal agencies, offices, and elements, some of which are involved in both the National Intelligence Program and the Military Intelligence Program. The result is an inevitable tension between the two offices.[36]

Before the 2004 intelligence reform, which created the office of the Director of National Intelligence, the task of protecting the interests of the policymaking community fell to the Director of Central Intelligence. Unfortunately, while he had statutory responsibilities that spanned the Intelligence Community, his actual authorities, though they varied a bit from President to President,[37] generally have been limited to the budgets and personnel over which he exercised direct control, that is, the CIA, the Office of the Director of Central Intelligence, and the Community Management Staff.[38]

Thus, as former Senator Warren Rudman testified to the Joint House/Senate Inquiry: "You have a Director of Central Intelligence who is also the Director of CIA; [however] eighty-five percent of [the Intelligence Community's budget] is controlled by the Department of Defense."[39]

The consequences of such a situation were noted in a joint report of the House and Senate intelligence committees:

> The inability to realign Intelligence Community resources to combat the threat posed by Usama Bin Ladin [*sic*] is a relatively direct consequence of the limited authority of the DCI [Director of Central Intelligence] over major portions of the Intelligence Community.[40]

The Intelligence Reform Act 2004 has given the Director of National Intelligence additional authorities beyond those assigned former directors of Central Intelligence (with perhaps the exception of Stansfield Turner)[41] and more commensurate with his responsibilities. The objective is to provide the Director of National Intelligence the tools needed to better manage the overall intelligence effort. In particular, the Act strengthens his budget authorities in several ways.

- He not only is to provide guidance to the Intelligence Community for the developing of their respective budgets and consolidate those budgets into a coherent national intelligence budget,[42] but also now has the authority, acting through the Director of the Office of Management and Budget, to direct how congressionally appropriated funds are apportioned to cabinet-level agencies with Intelligence Community elements.[43]

- He now may allot appropriations directly to subcabinet agencies and departments.[44] In theory this should allow him to better insure that agency spending is in line with his priorities.
- He also is now able to "participate in the development by the Secretary of Defense of the annual budgets for the Military Intelligence Program."[45] In addition, the Secretary of Defense must "consult" him before transferring or reprogramming funds made available to the Military Intelligence Program.[46]

However, while the Director of National Intelligence has overall responsibility for establishing objectives, priorities, and guidance for the Intelligence Community, his ability to insure that his priorities are unequivocally reflected in the tasking of those elements of the Intelligence Community that come under the authority of the Secretary of Defense is circumscribed. The Intelligence Reform Act 2004 notes the Secretary of Defense exercises tasking authority over agencies and departments under his authority in accordance with "arrangements *agreed upon* (emphasis added) with the Director of National Intelligence."[47] Thus, it remains to be seen whether such new authorities given the Director of National Intelligence will remedy most, much less all, of the problems that plagued the relationship between him and the Defense Secretary.[48]

The fact that John Negroponte, the first Director of National Intelligence, abandoned a cabinet-level position with a direct line to the President after a mere eighteen months to take the number two position at the Department of State suggests otherwise. Following Negroponte's announced departure, former Deputy Director of Central Intelligence John McLaughlin commented on the Reform Act of 2004. He wrote that key decisions were "cobbled together" in the heat of a presidential election campaign with "campaign talking points often driving the debate" and that the "robust budgetary authority along with clear direction and control over the nation's principal intelligence agencies" that he and other senior intelligence officials had sought were lacking. Indeed, according to McLaughlin, Congress had yielded to Department of Defense insistence that the most important agencies (the National Security Agency, National Geospatial-Intelligence Agency, and the National Reconnaissance Agency) remain in its chain of command.[49]

Moreover, bureaucratic tensions between the CIA director and the Secretary of Defense are likely to grow as the Department of Defense, in a further challenge to the CIA's National Clandestine Service, expands its espionage and covert activities. The operative questions here are: just where do the responsibilities of the Department of Defense end and those of the CIA's clandestine service begin? Will efforts be fully coordinated and information shared, especially in those areas of interest where the overlap undoubtedly will occur? Perhaps more importantly, should clandestine foreign intelligence gathering efforts be centralized for efficiency of effort?[50]

Another major bureaucratic problem, the so-called "legacy user bias," hinders the effective collection of intelligence.[51] Since the end of World War II collection efforts were focused on the Soviet threat. Personnel were hired and platforms designed to address the Soviet challenge. As new threats arose following the end of the Cold War, those charged with collecting intelligence on these new threats found themselves in competition with those who continued to monitor changes taking place in post-Soviet space, having to barter for the resources necessary to address the newly emerging threats. Presumably much of this may well be mitigated, if not eliminated, if the Director of National Intelligence can establish his authority over the Intelligence Community and provide clear guidance and enforce unequivocal priorities on a system that heretofore too frequently has operated as a number of independent fiefdoms.

Requirements and/or Priorities Ill-defined or Unclear

In theory, assigning requirements and priorities would not seem to be difficult. Ideally policymakers have a well-considered and well-defined understanding of their intelligence needs and priorities. In practice this is not always the case. The President deals with many issues that may have an adverse effect on America's security or economic well-being, and therefore seem to demand additional intelligence. Likewise cabinet officials and other senior policymakers address a number of issues that warrant additional information about foreign intentions and activities. This plethora of issues and the pressure of immediate events frequently serve to cloud vision and limit time for the thoughtful consideration of intelligence needs and priorities. Thus the policymakers themselves often do not have a clear understanding of their needs and associated priorities. Moreover, frequently assuming that the intelligence providers have read their policy statements and are aware of their objectives and concerns, policymakers often fail to see a need to provide clearer guidance of their intelligence needs and priorities.[52]

In the post-Cold War period, as intelligence needs and demands on requirements process have grown, so has the problem of establishing clearly defined and well-understood requirements and priorities. This is particularly true in an environment that classically has fewer resources than necessary to meet the vast informational needs of a superpower with worldwide interests, where conflicting requests cross agency boundaries, and where "turf" becomes an issue when one agency attempts to assign collection priorities for systems and people operationally controlled by another.[53]

Though President Clinton promulgated Presidential Decision Directive -35 to ameliorate the problem, the problem was not solved. In the aftermath of the 9/11 attacks, Intelligence Community officials testified before Congress that a lack of adequate separation between PDD-35 tiers made it difficult to choose between priorities. Priorities were too broad to be meaningful and the PDD-35 process was incapable of adapting to a dynamic threat environment.[54]

The joint House Permanent Select Committee on Intelligence/Senate Select Committee on Intelligence (HPSCI/SSCI) 9/11 report noted:

> As counterterrorism became an increasingly important concern for senior Intelligence Community officials, collection and analytic efforts did not always keep pace because other requirements competed with terrorism for attention, and real priorities often were not clear.[55]

Likewise the joint report noted, "The Director of National Security Agency testified that prior to September 11, other priorities frustrated his attempts to acquire capabilities to process modern communications used by terrorists and other intelligence targets: It required a significant redirection of investment for us to acquire the capabilities to exploit modern communications."[56]

Also overly broad priorities in some cases led to a large number of "Essential Elements of Information"[57]—the most critical information about an issue or country needed by policymakers in order to make a rational decision. The large number of Essential Elements of Information apparently burdened an overtaxed system and precluded some analysts from delving more deeply into areas they believed to be important.

A House Permanent Select Committee on Intelligence staff study signaled this problem over a decade ago.[58] The study noted that, as intelligence agencies and components rushed to fulfill higher Tier PDD-35 requirements, less pressing requirements were ignored, even when some of those agencies were better equipped to address the lower Tier requirements. The result, House staff members feared, might be yet another Rwanda or Somalia situation in which the United States had insufficient intelligence coverage of countries that might suddenly become top Tier priorities.[59]

Some intelligence officials contend that while the formal processes may not work effectively or even be followed by some, informal processes assist in making the system work. National intelligence officers do meet with senior officials as well as among themselves in efforts to define, further refine, prioritize, and coordinate collection requirements. Nevertheless, this process has not been completely successful in clarifying intelligence requirements and priorities. Dialogue among the various requirements committees remains insufficient.[60]

The addition of post-Cold War intelligence tasks related to such concerns as cyber crime or cyber warfare, drugs, and human trafficking complicates the problem. Thus, as new intelligence requirements are added to already burgeoning lists, priorities get confused. For example, which intelligence requirements have a higher priority: identifying drug routes in Central Asia or traffickers in human beings in Southern Europe, locating bin Laden or terrorists in Iraq, monitoring the nuclear activities of North Korea or those of Iran?

Communicating Requirements and Priorities

Communication in any bureaucracy is a problem. Like the "Whisper Game," the larger the bureaucracy, the greater is the problem. The U.S. government is no exception. In intelligence collection, the degree of distortion from original intent is a function of the number of channels through which decisions concerning requirements and priorities must travel before arriving at the desk of those responsible for collection. This is usually true even in the case of written guidance, which is still unlikely to be specific enough to cover every contingency. Each intermediary thus will interpret what he or she has heard or read based on their own peculiar understanding of the situation. The more vague the guidance, the greater the opening for individual interpretation by those through whose hands the guidance is passed.

Furthermore, when priorities change the change might not be effectively and fully communicated to the Intelligence Community. For example, following the August 1998 bombings of U.S. embassies in East Africa, the Director of Central Intelligence elevated the threat posed by Osama bin Laden to a "Tier O priority," the highest level of priority, and announced in writing in December: "We are at war . . . I want no resources or people spared in this effort, either inside the CIA or the [Intelligence] Community." However, this declaration only appeared in a memorandum from the Director of Central Intelligence to some members of his immediate staff and to CIA senior managers. The Intelligence Community as a whole and other important officials had only limited awareness of the directive. Some key players like the Deputy Secretary of Defense and the Chairman of the Joint Chiefs of Staff were unaware of the directive. The Director of the National Security Agency, who collects and processes foreign signals intelligence information for members of the policymaking and military communities, believed the memo only applied to the CIA. CIA officials, on the other hand, thought the memo was intended for the entire Intelligence Community, since they were already doing all they could and believed that the rest of the community needed to pull its weight.[61]

Translating Priorities into Collection Programs

The Intelligence Community has faced at least four serious problems as it attempts to manage collection activities across agencies and across disciplines. First, it has confronted a process problem. Typically, to ask another agency to gather information on a particular issue, analysts have had to forward their requirements to their own organization's collection managers or to discipline-specific Intelligence Community collection committees, which in turn sent collection requirements to specific collection agencies.

Each collection agency, operating with its own understanding of national intelligence priorities, which may not be particularly clear, may be in flux, or may be inconsistent with those of other agencies, then worked independently to satisfy the customers' needs.[62] Though agencies cooperated at times, there has been little or nothing in terms of well-coordinated joint action.[63] Such an environment has been ripe for significant collection omissions as well as cross-agency duplication of effort. To limit potential negative consequences, the process occasionally was overseen by the Assistant Director of Central Intelligence for Collection and his National Intelligence Collection Board. Members of this Board represented the collection agencies and met to discuss and review high-priority intelligence issues, as well as the efforts of individual collection agencies to meet customer needs. Nevertheless, the President's Commission on Weapons of Mass Destruction found this process to be haphazard and inadequate to meet contemporary intelligence requirements.[64] In October 2007, as a part of his 500-day plan, the Director of National Intelligence established the National Intelligence Coordination Center. The Center's purpose is to provide the Director of National Intelligence the means through which he can more effectively and efficiently direct and integrate collection assets and activities of all national, defense, and domestic intelligence organizations in order to ensure that standing and emergent strategic intelligence priorities are met.[65] The Department of Defense has the Defense Intelligence Operations Center to synchronize intelligence operations and collection in support of the Combatant Commands and to serve as an interface with the newly established National Intelligence Coordination Center and the Director of National Intelligence. It is, of course, too early to see if these Centers will fix problems identified by the President's Commission.

The second problem is institutional. While program managers attempted to translate previously identified collection requirements into programs within their own agencies, insufficient resources frequently forced them to make internal trade-offs to build coherent and sustainable programs capable of competing for funding within their own agencies. The cumulative effect within and across the intelligence agencies often has been failure to satisfy collection requirements. This problem was compounded by a lack of program management expertise. For example, the joint House-Senate intelligence committee's inquiry into the terrorist attacks of 9/11 noted that one of the effects of the downsizing, outsourcing, and transformation of the National Security Agency was a loss of critical program management expertise, systems engineering, and requirements definition skills.[66]

The third problem is how much information should to be collected to yield, with a high probability, the intelligence needed. The more information you collect, the more costly but also the more likely it is that the information collected will meet the requirement. However, the more information that is collected, the greater the burden on the already overtaxed processors, who must then sort through the large amount of frequently coded imagery and signals and other forms of data in order to separate the "chaff" from the relevant "wheat." On the other hand, if less information is collected for budgetary reasons or to reduce the processing burden, then the risk of missing the very intelligence required increases.[67]

Finally, neither a clear mechanism for deciding on the appropriate mix of intelligence collection assets nor a means for determining how well collection assets are performing against assigned tasks has existed. In the past, with no one firmly in charge of managing the collection process on any given case, there has been no one able to assign responsibilities across agencies, draw relevant intelligence from anywhere in government, track progress, and identify and eliminate obstacles. In short, there has been no "quarterback."[68] Thus there has been no integrated approach to collection, which significantly hinders the task of "connecting the dots."

Processing

As noted earlier, the Collection process involves identifying, prioritizing, tasking, and communicating requirements to collection agencies and then collecting and processing collected information before passing it to the analytical community. During the processing phase information collected is examined for intelligence relevant to the tasked requirements. This includes sorting through intelligence frequently gathered by human, signals, imagery, measurement and signature, electronic, or other means. It may require extensive decoding or translation. Unfortunately, as threats have become more diffuse and requirements have expanded in the post-Cold War period, demands for efficient processing and timely and effective forwarding for analysis have increased. This demanding environment needs well-developed technical programs and a well-trained cadre of individuals capable of processing and reporting the information received. In this regard, James Monnier Simon, Jr., a former senior CIA official who had been charged with managing the CIA's collection requirements, noted: "the time imagery analysts have is scarcer than the images themselves." He thus concludes: "it is futile for customers to task collection without the certainty that someone will look at it."[69]

Similarly Mark Lowenthal has noted that collection always outpaces the ability to process the information collected. Providing budgets commensurate with the processing requirements lacks the appeal of sexy high-tech satellites which are heavily supported by business and industry, generally a high priority in the President's budget requests, and frequently well-funded by Congress.[70]

THE WAY AHEAD

Such problems of strategic vision, global complexity, bureaucratic tensions, and near-term focus are likely to continue to plague the intelligence collection processes to a greater or lesser degree, depending on the personalities and capabilities of policymakers within a given administration. Nevertheless, in response to the report of the President's Commission on Weapons of Mass Destruction and the changes mandated by the Intelligence Reform and Terrorism Prevention Act of 2004, efforts are underway to reduce or eliminate many of the problems associated with setting and communicating priorities, as well as translating priorities into collection programs.

Pursuant to both the authorities and responsibilities granted to him by Executive Order 13355 signed in August 2004 and the Intelligence Reform Act passed in December of that same year, the Director of National Intelligence has established both functional and country-specific Mission Managers. As of this writing, Mission Managers have been designated for counterterrorism, counterproliferation, counterintelligence, Iran, North Korea, Cuba, and Venezuela. Mission Managers are the principal Intelligence Community officials overseeing all aspects of national intelligence related to their respective mission areas.[71] Each Mission Manager works in partnership with the National Intelligence Council, senior officials in the Office of the Director of National Intelligence and other senior officials in the Intelligence Community. Among Mission Manager responsibilities are:

- Understanding the full range of policymaker requirements and insuring that they have been conveyed to and coordinated with the Deputy Director of National Intelligence for Requirements.
- Setting collection priorities.
- Determining the state of collection against their assigned missions, identifying collection gaps, tasking collection activity, and evaluating collector responsiveness and success in filling collection gaps.

Additionally, the Director of National Intelligence has centralized collection responsibilities in the Office of the Deputy Director for Collection. His responsibilities include overseeing Intelligence Community collection activities via the National Intelligence Collection Board, the collection committees for Human, Signals, Geospatial, Measurement and Signature, and Open Source Intelligence, and Mission Managers.[72]

It, of course, is too early to tell the extent to which such arrangements will solve the many problems associated with setting and managing collection priorities. One thing is for sure, at present Mission Managers only cover a limited though important spectrum of U.S. intelligence requirements. Even within that limited spectrum, much will depend on the strength of the Director of National Intelligence and his ability to get the entire Intelligence Community to work together. As noted above, at this point it does not appear that either the President or Congress has given him sufficient authority to do so.

2

People, Technology, and Money

"Give us the tools, and we will finish the job."

—Winston Churchill

PEOPLE

Ultimately the successful collection and processing of information depends on the people and technology involved in the collection processes and the budgets required to support both. Arguably, the most important element in the collection of information is people.

In recent decades the increasing ability to gather information by technical means, such as spy satellites capable of intercepting communications or capable of photographing terrain features and military equipment and facilities, has resulted in a reduction in the perceived need for human sources of intelligence and a corresponding reduction of such sources.[1] Nevertheless, people still remain the key ingredient in the collection process.

Technical means are frequently insufficient to identify activities inside a building, or penetrate highly secure discussions, or to access planning and policy documents, technical manuals, weapons design notes, laboratory test results, weapons system blueprints, and the like. Nor can technical means actually acquire weapons systems or their components. Technical means are also unlikely to provide a sufficient understanding of the underlying beliefs and motivations of foreign leaders and/or the bureaucratic and organizational decision-making processes of foreign countries to enable the U.S. Intelligence Community to develop accurate assessments of a foreign government's more probable courses of action in given situations.[2] And in the context of global efforts to thwart terrorism, technical means have proven less effective in identifying and locating terrorists, identifying their future plans and potential targets, or in tracking and capturing their leaders. Frequently the key ingredient in the gathering of such information is people.

When we think of the people engaged in the processes of gathering intelligence, generally we think of those engaged in espionage. However, human resources are engaged throughout the collection processes. Language specialists monitor communications for relevant information. Interpreters play an intermediary role between foreigners who do not speak English or have only a cursory understanding of the English language and American officials charged with gathering intelligence. Translators translate foreign source documents so the Intelligence Community can extract important information. Others maintain the technical collection systems. Still others process and report on collected information. And there are those who manage all of the above.

There are the recruiters, who identify and recruit foreigners to serve as intelligence agents (spies) for the United States or to serve as "agents of influence"—tasked to influence the behavior of another government.[3] These foreigners may be dissidents living in their home country or refugees living abroad or in the United States—people who are willing to spy for or act on behalf of another country for ideological reasons, or for revenge against a regime that wronged them or for the money. They may be members of a foreign government or organizations the United States wishes to penetrate or close friends of members of those in governments or organizations. Or perhaps they have access to important classified information, such as weapons system designs or movements of individuals or are in a position to obtain such information. They may be individuals of exceptional promise in whom the U.S. Intelligence Community wishes to make a long-term investment, hoping that someday they will be in a position to assist in the gathering of intelligence. Or by virtue of their native language skills and appearance they are able to move easily about their home country gathering information on significant events. Recruiting such individuals can be a tedious and dangerous process that draws heavily on all the talents of the recruiters over a long period of time.

There also are those who work closely with foreign agents in the employment of the U.S. government, clandestinely passing on tasks and then collecting the information that has been gathered and passing it on to U.S. intelligence agencies. And those who work closely with friendly foreign intelligence agencies, encouraging those agencies to share information they have gathered.

Then there are those tasked overtly to gather information of interest to the Intelligence Community. They may be military or foreign policy specialists, members of U.S. governmental missions abroad, or members of the government who are frequently in contact with foreigners by virtue of their travels or professional associations. Their task, for example, may be to examine unclassified "open source" government publications, periodicals, journals, magazines, other relevant publications, radio or TV newscasts and informational programs, or query their foreign contacts on their views and the views of others about given issues or situations.

There also are some members of the business community, academicians and scientists who provide information to the Intelligence Community that they have gleaned from their travels abroad or from their professional and /or social contacts with foreigners. This information may have been provided by them voluntarily on an ad hoc basis, may have been actively sought out by the Intelligence Community based on the expertise and/or the nature of contacts of the provider, or may have been acquired in the course of a professional conference on issues of importance to the government. Indeed, government agencies frequently sponsor such conferences to enhance their understanding of a region, a country, or of specific issues or given situations. Interestingly enough, information obtained this way by government agencies that are not a part of the Intelligence Community may not necessarily be shared with members of the Community. Hence, although the Intelligence Community is a likely recipient of final reports by those agencies, especially those advancing policy recommendations, the recommendations may not be based entirely upon the common Intelligence Community view of the situation.

Finally, of course there are the "spies," those engaged in espionage—clandestine efforts to gather intelligence. These include Americans as well as foreigners employed by the United States to seek out protected information deemed important to U.S. foreign policy and security interests writ large. These so-called intelligence agents come from various backgrounds and organizations. They may be members of the U.S. military who gather intelligence on foreign military forces and capabilities. For example, during the Cold War, the U.S. Military Liaison Mission located in Potsdam in East Germany kept abreast of Soviet and East German troop movements and capabilities. Or they may be CIA agents disguised as military personnel. They may be members of American missions abroad (e.g., attachés and diplomats), members of intergovernmental organizations (e.g., United Nations, North Atlantic Treaty Organization, Organization for Security and Co-operation in Europe) or nongovernmental organizations (e.g., Red Cross, Amnesty International, etc.), or people engaged in businesses and industries operating abroad. They may be paid or unpaid foreign officials or individuals. An example of a high-ranking official working for of the U.S. Intelligence Community was Panamanian General Manuel Noriega. Noriega reportedly received approximately $100,000 annually from the U.S. government from the mid-1960s until the mid-1980s.[4] During that time he served as the head of Panamanian Defense Forces intelligence and from 1983 as Defense Forces Commander. Spies also may be third-country individuals with access to individuals or information in a country that is important to U.S. foreign or security interests.

Perhaps the greatest challenge that the Intelligence Community confronts is recruiting, training, and maintaining the human resources needed to acquire the information needed for effective decision making.

Insufficient Numbers of Trained Personnel

A common concern of the Intelligence Community is insufficient personnel to cover the tasks assigned. With the demise of the Soviet Union, some government officials came to the mistaken conclusion that there would be less need for the type of intensive efforts that went into collecting intelligence during the Cold War. Indeed, prior to his election as president, William Clinton promised to cut the intelligence budget by about a quarter.[5] However, global terrorism, increasing ethnic and national conflicts, blossoming drug and human trafficking, and the challenges of nuclear proliferation in general, and of tracking Soviet nuclear weapons and fissile materials upon that empires demise are among the many concerns that belied such wishful thinking.

Indeed, burgeoning intelligence requirements soon began to overwhelm declining Intelligence Community resources. Congressional investigations revealed that "[b]y the late 1990s, Intelligence Community coverage of many issues had become exceptionally slim and staffing was skeletal."[6] For example, National Security Agency officials, in testimony before Congress on the 9/11 attacks, acknowledged that the Agency had insufficient numbers of linguists to cover the growing terrorist threat. Those close to the counterterrorism problem stated they had been requesting personnel increases for years, mostly to little or no avail.[7]

However, personnel deficiencies were clearly not just limited to dealing with the growing terrorist threat. The CIA was unable to meet its broader collection goals. In the CIA directorate tasked with gathering intelligence overseas, personnel deployed abroad had been cut by almost one-third.[8] In part this reduction likely was due to former Director of Central Intelligence John Deutch's guidelines restricting recruitment of agents with poor human rights records.[9] However, budget cuts addressed below most certainly played a role.

Moreover, the CIA frequently relies on people who are willing to volunteer information to the U.S. government.[10] Thus, it must have people in the field capable of understanding, in full nuance, what they are being told by such sources and able to ascertain the veracity of the information,[11] so they can assess and pass on to analysts at headquarters their judgments about the quality of the information received. The Director of the CIA Language School testified to Congress that the language proficiency required to debrief volunteer sources and write reports about such information is very different than the level of language you need for daily social intercourse or to recruit someone. It doesn't take much imagination to glean from the highly edited version of her testimony that the United States currently has an insufficient number of well-trained people to do the job.[12] The Director further underscored the lack of personnel by noting: "With the progress in technology, we keep getting more material that needs translation, we don't have that capability."[13]

Reflecting a similar deficiency, according to the Chief of the FBI's Language Service Division, prior to 9/11, for lack of Arabic speakers, 35 percent of the Arabic language materials the Bureau derived from Foreign Intelligence Surveillance Act collection were neither translated nor reviewed.[14]

The House and Senate intelligence committees in their joint report on 9/11 concluded that the shortage of language specialists has been a perennial problem within the Intelligence Community.

> Prior to September 11, 2001, the Intelligence Community was not prepared to handle the challenge it faced in translating the volumes of foreign language counterterrorism intelligence it collected. Agencies within the Intelligence Community experienced backlogs in material awaiting translation, a shortage of language specialists and language-qualified field officers, and a readiness level of only 30% in the most critical terrorism-related languages used by terrorists.[15]

Likewise, translating, processing, and performing an initial analysis on intercepted communications not only requires a very high level of language expertise, including knowledge of the many dialects that might be used, but also requires a high level of knowledge of the target. For example, in attempting to determine what information is relevant to a particular intelligence collection task related to, say, an Islamic terrorist group, any evaluation of intercepted communications requires a considerable degree of subject matter expertise in Islam in general and Islamic extremism in particular in order to ensure the best possible interpretation.[16] Yet, according to the House-Senate joint report on the failures of 9/11, very few Arabic language specialists analyzing information collected by the National Security Agency have done any graduate work in Islamic Studies. Furthermore, at the time of the report the joint House-Senate committee noted that the "Language Readiness Index" for Agency personnel working on counterterrorism "campaign languages" was around 30 percent. The index reflects the percentage of the mission that is being performed by qualified language analysts.[17]

Echoing similar concerns, then National Security Agency director General Hayden, in his testimony to Congress, cautioned, "If these hearings were about the war that had broken out in Korea or the crisis in the Taiwan Straits that had taken us by surprise or if we had been surprised by a conflict in South Asia or if we had lost an aircraft over Iraq or if American forces had suffered casualties in Bosnia or Kosovo, in any of these cases I would be here telling you that I had not put enough analysts or linguists against the problem. We needed more analysts and linguists across the agency, period."[18]

Shortages of personnel involved in collection, of course, are not limited to linguists. There simply have been too many priorities for available resource levels. For example, commenting on Intelligence Community's failure to provide advanced warning of India's nuclear bomb tests in 1998, the report by Admiral David Jeremiah noted that the United States had little or no "human intelligence," meaning spies in India.[19] Furthermore, when the October 2002 National Intelligence Estimate was written the United States had little human intelligence on Iraq's weapons of mass destruction. One can assume that the lack of trained personnel involved in various other collection tasks, at least in part, was behind the President's Commission on Weapons of Mass Destruction conclusion that the

United States has "only limited access to critical information" in such high-priority intelligence targets as Iran, North Korea, China, and Russia.[20]

The problem frequently is compounded by ad hoc requests for additional information. For example, according to the director of the National Security Agency, the requirements system in place on the eve of September 11, 2001, consisted of some 1,500 standing requirements calling for some 200,000 detailed pieces of information. To these enormous requirements additional requests were received telephonically or via e-mail.[21]

Difficulty Penetrating the Target

Even with sufficient numbers of personnel overall, it is often difficult to gather timely information for lack of personnel able to penetrate the highest levels of a government or targeted group. Some governments have been successful at limiting enemy agents' access to protected information through denial and deception efforts. Indeed, denial and deception are two sides of the same coin.[22] Through effective internal security and counterintelligence efforts governments can deny access to information sought by an adversary's spies. They can also deceive collectors, as well as analysts, through misleading statements and actions. The objective of both is to preclude information that might jeopardize the nation's security from falling into the hands of a potential adversary.

During the Cold War, while Moscow was able to penetrate American intelligence and gather highly classified information, the United States had less success penetrating the Kremlin. There were few high-level Soviet defectors[23] and U.S. efforts to recruit "spies" with access to highly classified information were not generally fruitful.[24] Apparently the CIA even lacked a low-ranking "mole" in the Soviet government until just before Stalin's death.[25]

Governments also have been partially successful at limiting information obtained through satellite photography. Nongeosynchronous satellites fly a predictable path over the earth's surface. To limit the information obtained by such satellites, governments know when to conceal forces and equipment, thus, denying the adversary information about numbers, type, and locations. Unmanned aerial vehicles such as the Predator and manned aircraft equipped with photographic and other intelligence-collecting devices make it more difficult to forecast the timing and targets of intelligence-gathering missions. This complicates, but does not eliminate, the ability of a determined adversary to conceal forces and equipment. Even to the extent such platforms are able to collect physical information, they are often not able to differentiate between, say, a pharmaceutical plant and a chemical weapons factory, underscoring the unique role of the human sources in the intelligence enterprise.

Similarly, governments have become more adept at denying information gathered through signals, measurement, and signature intelligence methods. Security programs have increased awareness of government officials of the dangers of an adversary being able to piece together classified information by monitoring conversations or reading unclassified articles or reports written by government officials. Governments increasingly encourage personnel to limit classified discussions to specially shielded rooms where and when they are available. Governments also increasingly encrypt spoken and written communications and telemetric data transmitted during equipment testing. Furthermore, in the arena of tactical military operations, countermeasures, such as flares, chaff, and thermal blanketing are regularly employed to limit information obtained through measurement and signature intelligence on the disposition of military forces.

With the end of the Cold War, the problem of penetrating targets of intelligence has become no easier and for many new threats, even more difficult. For example, terrorist groups and other criminal organizations can be "relatively small, secretive, and tightly knit." Membership in the group may depend "on long acquaintanceships, family ties or previous criminal acts." Entrance into the group may even require proof of commitment in the form of performing a terrorist or other criminal act. Thus inserting a source into such groups can be a first-order challenge.[26]

Before September 11, none of the three agencies with primary responsibility for the collection of intelligence from human sources (the CIA, the FBI, and the Defense Intelligence Agency) had collected any information through those sources warning of the attacks on the World Trade Center or the Pentagon.[27] According to senior officials at the Counter Terrorism Center, prior to the 9/11attacks the CIA had no penetrations of the al-Qaeda inner circle.[28] The Defense Intelligence Agency did not fare any better.[29] This failure, in part, was a result of the difficult nature of the target. Information about al-Qaeda terrorist operations was not shared widely within the organization but rather held in confidence by bin Laden's trusted inner circle, a group with close bonds forged by kinship, wartime experience, and long-standing association.[30] As a result, the United States never obtained information that was sufficient for action against bin Laden.[31] Though the FBI did manage to collect some valuable information on Islamic radical activity in the United States,[32] it was confronted with similar difficulties in attempts to penetrate al-Qaeda and other terrorist groups operating inside the United States. Indeed, recruiting sources in radical fundamentalist communities within the United States may have been more difficult than recruiting abroad.[33]

Likewise, as the United States approached the decision to go to war with Iraq in 2003, it had little intelligence on Iraqi's nuclear, chemical, and biological weapons programs and apparently no human intelligence on Saddam Hussein's intentions[34] beyond that provided by members of the Iraqi National Congress, who were seeking the removal of Saddam Hussein. After 1998, the CIA had no dedicated unilateral sources in Iraq reporting on that country's nuclear, chemical, and biological programs. In fact, as of 2001, it had only a handful of Iraqi assets.[35] Perhaps of greater significance, Saddam Hussein's decision-making process was highly centralized, secretive, compartmentalized, and difficult to penetrate.[36] Saddam made "all key policy decisions," relying on a few close advisors and family members with little input from the bureaucracy, and usually acting quickly and decisively.[37] Such methods were apparently very effective in denying information to those outside Saddam's inner circle.[38] The result: Intelligence Community's judgments on Saddam Hussein's thinking and motivations were largely speculative[39] and thus vulnerable to manipulation.

On the other hand, while the Defense Intelligence Agency Human Intelligence Service had little success against al-Qaeda, according to the joint House-Senate committee report, it did enjoy some success in penetrating the Taliban in Afghanistan.[40]

The future ability to gather intelligence, however, may be even more clouded than the past. Today terrorists, drug dealers, those who traffic in human beings, and others, wishing to keep information secret, avoid using cell phones and discard them after they have been used. Some use hard-to-intercept digital or fiber-optic transmission systems. Many are gaining access to sophisticated encryption technologies.[41]

Deception also is commonly used to thwart access to information by collectors. An adversary, knowing when a photographic satellite is to pass overhead, may hide or camouflage equipment. Or he may assemble fake pieces of equipment to deceive collectors into thinking he has more equipment at that location than actually exists. Deception also can serve to frustrate the collection capabilities or covert efforts of an adversary. One example of such an effort occurred during World War II. In 1941 the Germans, in operation "NordPol"—North Pole—managed to catch and arrest allied intelligence agents working for British intelligence as saboteurs and in support of Dutch resistance. Using the agents' codes, the Germans were able to deceive British collectors. The British continued to send agents and supplies that were subsequently captured by the Germans. The operation, which largely thwarted British efforts, continued successfully for more than two years until 1944, when two agents escaped their captors.[42] Deception, for its success, frequently relies on playing on the attitudes, predispositions, biases, and preconceptions of the adversary. A classic example of one of the most successful efforts to deny accurate information to an adversary by deceiving collectors led to the infamous "bomber gap" of the 1950s discussed below.

Biases and Preconceptions

As a human enterprise, it is inescapable that intelligence collection processes are affected by the personal biases of those involved. This "mindset" problem, as Greg Treverton calls it,[43] is a significant obstacle to effective intelligence efforts. Bias is an inherent part of human observation and influences all human behavior. Until confronted with overwhelming evidence to the contrary, most human beings are predisposed to act in ways consistent with their current opinions and beliefs. They generally reject information that is inconsistent with their previous beliefs[44] or "squeeze" or alter the new information to fit their predispositions.[45] "Lack of imagination," a frequently heard criticism of the Intelligence Community since 9/11, is one effect of biases/preconceptions.[46]

Biases and preconceptions affect every aspect of intelligence collection, from tasking to processing to reporting. Indeed, policymakers and senior Intelligence Community officials are likely to seek information consonant with their beliefs about a given situation, to fail to seek information at odds with those beliefs, and to interpret information received in ways that reinforce their beliefs. For example, during the Cold War, American policymakers were eager to deter the Soviet Union from exploiting its conventional military superiority in Europe. They believed that the Soviet Union would be deterred from an attack on Western Europe if they could be convinced that any successful conventional attack would inevitably lead to the use of nuclear weapons. This was at the heart of the Western strategic concept of "flexible response" adopted by the North Atlantic Treaty Organization (NATO) in 1967. If the West were unable to contain and defeat an attack by Soviet conventional armed forces, the West would use tactical nuclear weapons before resorting to an all-out strategic attack on the USSR. However, since tactical nuclear weapons are incredibly destructive, the credibility of the concept was always in doubt. NATO was always confronted with the question: How do you save Western Europe from a Soviet attack without destroying it? Since the neutron bomb employed enhanced radiation while reducing the blast effect, the neutron bomb was seen as a partial answer to the question. Enemy forces could be eliminated without totally destroying Western Europe. As a result American policymakers assumed consciously or unconsciously that Soviet leaders thought that the neutron bomb increased the likelihood that the United States would respond with nuclear weapons in Europe in the event of a Soviet attack with conventional military forces, and little thought was given to tasking intelligence to ascertain exactly what Soviet leadership thought about the subject. The extrapolation that an adversary is likely to think and act like we would in similar circumstances, sometimes called "mirror imaging," can and does inhibit effective tasking.

Biases and predispositions also can affect adversely observation and subsequent reporting. The old adage that we see what we want to see and hear what we want to hear, though tempered among intelligence personnel by training and experience, is also inescapable. Reporting from the July 1955 Moscow air show illustrates this tendency. The Soviet air force had painted over the identifying numbers on a few of its "Bison" bombers and flew them over the reviewing stand several times. It is likely that American military and intelligence personnel observing the event were predisposed to believe the Soviet Union, engaged as it was in a strategic competition with the United States, was producing large numbers of strategic bombers. Thus it was easy to assume that the waves of bomber aircraft they observed represented a significant increase in Soviet strategic aircraft rather than a wily subterfuge. The result: a short but intense debate over the now infamous "Bomber Gap" between the USSR and the United States.[47]

Similarly, prior to the March 2003 War with Iraq, it was very likely that policymakers and intelligence officials were predisposed to believe reports from disaffected Iraqis that Saddam Hussein had weapons of mass destruction. U.S. officials had come to believe that Saddam had retained a substantial number of chemical weapons that he had produced prior to and during Iraq's war with Iran in the 1980s and that he was developing biological and nuclear weapons. Confirming information from dissident Iraqi groups, whether accurate or not, was consonant with those beliefs and given additional credibility since International Atomic Energy Agency inspections were not allowed for nearly four years prior to the war.[48] The fact that United Nations inspection teams, after reentering Iraq in November 2002 and using the best intelligence the United States and others could supply, could not find any weapons of mass destruction was not consonant with those beliefs and generally discounted.

Also largely discounted were International Atomic Energy Agency and Department of Energy views that the aluminum tubes Saddam had purchased were more likely for use as artillery shells than in centrifuges, as well as the revelation by Ambassador Joseph Wilson that information alleging that Iraq had purchased "yellowcake" from Niger could not be substantiated. U.S. officials apparently believed Iraq had renewed its efforts to develop nuclear weapons prior to 1991. Indeed, early in September 2002 President Bush declared that satellite photographs of new construction at Al Furat, the former Iraqi site for uranium enrichment by centrifuge, demonstrated that Iraq's nuclear bomb program has been resurrected. That same month both the United Kingdom and the United States released reports citing the reasons for concluding that Iraq was violating various weapons bans. Both reports mentioned the Iraqi purchase of aluminum tubes alleged to be intended for use in the enrichment of uranium. The UK report mentioned the "yellowcake." Yet both the International Atomic Energy Agency as well as the experts at the U.S. Department of Energy, which runs enrichment facilities, had already determined that the aluminum tubes were not likely to have been related to the manufacture of centrifuges for the enrichment of uranium. And both the International Atomic Energy Agency and Ambassador Joseph Wilson, who had been sent to Niger to investigate reports of Iraqi efforts to purchase "yellowcake," had determined that the information about Iraqi attempts to acquire yellowcake was based on forged documents.[49] Yet for the most part, U.S. officials chose to ignore such findings. They were not consonant with what they believed to be the case.

Credibility of Sources

Intelligence services collect information from a wide variety of individuals with an assortment of motives. In each case the problem is to insure that the information received is credible. Many of those individuals who provide intelligence are self-selected or "walk-ins." As noted above, they may be academics, businessmen and women, journalists, or tourists, motivated by patriotism and willing to share their knowledge of and experiences in other countries with the Intelligence Community. On the other hand, they could be unbalanced people, motivated by greed or seeking to break the monotony of their lives or defectors, motivated by ideology, or dissatisfied with their country's or another target country's policies or with their personal status or treatment. They may be members of another country's diplomatic corps, employees of international organizations, or foreign journalists similarly motivated.

In each of these cases, individuals come with their own predispositions, their own biases. Hence, their view of events is likely to be so colored. The task of the intelligence services is to sort the wheat from the chaff. Sometimes intelligence services are able to do so by examining that individual's track record of past reporting or by other corroborating information. If the information received from a particular individual has generally proved reliable in the past, if other information through human or technical means is supportive, then there is reason to attach a high level of credibility to the new information. In each case, however, intelligence officials are mindful that a foreign government or other foreign source may be, craftily and unknown to the individual, using the individual to pass on disinformation. This was a common practice of the Soviet Union during the Cold War, particularly with academics or journalists, who it was hoped would pass the information on to a larger audience.

Of even greater concern, among those willing to provide information to the intelligence services there are those individuals with their own agenda seeking to pass information, real or imagined, that will influence the actions of the recipient government. Among the more recent examples of this is the apparently fabricated information provided the United States by members of the Iraqi National Congress about Saddam Hussein's possession of weapons of mass destruction. Indeed, Iraqi National Congress leader Ahmad Chalabi is reported to have remarked that even if his information about Saddam Hussein's weapons was discredited, it had achieved its aim of persuading America to topple the dictator.[50]

There also are those who may be spies recruited by a foreign power or volunteer to become double agents.[51] One of the more well-known cases was that of Juan Pujol. Though Pujol, a Spanish citizen, was not in the employ of British intelligence at the time he offered to serve the German Abwehr (counterintelligence), it was not for lack of trying. Rabidly antifascist, he detested Nazi Germany. Through his wife, he had offered his services to British intelligence. But alas the British declined. Undaunted he decided to establish himself as a German agent before reapproaching the British to offer his services as a double agent. By then aware of his efforts, the British accepted his offer. Though many of his reports had significant errors, he managed to dupe the Germans. Indeed his reporting was so well received by the Germans that he was able to play a major role in the Allied invasion of France, helping to convince the Germans that Normandy was a feint and the Allies were going to launch a second invasion in the Pas de Calais region.

Focus on a Single Type of Intelligence or Source

In the absence of information, too often collectors are tempted to rely on a single type or source of intelligence. For example, in the waning days and weeks of 1941 there were many indicators of a possible Japanese attack on Pearl Harbor (see Chapter 3). However, concentrating on "what appeared to be the highest Japanese code and cipher system," Army and Navy cryptographers gave "low priority to the processing of traffic to and from Tokyo and its consulate in Hawaii." Had more of that information been made available to analysts and policymakers from such traffic, it might "have raised the degree of awareness that Oahu was a possible target of attack."[52]

Quality of Foreign Liaison

Intelligence agencies often augment their capabilities through cooperation with the intelligence and law enforcement agencies of foreign governments and nongovernmental organizations. These cooperative efforts provide critical advantages. They serve as "force multipliers," supplementing U.S. capabilities with those of other governments and nongovernmental entities. They frequently provide access to foreign agents with language skills, networks of contacts, and cultural backgrounds that enable them to operate more effectively in the targeted environment than U.S. intelligence agents. They are often very useful in augmenting American efforts in remote or hostile parts of the world where U.S. access is limited or where a foreign government has already been successful in penetrating the targeted state or group.[53] One of the better known liaison operations with a nongovernmental organization was the liaison between the U.S. Office of Naval Intelligence and Mafia groups for counterespionage efforts against the fascist government of Sicily during World War II.[54]

During the Cold War U.S. cooperation with foreign intelligence services spanned a spectrum of foreign policy and security concerns, from Soviet and Warsaw Pact political intentions and military capabilities to efforts to better understand political, economic, and military developments in other parts of the world. This policy of foreign interagency cooperation continued, and in some cases increased after the Cold War. For example, by the mid-1990s, as the threat of terrorism became more pronounced, U.S. intelligence officials recognized that unilateral CIA operations were not sufficient to penetrate and counter terrorist organizations.[55] As a partial remedy, the CIA and other Intelligence Community agencies,[56] with some success,[57] strengthened their liaison relationships with existing partners and forged new relationships to fight al-Qaeda and other terrorist groups.[58]

Despite the advantages of working with foreign intelligence organizations, there are factors that affect the results of that effort. First, success frequently depends on the willingness of other governments to work with the United States, not only in sharing information but also in undertaking tasks at the behest of the United States. Governments can be highly sensitive about sharing information with the United States—a problem even common with governments that have long been close partners. They may be reluctant to share intelligence information in order to protect sources and methods or because shared intelligence might implicate their citizens. Governments may also be reluctant to share information because they fear leaks of information revealing the role played by their intelligence services in assisting the United States could prove politically embarrassing.[59] The presidential commission on weapons of mass destruction noted that the inability to obtain information from foreign liaison services hampered Intelligence Community efforts to determine the exact nature of the threat from such weapons.[60]

Second, success at gaining timely information through cooperative efforts with foreign intelligence agencies may be hampered by the excessively bureaucratic nature of the foreign government itself or by constitutional or legal restrictions on their intelligence operations that governments themselves can do little about. For example, to guard against abuses of power, the German intelligence apparatus is deliberately fragmented complicating coordination and information sharing. Moreover, before 9/11 it was not illegal in Germany to be a member of a foreign terrorist organization or to raise funds for them.[61] Thus there was no legal constitutional authority for Germany to act against such individuals.

Third, some foreign services lack the resources to fully investigate and evaluate their own intelligence agents and officials. Thus, there is always the concern that operatives working for an adversary may have penetrated foreign intelligence services and thus can provide advance warning of U.S. efforts. Moreover, as the Cold War experience and recent examples have underscored, even those nations that do have sufficient resources to properly investigate and evaluate their intelligence agents have, on occasion, been successfully penetrated.

Fourth, whether the result of having been penetrated by operatives in the employment of another country or because of lax security procedures, information shared with some foreign intelligence services leaks out and is thus compromised.

Fifth, the same agent may be used by several foreign intelligence services with which you have a liaison relationship. Unless you are privileged to know the source of their information, it may seem that the information you are receiving is collaborated by several sources.

Finally, foreign governments have their own concerns. No foreign intelligence services come close to the size and complexity of the U.S. Intelligence Community. As a result, requests for assistance by U.S. agencies can easily overwhelm foreign intelligence services. If a foreign government does not share America's urgency about a particular issue, the time it is willing to devote to that issue may be restricted. It also may be reluctant to assign valuable but limited assets to the problem. Thus the quantity and/or quality of information received may be adversely affected. For example, prior to 9/11, several European governments were apparently indifferent to the threat posed by al-Qaeda. According to then Deputy National Security Advisor Steve Hadley, European support varied according to their perception of the threat. Likewise, the former chief of the Counterterrorism Center's bin Laden unit testified before Congress that European intelligence services had minimal interest in bin Laden and offered little assistance.[62] The problem, of course, can be further compounded when working with intelligence services with fewer resources than those of our European allies.

TECHNOLOGY

Technology has always played a role in the gathering of intelligence, particularly as an adjunct to human intelligence. For example, telescopes and later binoculars allowed observers to see at distances greater than with the human eye alone, balloons took men aloft to observe events not visible from the ground, photographic equipment allowed spies to record information available in secret files and so on. However, with the advent of the Cold War, technology became more important in U.S. intelligence collection efforts.

Technical advances allowed the Soviet Union to place listening devices, cameras, and even tiny sensors in many hidden locations. The listening device placed in a two-foot replica of the Great Seal of the United States that was presented to U.S. ambassador Averell Harriman in 1946 by Soviet school children was an early Cold War example of the use of technology to uncover secrets. The ambassador hung the seal in his office at his Spasso House residence in Moscow and presumably the hidden microphone yielded a wealth of classified information to Soviet listeners until it was discovered in 1952. Equally successful was the effort by Soviet technicians to implant a small sensor in IBM Selectric typewriters prior to delivery to the U.S. embassy in Moscow. Discovered in 1984, the implant allowed the Soviets to secretly capture all keystrokes typed on those IBM Selectric machines and transmit the information to a nearby listening post.[63]

Another well-known incident was the bugging of the new U.S. embassy in Moscow as it was being constructed in the 1980s. Thousands of cleverly designed bugging devices were placed everywhere by Soviet workers—inside walls and ceilings, foundations, even in the surrounding sewage network.[64] Perhaps equally significant was the bugging of the seventh floor conference room just down the hall from Secretary of State Madeleine Albright's office at the U.S. Department of State, discovered in the late 1990s.[65]

Less well known was the use of bugs to monitor lesser officials during their travels to the USSR and all Soviet satellite countries. Indeed U.S. government officials who traveled to the Soviet Union had to assume that the table they were seated at in a restaurant[66] or the room they stayed in was bugged—and that included Spasso House, the residence of the U.S. ambassador or embassy residences such as those occupied by the defense and other military attaches. Indeed, during a 1979 trip to the Soviet Union to ascertain Russian thinking on future strategic arms limitation talks, the author was unable to get appointments with anyone other than those at the Institute for USA and Canada Studies, despite having made requests months in advance to speak with researchers from the Institute of World Economy and International Relations, then headed by Nicolai Inozemtsev, a close advisor to then Soviet leader Leonid Brezhnev. In response, the author and his wife staged a "talk to the walls" in the Hotel Rossiya, located just opposite the Kremlin off of Red Square. Complaining that since he was only allowed to speak to Institute of USA and Canada Studies functionaries tasked to study and report on U.S. thinking, the information provided little insight into Soviet thinking and would therefore be immediately discounted in the United States. The next day he was granted lengthy interviews with Institute of World Economy and International Relations researchers. They had been listening.

A similar event occurred earlier on the same trip at the Orbis Hotel in Warsaw. The author's visa to the USSR had been delayed with the prospect of not arriving at all. Prior to departing for breakfast on the day before our scheduled departure for Moscow my wife and I spoke of the prospect of being forced to skip Moscow, visiting Krakow before continuing on our trip to other East European capitals. Upon our return from breakfast, sitting on the already made bed was a brochure on Krakow in Russian. They had been listening.

However, by the 1970s technology was advancing well beyond hidden microphones and cameras in hotel rooms. Advances in missile and space satellite technologies coupled with advances in photographic, sensor, imagery, and communications technologies frequently allowed the United States to locate everything from troop movements to submarines undersea[67] to Soviet strategic nuclear missiles. Advances in electronics, among other things, permitted the United States to listen in on communications, intercept electronic and data transmissions, and often ascertain the nature and even the specific capabilities of military and civilian hardware of potential adversaries.[68]

Similar technologies allowed the Russians in 1996 to identify, locate, and kill Chechen rebel leader Dzhokhar Dudaev. By matching Dudaev's "voice signature" to existing samples of his speech while he was using his satellite phone the Russians were able to locate him and then direct a precision-guided bomb to kill him.

As technological advance imposed on technological advance, technology has come to be viewed increasingly as a major, and perhaps, by many, the major solution in the intelligence game. Billions of dollars have been invested in intelligence technologies, sometimes at the expense of investments in other Intelligence Community efforts, including Human Intelligence.

Today, technology is used to gather intelligence from space, airborne and seaborne platforms, ground stations, and even from the office desktop via computer. Indeed, continued improvements in computing technology, coupled with the ever-expanding use of Internet search engines, provide states and terrorist groups new opportunities to acquire sensitive or secret information and have produced a new breed of intelligence collectors—the so-called cyber spies. According to reports, cyber spies have penetrated the networks of several governments, including purportedly secure computer networks in the United States, collecting "sensitive," if not classified information. Computer networks known to have been attacked by cyber spies include those in the Foreign, Economics, and Research and Development ministries and the Chancellor's office in Germany, government agencies in Taiwan,[69] and in the United States those of Lockheed Martin, Sandia National Laboratories, the Redstone Arsenal, home of the U.S. Army's Aviation and Missile Command, the National Aeronautics and Space Administration (NASA), and the World Bank. In one instance counterespionage efforts revealed that a Chinese group had acquired numerous aerospace documents with hundreds of detailed schematics describing propulsion systems, solar paneling, and fuel tanks for the Mars Reconnaissance Orbiter, the NASA probe launched in August.[70]

Nevertheless, technically acquired intelligence, though profoundly valuable, has always had limitations. Sometimes it simply isn't possible through technical means to gain needed intelligence. For example, during the Cold War, while the United States was often able to locate Soviet military forces, it was less successful in determining Soviet intentions.[71] Moreover, while technical capabilities frequently allowed the United States to see and listen, countertechnologies often limited their effectiveness.

Measure versus Countermeasure

The technological race is and always has been a race between measure and countermeasure. When one side gains an advantage through the development of some technology the other frequently employs technical countermeasures, deception, camouflage, or brainpower to reduce or eliminate that advantage. During World War II the Germans relied on a device called the Lorenz cipher to code high-level messages and the Enigma machine to code messages sent to their military units. Through Polish and British efforts the codes used by the Germans on their Enigma machines were broken. The information obtained was invaluable in the war effort.[72] Similarly, the United States was able to break codes encrypted by the Japanese "Purple" machine, leading to a major defeat for Japan's navy at Midway. The code name given to the intelligence derived from this code-breaking effort was "MAGIC." The Japanese did not find out that the United States had broken the codes of the Purple cipher machine until after the war.

Simple Countermeasures

Sometimes intelligence technologies can be thwarted by the simplest of methods. Balloons and later aircraft using human and photo-observation to gain tactical intelligence on the disposition of enemy forces were frequently thwarted by the use of smoke or camouflage. During World War I, the United States, on occasion, encoded messages in Native American languages to avoid interception by adversary intelligence services. Similarly, during World War II, the United States was able to successfully avoid Japanese efforts to tap into American wartime communications through the use of Navajo code talkers. The Japanese never broke the code.[73] Indeed, this method of encryption was so successful that it was employed again in the Korea and Vietnam conflicts.[74] During the war in Vietnam, the United States equipped their aircraft with technologies that enabled them to locate and attack North Vietnamese surface-to-air missile sites before they could launch their missiles by identifying their electronic signature. The North Vietnamese often responded by optically tracking approaching American aircraft, turning on their electronic tracking equipment only as the missile was launched and then shutting down their sites shortly thereafter. Thus they were able to make it more difficult for U.S. aircraft to successfully attack their missile sites or avoid their surface-to-air missiles.

As U.S. intelligence capabilities have become better known, states and non-state actors are employing a variety of techniques to thwart American efforts. Hiding equipment or using camouflage has been employed to deny information to imaging satellites. Alternatively, equipment or dummies can be amassed to deceive the adversary about the size or dispositions of one's forces. Limiting or eliminating communications or relying on landlines instead of open-air transmissions can deny useful information to signals intelligence efforts. Conversely, increasing the level of communications and/or altering the content can be used to deceive an adversary.

Technology versus Technology

Sometimes technical countermeasures are called on to defeat advancing intelligence technologies. Radar, designed to provide tactical intelligence on approaching enemy aircraft, ships, and missiles, has been countered by changes in the design of such weapon systems, incorporating new "stealth" technologies. However, "stealth" technologies are now becoming less effective due to algorithms used to process the data received by the radars, as well as the use of passive radar arrays and low-frequency radars.[75] As the ability to intercept communications, even conversations taking place inside guarded buildings, improved, countries frequently employed reasonably successful countermeasures. They monitored the wire lines through which messages were transmitted to detect wire tapping or replaced the wire with fiber-optic cable, which poses a significantly more complex problem to those attempting to intercept messages. They used electromagnetic noise generators to prevent adversaries from gaining information through the electromagnetic emanations of cipher machines or shielded equipment or entire rooms to protect both electronic and voice communication, thus allowing officials to engage in open discussions and operate communications equipment without fear of compromise.

As airborne and satellite surveillance capabilities improved, the countries developed mobile missiles that could move to locations hidden from the view of overhead satellites. Likewise by measuring the differences in emitted radiation, thermal-imaging technologies can provide intelligence on everything from an adversary's military forces to his operation of plutonium production plants. As a countermeasure, adversaries can use flares, or smokescreens of hot fragments, or special camouflage nets or thermal blankets that dissipate heat slowly to offset the advantages of thermal imaging.

Post-Cold War Challenges

In the wake of 9/11 and the intelligence failures associated with the 2003 war with Iraq, the deficiencies of technically gathered intelligence have again been highlighted. During the Cold War, Imagery Intelligence was excellent for locating fixed missile sites, air bases, surface ships, and significant military formations. Imagery Intelligence has been less helpful with post-Cold War period tasks such as locating weapons of mass destruction in Iraq and tracking transnational organized criminal groups or terrorists. Measurement and Signature Intelligence, through the use of optical, acoustic, or seismic sensors, can locate and identify such targets as aircraft, submarines, surface ships, and ground force hardware, and even identify seismic events such as nuclear explosions. Since terrorists seldom use aircraft, submarines, etc., Measurement and Signature Intelligence has been less helpful in the fight against terrorism and played a negligible role in Iraq.[76] Even Signals Intelligence—the interception of radio, telephone, and computer communications—which has historically been a primary source of good intelligence,[77] has been markedly less successful in the post-Cold War period. These deficiencies are largely a function of the changed nature of the threat, the sheer volume of communications, a failure of collection technologies to keep pace with the rapid pace of technological change, and adversaries who are getting better at denial[78] and deception.

Today's threats are more diffuse. In the world of the twentieth century, the actions of states, with their fixed government complexes and military installations, were our principal and arguably our only real security concerns. Serious twenty-first-century security threats come from diverse and highly mobile groups operating from anywhere on the globe.

Moreover, while the communications revolution has led to a blossoming of worldwide communications and an abundance of new opportunities for information collection in support of actionable intelligence, the very success of this revolution has complicated collection efforts. Lt. General Michael Hayden, former director of the National Security Agency, summed up the growing problem: "Forty years ago, there were 5,000 stand-alone computers, no fax machines and not one cellular phone. Today, there are over 180 million computers—most of them networked. There are roughly 14 million fax machines and 40 million cell phones, and those numbers continue to grow."[79]

Today, millions of people around the globe use these technologies to conduct daily personal and public business. Among these multitudes are organized crime groups and terrorists who also use these technologies to recruit new members, marshal resources, transfer funds, and coordinate their activities on a global scale.[80] This proliferation of communications further burdens attempts to develop computerized programs that can sift the massive amount of global communications for information that might be relevant to U.S. security concerns. As a result, a substantial amount of information that is collected never gets processed or exploited.

Lamentably, organized crime and terrorist groups also have access to many of the information processing technologies currently available to governments. Today's laptop computer is comparable to the computational power available to the entire Department of Defense in the mid-1960s. Terrorists can use this power to run widely available state-of-the-art encryption software.[81] Using less advanced technologies, they can embed messages into digital photographs and music chips. They can use "spread spectrum" radios that randomly switch their broadcasting and receiving signals, allowing terrorists to obscure their messages or make them invisible.[82] Testifying before Congress, then National Security Agency director Lt. General Hayden lamented the fact that terrorists now have access to the three-trillion-dollar-a-year communications industry.[83]

Of course, the Intelligence Community is not idle. It is identifying architectures and technologies to enable it to separate the wheat from the chaff. But the critical question is, "whether it is moving at a rate that exceeds what adversaries are doing to frustrate the upgrades."[84]

In its report to the President on the September 2001 terrorist attacks, 9/11 Commission members concluded: "The challenge of technology . . . is a daunting one. It is expensive, sometimes fails, and often can create problems as well as solve them."[85]

BUDGETS

A nation with worldwide interests must make commensurate investments if it is to acquire the information necessary to protect those interests. Following the Cold War, freed from decades of confrontation with the Soviet Union and the threat of nuclear war, many believed a new era of security would allow some national security expenditures to be shifted to support "higher priority" domestic programs. The so-called peace dividend led to cuts in national security expenditures. Though there were sizeable increases in the counterterrorist budgets in most agencies, those budget cuts reduced support to the U.S. National Foreign Intelligence Program (redesignated the National Intelligence Program in 2004) from fiscal years 1990 to 1996. From 1996 to 2000, except for some supplemental appropriations, the intelligence budget remained flat.[86]

These budget cuts compounded the difficulties faced by intelligence agencies just as the entire intelligence system needed to be revamped to address newly emerging threats. The existing system was primarily focused on countering a

Soviet strategic missile attack on the United States or a thrust into Western Europe. Costly but necessary investments were made in satellite-borne systems capable of monitoring Soviet military capabilities. However, emerging post-Cold War threats demanded, inter alia, resources to rebuild neglected human intelligence capabilities. Furthermore, policymakers demanded the Intelligence Community move into the digitized future to operate effectively in computer-to-computer communications environments and against modern communications systems. At the same time they demanded capabilities be maintained against older systems, spanning the radio spectrum from high-frequency to ultra-high and very high-frequency (line of sight) systems. Such demands placed additional pressures on the Intelligence Community's already limited fiscal resources.[87]

The 1990s budget cuts and the reliance on supplemental appropriations[88] reduced Intelligence Community capabilities, including reductions in operations personnel and facilities abroad,[89] fewer supporting efforts at home and abroad, and a decline of coverage and expertise as personnel were moved from crisis to crisis[90] as management attempted to respond to residual concerns left over from the Cold War and the newly emerging threats.

Budget cuts even had an adverse effect on America's counterterrorist efforts, despite the significant budget increases for counterterrorism programs during the post-Cold War period.[91] For example, the CIA's Directorate of Operations cut personnel deployed abroad and closed some facilities outside the United States, some in places conducive to collecting information on terrorism.

Also spending was limited in areas such as training and communications, which supported America's intelligence efforts.[92] George Tenet, former Director of Central Intelligence, in testimony before the 9/11 Commission complained that in 1997 when he became the Director "the infrastructure to recruit, train and sustain officers for our clandestine services . . . was in disarray." He further stated that in 1995, the year he became Deputy Director of Central Intelligence, there were only twenty-five new case officers graduating from the CIA's case officer training program—too few even to replace those who were retiring or resigning. The result: fewer case officers were available to recruit foreign spies and direct their intelligence production.[93]

Budget cuts also weakened the U.S. ability to protect its classified information and communications, directly or indirectly affecting its ability to collect intelligence. James Gosler, a former CIA official and National Security Agency visiting scientist, referring to the vulnerabilities of both hardware and software, notes that in the modern world technology development and production are global endeavors, with personnel from dozens of countries participating in the production of information technologies used by the U.S. and other governments. "Opportunities to clandestinely influence a component during its global path to birth are simply endless."[94] You can't trust software coding not produced in-house and even then software designed by expert programmers may behave "unpredictably under certain circumstances."[95] Similarly hardware produced offshore "could result in the intentional insertion of unknown vulnerabilities into vital pieces of equipment and result in the exploitation by a foreign government."[96] Indeed, in many cases it is reasonable to assume as Gosler suggests: "Today our adversaries develop our software, fabricate our microelectronics, assemble the components on our printed circuit boards, and remotely maintain our systems."[97] All of which increases the potential vulnerability and reliability of U.S. communications capabilities and thus threatens to undermine U.S. intelligence collection efforts.

A 1999 publication of the Computer and Telecommunications Board and National Research Council concluded there is inadequate funding for research in information security. In light of this finding, James Gosler's relatively recent contention, "There is no clear indication of a national investment strategy for information assurance,"[98] is even more troubling.

Throughout the Senate and House joint intelligence committee's inquiries into the pre-9/11 intelligence failures, Intelligence Community witnesses cited a lack of money and people as a primary reason for lack of intelligence on al-Qaeda.[99] For example, then Director of Central Intelligence Tenet told the committee that in earlier questioning before another committee of Congress he had been asked about budget shortfalls. He answered, "I'm short $900 million to $1 billion every year for the next five years." He further noted: ". . . we told that to everybody downtown for as long as anybody would listen and never got to first base. So you get what you pay for. . . . "[100]

Since 9/11 the situation has improved dramatically. Though the exact size of the intelligence budget remains secret, since 1998 the intelligence budget (excluding that for tactical military intelligence) has grown from around $15 billion to over $44 billion—an increase of about 140 percent in inflation-adjusted dollars.[101] This is a healthy trend that must be sustained. Every dollar used to deliver high-quality intelligence, given sound leadership, will have a direct effect on the quality of U.S. foreign policy, save American lives, and reduce the probability of costly, ill-conceived wars.

Part II

Analysis

Analysis translates raw collected information into finished intelligence and is the intermediate step between collection and exploitation. Part II examines the analysis processes and obstacles that confront those tasked to consolidate and analyze information obtained from the various collection methods.

The analysis of frequently incomplete and often obscure information gathered in the most difficult of circumstances is an extraordinarily complex task. In some respects the task of the analyst could be likened to a driver attempting to find an unknown location in heavy fog and mist. Landscapes are blurred. Signs along the way that might provide direction are often difficult to detect until perhaps the last minute. Even then they might be too obscure to provide useful information about what lies ahead. Even roadblocks may not be easily identifiable. And, if the road is to be traveled successfully, the uncertainty may demand a snail's pace with an arrival too late to make a difference.

Chapter 3 addresses the challenges Intelligence Community management faces in providing policymakers with timely, meaningful, and accurate analysis. These challenges include clarifying requirements, tasking, resource allocation, education and training, sharing and coordination, and stimulating critical thinking.

Chapter 4 outlines the principal tasks of analysts as well as major impediments to success: for example, too little or too much information, denial and deception, cognitive bias, "worst case" analysis, lack of strategic thinking, and politicization of analysis.

3

Analysis: Challenges of Management

> "Management by objectives works if you first think through your objectives."
>
> —Peter Drucker

It should come as no surprise that criticisms of U.S. intelligence effort in the wake of 9/11 and the run-up to the Iraqi war have focused heavily on intelligence analysis. Providing decision makers with timely and meaningful analysis is arguably the most demanding, yet most crucial, aspect of the entire intelligence effort. Analysis, however, has had a rocky past.

Following World War II, President Harry S. Truman, conscious of the need for the United States to be well informed on world happenings, set about creating a permanent peacetime intelligence apparatus. In September 1945 President Truman abolished the Office of Strategic Services[1] and within four months signed a Presidential Directive establishing the Central Intelligence Group and the position of Director of Central Intelligence. The Central Intelligence Group was to operate under the direction of the National Intelligence Authority. The following July Congress passed the National Security Act of 1947, which among other things, replaced the National Intelligence Authority and the Central Intelligence Group with the National Security Council and the Central Intelligence Agency. It was clearly the intent of Congress that the newly reorganized Intelligence Community not only provide timely "facts" on the capabilities and activities of foreign governments, foreign organizations, and foreign persons, but also undertake analyses of available information in order to provide policymakers with "estimates" of foreign "intentions." Nevertheless, since then the production of analytical products by the Intelligence Community has had a checkered existence.

Not all presidents, policymakers, or directors of Central Intelligence have been as committed to analysis as Congress had intended in 1947. Indeed, President Truman had an evident preference for "current intelligence." Rear Admiral Sidney Souers, the first Director of Central Intelligence, once remarked that what Truman wanted from his intelligence apparatus was for it "... to keep him personally well-informed of all that was going on in the outside world."[2] Rear Admiral Roscoe Hillenkoetter, the third Director of Central Intelligence, noticed a similar Truman emphasis on the Daily Summary at the expense of long-term analytical efforts.[3] Indeed, when summoned to Capitol Hill to explain why the CIA had failed to "predict" the North Korean attack on South Korea in June 1950, Hillenkoetter managed to convey to Congress not only that the current intelligence people on the very day of the attack put out a report containing indicators of an attack, but also the fact that his job, as the National Security Council had defined it, was to collect and disseminate, not to evaluate.[4] Admiral Stansfield Turner summed up Truman's approach to intelligence by noting: "... Truman wanted the CIA to provide him with a "newspaper" that gave him the facts without independent judgments...."[5] Truman was not the only President to emphasize current intelligence over longer-term analysis, but no President distrusted and despised the CIA more than Richard Nixon. He believed the Agency was staffed by a bunch of Ivy League Liberals. Indeed, when a CIA analysis concluded that "... it was highly unlikely that [the Soviets] will attempt within the period of the estimate to achieve a first strike capability," it has been reported that Henry Kissinger directed Director of Central Intelligence Richard Helms to remove the paragraph that speculated on Soviet intentions. This was, according to Stansfield Turner, a blunt way of informing Helms that in the Nixon administration, the CIA was to provide information only.[6] "The problem, according to Richard Helms, was that Nixon did not want 'an independent intelligence service,' but instead a CIA supportive of his policies."[7] As a result, "the national estimates function fell into comparative dispute and neglect."[8]

Likewise, several directors of Central Intelligence have been variously described with "disinterest in analysis" (Allen Dulles under Presidents Eisenhower and briefly Kennedy), "heart... not in analysis" (Richard Helms under Presidents Johnson and Nixon), and "... more interested in managing the covert action and espionage side of the CIA" (William Casey under President Ronald Reagan).[9]

In general it would be fair to conclude that over the decades since the creation of the post-World War II intelligence system, "analysis" has more often than not played second fiddle to collection, as has analysis of current intelligence vis-à-vis long-term estimates.[10]

ORGANIZATION

While preliminary assessments are undertaken by the various collecting agencies as they process gathered intelligence, the United States has three principal agencies engaged in providing government officials with comprehensive analysis of intelligence garnered from all sources—the CIA, Defense Intelligence Agency, and the Department of State's Bureau of Intelligence and Research.

The CIA provides analyses of intelligence about foreign policy and national security issues to national policymakers, defense planners, law enforcement officials, and the military services, while the Defense Intelligence Agency's principal task is to provide comprehensive all-source analyses of foreign military intelligence to the military services, defense and national security policymakers, and defense planners. The primary mission of the Department of State's Bureau of Intelligence and Research is to support U.S. diplomatic efforts.

All three agencies produce numerous oral briefings and written reports, which may be short—one page or less—or lengthy studies. These reports may involve current intelligence of immediate importance to policymakers or long-range assessments. All three agencies also participate in the drafting and production of National Intelligence Estimates, which reflect the collective judgments of the Intelligence Community.

During periods of international crises or when intelligence support is critical to high-level negotiations, Interagency Task Forces are often created to provide necessary intelligence support. Under such circumstances the Director of National Intelligence directs a particular agency to serve as executive agent responsible for overall management of the effort and the final product. Task forces frequently include members from all three all-source analysis organizations as well as experts from other intelligence organizations. They produce and disseminate situation reports, daily intelligence updates, and other products to appropriate members of the policymaking community.

Should an international crisis involve or be likely to involve the use of U.S. military forces, the Director of National Intelligence would establish an Intelligence Task Force dedicated to providing round-the-clock intelligence support to operational and combatant commanders. In cases of lesser involvement of the U.S. military, the Director for Intelligence in the office of the Joint Chiefs of Staff establishes a Working Group. These task forces and working groups are usually composed of analysts and other experts from the Defense Intelligence Agency, the military services, and other interested agencies throughout the Intelligence Community.[11]

MANAGEMENT

Of course successful analyses depend in the first instance on effective management not just from within the Intelligence Community, but also by the policymakers themselves. Indeed management of analysis begins with the users—the White House, other executive department policymakers, and Congress. It also includes agency heads (the directors of the CIA and the Defense Intelligence Agency), heads of analytical components such as the Assistant Secretary of State for

Intelligence and Research, the head of the Defense Intelligence Agency's Directorate of Analysis, and the head of CIA's Directorate of Intelligence, as well as of the various supporting offices that conduct analysis (e.g., the CIA Offices of Terrorism Analysis or Russian and European Analysis). It falls to the White House and other senior policymakers, including Congress, to communicate to the Intelligence Community their specific analytical needs and to manage the overall intelligence product by identifying shortfalls in analysis, including any need for additional clarification or greater detail. It also falls to these senior officials to provide feedback on whether the specific products produced by the Intelligence Community are providing them with the information they require. Managers within the Intelligence Community's analytical agencies must then clarify requirements, set priorities for their analysts, assess overall workloads, assign analysts specific tasks, identify resource shortfalls, insure that their analysts are adequately trained to deal with the tasks assigned, see to it that their analysts have access to critical information, coordinate their agencies analytical activities with those of other agencies, and perhaps above all, stimulate critical thinking. In the absence of effective management, available resources are not likely to be deployed in an efficient and effective manner.

Identifying Requirements and Prioritizing Tasks

As with collection, requirements drive the analytical effort. The intelligence analyst must have a clear understanding of the needs of the policymaker—for example, what information is needed, by whom, how soon, in what form, and to what purposes. In other words, the problem needs to be well framed if the analyst is to have any hope of providing timely responses to decision maker needs.

Intelligence requirements and priorities identified by policymakers in formal U.S. policy documents, which tend to be expressions of longer-term areas or issues of importance or interest,[12] are not necessarily the same as policymaker needs on any specific day, week, or month. Likewise intelligence needs and priorities identified for the collection agencies may not always be the same as those for the analytical community. An immediate crisis or pending policy decision may demand analysis of existing data and may take priority over longer-term requirements. It therefore falls to policymakers to make such requirements and priorities known to the Intelligence Community. For example, if the information requested about the economy of country "X" is in support of an upcoming presidential visit to that country, then the analyst knows the time available to him for analysis. He also knows that the kind of detailed, intricate examination that might have been required during the Cold War to support an analysis of the ability of the Soviet Union's economy to undergird a massive effort to develop a ballistic missile defense system is not required. However, he still would need to know more about what information is required and for what purposes. Is the information requested to be used to provide the President and/or his staff with some general knowledge about the overall economy of Country X? Or, for example, is it to provide a basis for understanding whether the country in question has the ability to effectively utilize economic assistance that might be contemplated to stimulate economic growth within some specified time frame? In other words, does the President need a snapshot in time or an understanding of potential future conditions? In the latter case, the analyst might have to examine such complex questions as the ability of the industrial infrastructure and labor force to take advantage of additional economic assistance, including an examination of such issues as the pace of innovation, the prospects for technological advance, and so forth.

In the absence of unambiguous guidance from policymakers, which is seldom forthcoming, it falls to agency managers,based on their interaction with policymakers and their best understanding of both the short- and longer-term needs of decision makers, to clarify requirements, align priorities, provide analysts with initial guidance, and issue any necessary subsequent clarifications. Agency managers then can further refine the process by encouraging analyst–policymaker dialogue.

The problem is compounded, however, by the existence of multiple policymakers at a variety of levels and by the need to balance the pressing demands of policymakers' short-term requirements against the longer-term requirements spelled out in policy documents. In an environment where there are never enough analysts to meet the requirements of all policymakers all the time, inevitably questions arise as to whose needs and what needs take priority. While it may be perfectly clear to the Intelligence Community, for example, that the needs of the President take priority over those of other policymakers, which Cabinet official's requirements should take precedence? And do their short-term requirements always take precedence over the longer-term ones? What about the needs of Congress? Intelligence agencies are part of the executive branch and exist, in large part, to serve the needs of that branch of government. However, Congress, as policymaker, is increasingly a consumer of intelligence. Congress makes policy through legislation and is constitutionally the ultimate decider on war and peace. It also is the Intelligence Community's bill payer.[13] Thus agency managers face the daunting daily task of deciding whose needs take precedence and therefore what tasks should be addressed by their analysts and when.

Allocating Resources

Once requirements and priorities for analysis have been set, agency managers assess existing workloads, allocate agency resources, and identify resource shortfalls. This is not as easy as first meets the eye. Anyone involved in management knows that when additional requirements appear on top of old, the first cry of the rank and file is for additional personnel resources and/or funds to meet the additional demands. Yet improvements in efficiency may be a better answer than additional personnel or funds, both of which will require time to acquire and place additional demands on management. For example, greater clarity of needs and priorities can help analysts better define their tasks. Improved technologies for the quick sharing of information can lead to greater access to information. And both are very likely to reduce "tasking to response time" and thus free up resources for other tasks. Likewise, close coordination with collectors and with other intelligence agencies involved in all-source analysis can result in increased efficiencies. The former affords analysts an opportunity to better understand the strengths and weaknesses of the various collection efforts and thus reduce or eliminate unnecessary speculation about the quality or utility of information received. The latter permits analysts to supplement their own information with that available to other analysts, as well as to test their preliminary judgments against those of others.

There are, however, times when additional personnel, equipment, or funding are called for. Once shortfalls have been identified and articulated to senior decision makers in the affected agency, they have a responsibility to address those shortfalls, if it is within their means to do so. If shortfalls cannot be addressed within the agency through a reallocation of resources and these shortfalls will significantly affect the analysis of critical intelligence, agency heads have a responsibility to bring these issues to the attention of the nation's senior executive, the President, who then must chose either to remedy the shortfalls or accept the risks to the foreign policy interests and security of the nation inherent in failing to do so.

Education, Training, Access, and Coordination

With worldwide interests and the increasing wide array of challenges that confront U.S. policymakers, today's intelligence managers confront the daunting task of ensuring that they have personnel adequately trained to address current and future tasks. Whether it is ethnic strife, drug or human trafficking, the illicit trade in biological, chemical, and radiological materials and know-how, the development of nuclear weapons by such states as North Korea and Iran, or the activities of terrorist organizations like al-Qaeda, the Intelligence Community must be prepared to provide decision makers with timely intelligence, sometimes on a moment's notice.

This requires a cadre of technically, linguistically, and culturally educated and trained specialists who are well versed in their functional, regional, or country specialty and capable of intense and detailed analysis. It also requires a cadre of analysts who know how the Intelligence Community works—where critical information can be found, how to access it, the strengths and limitations of the various collection efforts, etc. and who can coordinate their efforts with collectors, other analysts, and with the policy community in order to produce a quality product that meets the needs of decision makers. Here managers play a major role in making sure initial and follow-on training cover all aspects of the intelligence effort. They can also work closely with analysts to insure that analysts have access to needed information, stay closely connected with intelligence collectors, regularly interact with analysts from other agencies and, where and when possible, stay in contact with those policymakers whose tasks they are attending.

Imagination

Finally, effective analysis requires people capable of thinking critically and imaginatively in an environment that is all too frequently characterized by fragmented data and plagued by conventional wisdoms. Here managers also play an important role. It is easy, of course, to say to an analyst that he or she needs to think critically and imaginatively. It is much more difficult to demonstrate what is meant by asking critical questions that challenge conventional wisdoms. However, by so doing managers demonstrate that pat answers reflecting conventional wisdoms are only welcome if supported by careful analysis of a variety of possibilities.

CHALLENGES OF MANAGEMENT

Clarifying Requirements and Setting Priorities

In many respects analysis is tormented by the same absence of clarity of requirements and priorities that characterizes the collection effort and for many of the same reasons. A failure of strategic vision in an increasingly complex world leaves policymakers with only a vague and disjointed sense of what kinds of information and analyses are needed. The pressure of events drives policymakers to focus on near-term issues and to favor current intelligence and analysis of contemporary issues over in-depth analysis of longer-term strategic issues. As one observer put it: "We need to accept the fact that this country does not have an actionable national security policy that the Intelligence Community can use to *program* [emphasis added] analytic and collection resources."[14]

However, another factor—technology—unwittingly has intervened. Today, as a result of advances in communications technologies, policymakers are exposed to a vast amount of information that helps shape their views.

Sherman Kent, widely recognized as the single most influential contributor to the analytic doctrine and intelligence tradecraft, noted in a 1968 article in *Studies in Intelligence:*

> There are a number of things about policy-making which the professional Intelligence officer will not want to hear. For example, not all policy-makers can be guaranteed to be free of policy predilections prior to the time they begin to be exposed to the product of the intelligence calling. Indeed, there are some policy-makers who could not pass a rudimentary test on the "facts of the matter" but who have the strongest views on what the policy should be and how to put it into effect.[15]

Perhaps Kent's commentary provides some insight into why, for example, the administration of President George W. Bush did not call for a National Intelligence Estimate of Iraqi weapons of mass destruction prior to the invasion of Iraq in March 2003.[16] During the Cold War if a policymaker wanted to know what was happening in the Kremlin, or in Hungary during and after the revolution, or in

Czechoslovakia during and after the Prague spring, or for that matter anywhere in the communist world, and perhaps to a lesser extent in any number of foreign nations, he or she was almost completely reliant on the Intelligence Community for answers. There was no global mass media to provide instant coverage of world events, no World Wide Web with its massive amount of data, no Intelink[17] with intelligence reporting available at the click of a mouse, no e-mail, and only a few fax machines operating mostly near the end of the Cold War.

Today analysis produced by intelligence experts competes with a wide variety of sources of information available to policymakers—information that, for whatever its accuracy, tends to shape policymaker views on many of the issues he or she confronts. In today's world it is almost a given that policy-level consumers of intelligence are "well informed in his or her area of interest and not dependent on an intelligence analyst for a continuing stream of routine, updating information."[18] This too often results in a perceived lack of need on the part of the policymaker for additional information and analysis from the Intelligence Community.

On the other hand, sometimes there is simply a failure of organizational leadership within the Intelligence Community itself that results in an absence of clarity on requirements and priorities. As was noted in Chapter 2, following the August 1998 bombings of two U.S. embassies in East Africa, the Director of Central Intelligence elevated the threat posed by Osama bin Laden to the highest priority. Within a few months he further raised the status by declaring: "We are at war . . . [and} no resources or people [should be] spared in this effort." The decision was announced in writing in December 1998 and appeared in a memorandum from the Director to CIA senior managers. But the Intelligence Community as a whole had only limited awareness of the decision. Even within the CIA, whose senior managers were addressees on the Director's decisional memorandum, resources were not marshaled effectively to deal with the threat posed by bin Laden and the al-Qaeda organization.[19]

The joint House-Senate intelligence committee's report on 9/11 concluded that this failure to communicate a critical change in priorities to the broader Intelligence Community was "a relatively direct consequence of the limited authority of the DCI [Director of Central Intelligence] over major portions of the Intelligence Community"[20] and a reflection of an "absence of authoritative leadership"[21] within the Community. Nevertheless, a prima facie case can be made that it also was a failure of the personnel leadership of the Director of Central Intelligence, both as the nation's senior intelligence official and in his capacity as Director of the Central Intelligence Agency. As the nation's senior intelligence official, he had a responsibility to follow through on a memorandum of such critical importance to make sure that it had been both received and well understood by the major players in other intelligence agencies. In his role as Director of the CIA he had a responsibility to insure his staff understood the full ramifications of the memo. It also was a failure of those managers who did receive or were aware of the decision of the Director of Central Intelligence to insure that all elements under their direction were well informed of his priorities. The absence of personal leadership not only limited the Intelligence Community's ability to identify and coordinate collection efforts, but also its ability to channel and coordinate its analytical efforts toward this emerging high priority threat.

Personnel Resources, Training, and Experience

From a policymaker's perspective, ideally the Intelligence Community would be staffed so that on any given day, someone within the Community would be able to answer, with some significant degree of expertise, a specific question about a specific issue or country. The ability to do that is sometimes called "global coverage."[22] This, of course, has never been the case. To be sure, there are days when the pressure of policymaker requirements is less demanding on resources. Former Deputy Assistant Secretary of State for Intelligence Mark Lowenthal has noted: "There never are complete lulls," and "there is no reserve analytical capability."[23]

An insufficient number of personnel to meet analytical demands has been a perennial Intelligence Community problem—a problem exacerbated by the budget cuts of the 1990s. In an article published in 1997 in the CIA's in-house *Studies in Intelligence*, intelligence official Russ Travers contended: "Generally speaking, fewer analysts have less time to read more traffic and still fewer can keep up with their part of an increasingly complicated world; analysts have little opportunity for reflection, much less time for research."[24] He further argued that an underinvestment in analysts has left the analytical base dangerously thin.[25] The joint House-Senate select committee on intelligence noted in their examination of failures leading to the attacks on 9/11 that lack of analytical personnel was one of the factors that limited the effectiveness of efforts designed to uncover the terrorist plots,[26]

Insufficient personnel to cover assigned tasks levies a heavy burden on managers attempting to set priorities and allocate resources, It also renders nearly impossible attempts to balance tasking between the ever pressing demands by policymakers to meet their immediate needs and the requirement to insure that issues associated with long-term strategic concerns do not go uncovered. Indeed, one of the ways priorities are set is in response to crises. Danish humorist Robert Storm Petersen is reported to have remarked that "a crisis is a situation where nobody knows what it is that they have to do in a hurry." It is, of course, precisely the absence of a clear understanding of the situation and the presumption of a need to act quickly that drives the urgency of a situation and affects intelligence priorities. Crisis-driven priorities represent the ultimate victory not only of current over longer-range intelligence,[27] but also of tactical considerations over strategic. As a consequence, in the period preceding the 9/11 attacks, the Intelligence Community was far more oriented toward tactical analysis of al-Qaeda and support of its operations against al-Qaeda than on the strategic analysis needed to develop a broader understanding of the threat and the organization. No National

Intelligence Estimate was produced on al-Qaeda's threat to the U.S. Analyses aimed at identifying the scope and nature of threat posed by al-Qaeda, both internationally and domestically, were inadequate. An August 2001 CIA Inspector General report noted that analysts assigned to the Counterterrorism Center only had time to focus on crises or short-term demands, lacking "the time to spot trends or knot together the threads from the flood of information." Similarly, the FBI was performing little, if any strategic analysis. The Chief of the FBI's National Security Intelligence Section testified before Congress that the FBI had "no analysts" dedicated to strategic analysis prior to September 11. In fact, as of that date, the FBI had only one strategic analyst working on al-Qaeda issues.[28]

Reflecting similar concerns as the joint House-Senate committee on 9/11, the President's Commission on Weapons of Mass Destruction, while underscoring the need for strategic collection and analyses, concluded: "The Intelligence community we have today is buried beneath an avalanche of demands for "current intelligence"—the pressing need to meet the tactical requirements of the day."[29] The decline in the U.S. Intelligence Community's commitment to strategic analysis, according to Douglas MacEachin, former CIA Deputy Director for Intelligence, is one of the Intelligence Community's fundamental problems.[30]

However, lack of analysts is not the only personnel issue the Intelligence Community confronts. Education, training, and experience are often thought of as partial "offsets" to the lack of personnel, since well-educated, trained, and experienced analysts can often deal with a problem in the fraction of the time it might take a new entry into the analytical workforce. Unfortunately, these areas also suffer shortcomings.

Education and training, of course, are very important to success in business, industry, and government, but they are especially problematic for the Intelligence Community. In an environment of scarce personnel resources, questions like whom do you train, how long, how often, for what current and future tasks, and what do you leave undone while they are in the training process must be addressed. Clearly new hires come with a basic education, but must be provided the skills essential to the analytical tradecraft. Initial training also should undoubtedly include an understanding of their own organization, its values, standards, and expectations, where they fit within their organization, and where their organization fits in the overall scheme of things. New analysts should also be provided with a basic understanding of how the Intelligence Community is organized and how it functions, including an understanding of the various intelligence collection resources, their capabilities and limitations, how collected material is accessed, and the appropriate relationships between collectors, analysts, and policymakers.

What about follow-on education and training? How much is needed, on what issues? Should an analyst be sent off for additional education on the history, culture, traditions, attitudes, and beliefs of the peoples in the countries or regions for which he or she has responsibility, or for additional language training, or perhaps for additional education to deepen his or her understanding of his or her functional area of responsibility? Or, should any additional education and training focus on broadening an analyst's understanding of the wider set of issues confronting the Intelligence Community? The former would assist in developing specialists with keener insights and a sharper understanding of the complexities of given sets of issues. The later would result in the development of "generalists" with a better understanding of just how his or her work at a given time fits in with work done elsewhere, both inside and outside of the Intelligence Community, and how the analyst's work meets the needs of the policymaking community. It also would be sound preparation for any management tasks likely to befall the analyst as his or her career develops.

Adding further complexity is the problem of determining what kind of education and training will be necessary to meet future needs. How prescient would managers have had to have been even just a decade ago to foresee the need for a significant increase in the number of Afghanistan savvy analysts, with Afghanistan's mix of Pashtuns, Tajiks, Hazaras, Uzbeks, and a handful of other cultures and their 30-plus spoken languages and dialects?—or for analysts knowledgeable about Iraq and its competing ethnic and religious groups?—or for that matter a vast increase in Islamists and Arabists, both necessary if the United States is to have any hope of understanding the passions of Islamic fundamentalism and Arab nationalism?

And how about managers? Those who manage Intelligence Community assets below the level of political appointees are frequently selected from within the Intelligence Community. However, a highly skilled analyst does not necessarily make an effective manager. Most assuredly any manager on the analytical side of the Intelligence Community must understand well the analytical skills required. Beyond that, however, there are sets of management tools and interpersonal skills that are essential if he/she is to be effective. Providing Intelligence Community executives with such skill sets surely warrants a considerable amount of attention if the efficient and effective use of Community resources is to be the norm.

Commenting on the education and training within the Intelligence Community, Lowenthal contends that neither the initial training an analyst receives nor that which is provided mid-career is adequate. According to Lowenthal, in their initial training analysts are trained in the basic skills they will need, some of which goes fairly well; some does not. Unfortunately analysts are trained in "stovepipes," that is, within their own analytical units, The net result is that at the very outset of their career analysts come away thinking more about their home agency than about the broader intelligence community. A second major problem with initial training, according to Lowenthal, is that analysts fail to come away with a good understanding about what happens during the collection phase. "Even senior analysts exhibit a surprising amount of ignorance about what happens in collection as a whole or in specific collection disciplines." In a further indictment of Intelligence Community training he notes that mid-career training isn't as coherent as initial training. Whether an analyst will receive additional training frequently depends on the initiative of the analyst and on the analyst's supervisor's willingness to allow an analyst to go "off line." Again unfortunately, a supervisor's instinct is to keep as many analysts on hand as possible, especially during stressful and demanding periods.[31]

In January 2002 the FBI completed an internal study and found that 66 percent of the FBI's 1200 "Intelligence Research Specialists" (i.e., analysts) were unqualified—a problem compounded by the lack of training. The Chief of the FBI's National Security Intelligence Section in testimony before Congress said that while training was available on an ad hoc basis, "there was no standardized training regime other than a two-week basic course. . . . " He further noted that while the development of a standardized curriculum, linked to job skills, and career advancement was being planned, "it was never implemented."[32]

Echoing similar concerns, former National Security Agency Director and Assistant Chief of Staff for Army Intelligence William Odom in testimony to Congress had this to say:

> While the Intelligence Community's system of education and training is extensive, diverse, specialized—and fragmented . . . it lacks three key elements. First, nowhere is a common doctrinal understanding of intelligence functions and processes documented and taught to all Intelligence Community management and executive leadership personnel. Second, the teaching of Community-wide resource management has been generally neglected. Third, there is no educational emphasis on senior executive leadership and staff training.[33]

Experience, the other "force multiplier" also seems to be a commodity increasingly in short supply. As important as formal education and training are in providing a framework for competent analysis, no amount of training can replace the knowledge that comes from dealing with a specific set of issues, a country, or region on a daily basis over time. Unfortunately retirements and turnovers have taken their toll on the level of experience within the Intelligence Community. While the Intelligence Community has begun to beef up its rolls, the last big buildup of personnel in the Intelligence Community occurred in the early to mid-1980s during the Reagan administration. Many people hired during that period and before have reached retirement age and are now leaving the intelligence services.[34]

The result has been a decline in expertise. According to former CIA Deputy Director of Intelligence Jami Miscik, 40 percent of the analysts in the directorate of intelligence had worked for only one Director of Central Intelligence George Tenet, who resigned after seven years.[35] The overall average length of experience in the CIA is only eight years. The problem is worse elsewhere. A senior supervisor at the Counterterrorist Center testified before the joint House-Senate inquiry into the 9/11 failures that the Center did not have enough analysts with sufficient experience to produce sophisticated in-depth analysis in the quantities needed. Before 9/11, analysts at the Center had but three years experience on average.[36]

A former counterterrorism analyst at Defense Intelligence Agency noted that one of the consequences of the shortfall in experience and knowledge is the inability to place current intelligence reporting in the context of historical perspectives. For example, in the period leading up to the 1998 East Africa bombings and the

2000 attack against the *USS Cole* in Yemen, analysts made at least two serious errors. First, nearly across the board, terrorism analysts incorrectly assessed that a terrorist group would not conduct an attack in an area where it was able to operate with relative ease. Secondly, there apparently was a reluctance to correctly assess and evaluate the nature of cooperation between Islamic extremist groups. Both errors occurred despite more than a decade of credible reporting to the contrary.[37]

The combined effects of shortfalls in personnel, training, and experience have played a deadly roll in Intelligence Community failures in recent years. The joint House-Senate committee report on 9/11 concluded:

> Prior to September 11, the Intelligence Community's understanding of al-Qa'ida [*sic*] was hampered by insufficient analytic focus and quality, particularly in terms of strategic analysis. . . . The quality of counterterrorism analysis was inconsistent, and many analysts were inexperienced, unqualified, under-trained, and without access to critical information. As a result, there was a dearth of creative, aggressive analysis targeting Bin Ladin and a persistent inability to comprehend the collective significance of individual pieces of intelligence.[38]

Access, Sharing, and Coordination

Successful analysis depends highly on access to information relevant to the assigned tasks. However, access to information, its sharing among analysts or other intelligence agencies, and the willingness and ability to coordinate available information within the Intelligence Community have been perennial problems. Indeed, the greatest strategic intelligence failure in U.S. history was the case of the Japanese attack on U.S. military bases on the Island of Oahu, Hawaii, in 1941. Many factors contributed to that failure, among which were the success of Japanese deception efforts, the corresponding inability of the United States to collect information concerning Japanese intentions, and failures of analysis (addressed in Chapter 4).[39] Nevertheless, failure to share available intelligence played a significant role, see Boxes.

What the United States Knew from Intercepts of Japanese Messages

On September 24, 1941, Japan requested its consulate in Honolulu to report on vessels in Pearl Harbor using a grid system. It also requested reports on warships and aircraft at anchor, tied up at wharves, buoys, or docks and when two or more vessels were moored along the same wharf.

On November 15 Japan instructed its Honolulu consulate, that since relations with the United States are most critical, to make the "ships in harbor report" irregular, but at a rate of twice a week.

On November 19 Japan sent a message anticipating that relations with the United States might well reach a breaking point. If that occurred, Japanese offices abroad would receive the message "HIGASHI NO KAZE AME," or "East Wind Rain." Upon receipt, recipients were to destroy all code papers—surely a signal that war was on the horizon.

On November 22 Japan informed its Ambassador in Washington that U.S.–Japanese negotiations had to settle by November 29 because "after that things are going automatically to happen."

On December 1 Japan had changed ship call signs of the Imperial Navy, only one month after the previous change had been made. This change broke with the standard Japanese practice of changing ship call signs every six months.

On December 2 Japan ordered its embassies and consulates in Washington, London, and in several other locations to destroy all but the most important codes, ciphers, and classified documents.

Japanese aircraft carriers were out of port and their location was unknown and the United States had lost track of their submarines.

See Richelson, *A Century of Spies*, 118–119 and Harold P. Ford, "The Primary Purpose of National Estimating," at www.au.af.mil/au/awc/awcgate/nic/purpose_of_estimating.pdf, 69–70.

What the United States Knew from Other Intelligence Sources

Japan had paid particular attention to the successful November 1940 British aircraft carrier-based aerial attack with torpedo bombs on the Italian fleet located in the Harbor at Taranto, Italy, and that there had been unconfirmed reports that Japan was practicing simulated aerial torpedo bomb attacks against ships in harbor.

U.S. Ambassador to Japan Joseph Grew had reported in January that the Peruvian minister had learned "from many sources" that in the event of trouble with the United States, Japan "intended to make a surprise attack against Pearl Harbor with all their strength and emphasizing all their equipment."

Japanese agents had been reporting in detail on local U.S. military installations at Pearl Harbor, Clark Field in the Philippines, and elsewhere. And by December 5 the United States knew that Japan had instructed its consulate in Hawaii on November 28 to report upon the entrance and departure of capital ships and the length of time they remained at anchor.

See Ford, "The Primary Purpose of National Estimating," 70.

A wealth of information was available to U.S. intelligence before Japan attacked Pearl Harbor. But it was scattered around the many intelligence entities. Much of it was "never shared, brought together, and assessed." Thus it has been argued, "Tragedy ensued because there was no mechanism to collect and cooperatively examine every scrap of pertinent all-source intelligence."[40]

The terrorist attacks of September 11, 2001, though in many ways just as shocking to America, certainly were not of the same scale or magnitude as the Japanese December 7, 1941, attack. On the other hand, the war in Iraq has not had the shock effect of either the Pearl Harbor or 9/11 attacks, but has resulted in U.S. and coalition casualties that have been significantly higher than either of the other two events. The one thing that Pearl Harbor, the attacks of 9/11, and the war in Iraq have in common is that they each represent major intelligence failures and that those failures can be linked at least in part, often in large measure, to a failure to share information and coordinate intelligence efforts.

The joint House-Senate committee report on the terrorist attacks of September 11, 2001, noted:

> Even after the first World Trade Center attack in 1993, the Millennium plot, and attacks against U.S. embassies in East Africa in 1998 revealed that global Islamic extremists were capable of reaching into the United States, there was little sustained effort by the FBI, NSA [National Security Agency], and CIA to work together to collect and share information about contacts between foreign persons in the United States and those abroad.[41]

The 9/11 Commission Report was more pointed as it summed up reasons the United States missed opportunities to thwart the attacks of 9/11: "Information was not shared. . . . Analysis was not pooled."[42]

Similarly the President's Commission on Weapons of Mass Destruction reported that its study of intelligence failures that led up to the 2003 war with Iraq "highlighted a familiar challenge; that of ensuring effective sharing of information." The Commission went on to note:

> In the Iraq case, the information sharing problem manifested itself in three specific ways: intelligence was not passed (1) from collectors to the analysts; (2) from analysts to the collectors; and (3) from foreign liaison services to the Intelligence Community.[43]

Although there is evidence that this situation is improving,[44] nevertheless, it remains a serious management problem. Access to and the sharing and coordination of intelligence are affected by a number of factors.

First and foremost among these factors is the need to protect information from unauthorized disclosure. Information about what intelligence the United States has collected, how it has collected it and from whom—even that it has the ability to collect certain kinds of information—is among its most highly classified secrets. An adversary may know that you have spy satellites, listening posts, reconnaissance aircraft, etc., but he may not know what the focus of your efforts are or how effective they are—what detail they can see, what they can hear, what they can measure. Such information might well aid them in the development of effective countermeasures. Moreover, the very success of the clandestine services to gather intelligence from human sources depends on the ability of the Intelligence Community to recruit sources. Should information be revealed that could somehow be linked to specific sources, the number of individuals willing to serve as clandestine intelligence agents for the United States would be greatly limited.

As a result, since it is often difficult to separate content from sources and methods, it has been a long-standing Intelligence Community practice to narrowly limit disclosures of intelligence information in order to protect its sources and methods. Information within the Intelligence Community is classified according to the standards set by the U.S. classification system. The lowest level of classification is Confidential, followed by Secret, then Top Secret. The level of classification depends on the level of potential damage its unauthorized disclosure might cause to U.S. national security.[45] For example, information labeled CONFIDENTIAL is information whose unauthorized disclosure "could be expected to cause damage to the national security" while information labeled SECRET or TOP SECRET, if leaked, could be expected to cause, respectively, "serious damage" or "grave damage" to U.S. national security. SECRET and, especially, TOP SECRET materials usually include numerous handling restrictions. They also may be further labeled CODEWORD—signaling specific sensitive compartments or bodies of intelligence based on their sources.[46] Access to SECRET or TOP SECRET/CODEWORD intelligence is severely limited in order to protect against exposure to skilled and technologically sophisticated adversaries.[47] An individual's ability to access any level of classification depends, in the first instance, on their "need to know."

However, collectors and analysts frequently aren't sure just how much another analyst from within or outside his or her agency or even management really needs to know. As a partial solution to this problem employees from one agency are often detailed to another. For example, in the past the Departments of State, Transportation, Treasury, and Energy and the Immigration and Naturalization Service, Customs, and other organizations detailed personnel to the CIA's Counterterrorist Center, the FBI and, to a lesser extent, the National Security Agency.[48] However, despite these efforts to overcome barriers to the sharing of intelligence, host agencies frequently restrict the access of those who were sent to such assignments to information and databases for policy or security reasons.[49] Indeed, where there may be concerns about the compromise of sources and/or methods, collectors and analysts may well choose to interpret just what other individuals "need to know" rather narrowly. This may result in an editing or truncating of information before it is forwarded and thus the elimination of intelligence that may be essential to a more accurate understanding of a given situation.

Such actions can have a doubly pernicious impact. For example, to protect disclosure of sources or methods, the CIA sometimes limits the information it shares with National Security Agency. On the other hand, that Agency, overwhelmed with the information it gathers and with neither time nor personnel to analyze all information for relevance, focuses its attention on issues based on such factors as their priority, level of customer interest in a particular subject, and the perceived value of the information. When the CIA withholds or truncates the information it forwards to National Security Agency, it may be filtering out some information that would enable the Agency to make well-informed decisions on how to direct its efforts and what to report out to the CIA and other intelligence agencies. The impact may well be that information necessary to "fill in the dots" never is received by all-source analysts at CIA, Defense Intelligence Agency, or the Department of State.[50]

William Odom, former director of the National Security Agency and Assistant Chief of Staff for Intelligence, commenting on the effect that the need to protect sources and methods has within the clandestine services, notes that case officers are very aware of the fact that when an agent has been recruited, the agent has essentially placed his life in the case officer's hands. As a result, "When telling the unvarnished truth to management might risk [an] agent's well-being, or even his life, the decision to divulge the whole truth is not easy. The moral dilemmas are painful."[51] He further notes that the problem does not stop at this level.

> As a case officer's career progresses, he may be promoted to a management position. There he stands between case officers and higher management. The same inclination to play games with facts come into play. The problem repeats itself right up to the top on any clandestine human intelligence. Moreover, as time passes, such behavior creates an accumulation of distortion in what top management knows. . . .[52]

Thus the need to protect methods and sources often limits the information available to analysts and what analysts are able or willing to share with other analysts from other agencies, and in some cases represents a serious obstacle to successful all-source analyses. In a written statement to the joint House-Senate committee on 9/11, the Director of the Defense Intelligence Agency noted: "In my opinion, one of the most prolonged and troubling trends in the Intelligence Community is the degree to which analysts—while being expected to incorporate the full range of source information into their assessments—have been systematically separated from the raw material of their trade."[53]

The problem is further compounded when dealing with foreign intelligence agencies, which for similar reasons do not share all the information at their disposal. One of the more prominent of recent cases was related to the failure of the U.S. Intelligence Community to correctly assess the nature of Iraq's biological weapons program prior to the U.S. invasion of Iraq in 2003. Virtually all the Intelligence Community's information on Iraq's alleged mobile biological facilities came from an Iraqi chemical engineer codenamed "Curveball" by way of the intelligence liaison services of another country. The foreign intelligence service involved shared the information it had obtained from Curveball both with U.S. and British intelligence services. As virtually the sole source of such information, it would seem imperative that U.S. intelligence officials gain access to this individual in order to test reliability of the source and the veracity of the information.

However, the foreign liaison service would not provide either the U.S. or British intelligence services with direct access to him.[54]

Protection of information from unauthorized disclosure is not the only barrier to access, sharing, and coordination of intelligence among analysts and Intelligence Community agencies. Pride and allegiance to one's own agency and the race for scarce resources often inhibit the free flow of intelligence between and among analysts and agencies. This is sometimes referred to as the "bureaucratic turf" problem. Agencies within the Intelligence Community each have their own missions—missions that those who work within these agencies have come to believe in and identify with. Thus agencies and analysts often have an agenda that goes beyond the gathering and analyzing of intelligence. For example, analysts within these agencies are responding to higher agency authorities that frequently may be seeking additional funds for their intelligence programs. In which case, they may wish to demonstrate how effective they have been vis-à-vis other agencies and how important they are to policymakers by tightly circumscribing the number of people who have access to information they possess. Or an agency may be seeking funding for additional forces or weapon systems. In such circumstances an agency and its intelligence analysts may believe it is in the agency's and indeed in America's best interests not to share their intelligence, as that might open it up for outside analysis by other agencies that might draw different conclusions from the same information. This may be especially true say within the Department of Defense, where many may feel it is better to be militarily prepared for the worst possible case and thus safer to overestimate than underestimate the enemy's capabilities.

The absence, underutilization, or unreliability of existing technologies also has impeded access to and the sharing and coordination of the intelligence efforts. For example, the National Security Agency could not demonstrate during the congressional inquiry on 9/11 that it had the analytic tools nor could it identify technological upgrades that would assist its analysts in identifying critical intelligence from the large volume of information it collects. This situation has had two significant effects. First, National Security Agency language analysts have been forced to conduct the bulk of their work with pencil and paper. Perhaps more importantly, many of that Agency's analysts developed their own personal databases on index cards that cannot be made readily available to analysts at other agencies.[55]

Similarly, the FBI put into operation its Automated Case System in 1995 to replace written reports and indices. The automated system was designed to enable agents to send leads to other FBI offices and units and to have access to a vast array of electronic data. However, a number of studies have concluded that the system is "limited in its search capacity, difficult to use, and unreliable." Indeed, the Chief of the FBI's Radical Fundamentalist Unit testified before the joint House-Senate intelligence committee that, since Automated Case System is unfriendly, unreliable, and unworkable, many agents rely on e-mail and paper copies to transmit important data, instead of using the system to manage their cases. Because of such limitations, many FBI agents have shied away from using Automated Case System. As a result, according to some FBI personnel, routine leads, on which there were no automated communications, might have "fallen through the cracks."[56]

One evident consequence of this lack of automated technologies capable of facilitating and expediting the sharing of information was the failure associated with the so-called Phoenix Electronic Communication. In July 2001 an agent in the FBI field office in Phoenix, Arizona, sent an "Electronic Communication" to the Osama bin Laden and the Radical Fundamentalist units at FBI Headquarters and to several agents on an International Terrorism squad in the FBI New York office. The Communication outlined his concerns about a coordinated effort by bin Laden to send students to the United States for aviation training, noting that there was an "inordinate number of individuals of investigative interest" taking such training in Arizona and speculating that this was part of an effort to establish a cadre of persons, trained in aviation, who could conduct terrorist activity. He also suggested several steps that might be taken. However, several of the addressees, especially at the supervisory level, failed to receive the information before 9/11.[57] Moreover, the Phoenix agent had "no easy or reliable way of querying a central FBI system to determine whether there were other reports on radical fundamentalists taking flight training or whether FBI field offices were investigating similar cases."[58] Hence, he had no idea that another FBI field office had voiced concern about Middle Eastern men taking flight lessons in 1998 or that an operational unit in the Counterterrorism Section at FBI headquarters had directed twenty-four field offices (including the one in Phoenix) to pay close attention to certain Islamic students engaged in aviation training in 1999.[59]

According to The FBI's Deputy Assistant Director for Counterterrorism, prior to 9/11 "one of the FBI's "major deficiencies" was in the area of information sharing, "not only with other agencies but within the Bureau itself." He largely attributed this lack of sharing "to inadequate information technology."[60] Similarly FBI Director Robert S. Mueller III acknowledged that over the years, the FBI "[f]ailed to develop a sufficient capacity to collect, store, search, retrieve, analyze, and share information."[61] Moreover, database incompatibilities have exacerbated the problem. For example, the Automated Case System and most other FBI databases are classified at the Secret level. However, much of the information disseminated throughout the Intelligence Community is classified Top Secret. Therefore, it is not easily available to the FBI. Similarly, the CIA places some human intelligence information in a special compartment at the Secret level and that information cannot be shared within FBI databases. In September of 2002 in testimony before Congress the Chief of the FBI's Radical Fundamentalist Unit described the situation.

> ...[C]ommunications coming into our building from NSA [National Security Agency], from CIA cannot be integrated into existing databases. So if an analyst is working, say, on a subject in Phoenix division and they run that person's name

> through our databases, they will not retrieve information on that person that other agencies may also have. It is required of them to get up, walk over to a different set of—or different computer that has access to a different database to search the name in that database; and the two databases will never come together and be integrated. So it is a setup for failure in terms of keeping the strategic picture of what we are up against. Although some FBI personnel have access to separate Top Secret Intelligence Community networks, the FBI's computer systems are not linked to Intelligence Community systems or even to the Department of Justice.[62]

The sharing of information among Intelligence Community agencies is also affected by a phenomenon known as the "Wall." The Wall is actually a series of barriers or restrictions that have developed over time as a result of legal, policy, institutional, and personal factors. These barriers have separated foreign intelligence from law enforcement entities and thus, either directly or collaterally, foreign from domestic activities, and the FBI from the CIA. They also have separated communications intelligence from other types of intelligence, the Intelligence Community from other federal agencies, and national security information from other forms of evidence. As a result, the free flow of information among intelligence agencies and between intelligence agencies and law enforcement entities has been significantly hampered.[63]

For example, when the National Security Act of 1947 established the CIA, it charged the CIA with collecting intelligence through human sources and other appropriate means. But in order to avoid establishing a single organization that was responsible for both foreign and domestic intelligence and to preserve the jurisdiction of the FBI, the CIA was specifically precluded from having any "police, subpoena, or law enforcement powers or internal security functions." Hence, the first "wall" was established separating the gathering of foreign intelligence from domestic law enforcement. As a direct effect of the legislation, generations of intelligence professionals have been trained to believe that the CIA should not play an internal security role. Thus, collaterally, the legislation also had the effect of creating additional "walls" by separating foreign from domestic activities and, in turn, the CIA from the FBI, with both agencies carefully guarding the information—the CIA restricting the flow for fear that it might fall in the hands of foreign agents and thus reveal sources and methods and the FBI holding information tightly to preserve confidentiality, protect witnesses, and maintain the secrecy of grand jury information, all of which are essential to the successful investigation and prosecution of crimes.[64]

In the mid- to late 1970s Congress was concerned over the illegal domestic spying activities of the CIA and FBI that were revealed by the Rockefeller, Church, and Pike commissions. However, Congress also recognized the interests of the CIA in gathering of intelligence from foreign governments to protect the security of the nation could coincide with the interests of domestic law enforcement officials, particularly in cases of espionage and terrorism. As a result, Congress passed the Foreign Intelligence Surveillance Act of 1978. The Act allowed information obtained through surveillance, which targets foreign powers, to be shared with law enforcement officials, but only if the surveillance was targeted to collect foreign intelligence information.[65] As a result, by the early 1980s the intelligence and law enforcement communities often worked together in counterintelligence and counternarcotics investigations.

However, law enforcement agencies soon became aware of the fact that if, on the basis of national security, the government withheld information from defense attorneys seeking the discovery of investigative information relating to the guilt or innocence of their clients, defense attorneys could move to have the case dismissed. This led Intelligence and law enforcement officials to develop procedures that would permit the dissemination of intelligence for use in law enforcement while protecting intelligence sources and methods. These procedures added to the "walls" and as additional "walls" were erected, an environment was created in which access to and the sharing and coordination of intelligence was restricted.[66] It was just such an environment that resulted in the CIA not providing relevant information to the FBI's investigation of the bombing of the *USS Cole*. The CIA (perhaps overly risk-averse in dealing with Foreign Intelligence Surveillance Act-related matters) did not provide FBI New York field office criminal agents investigating the *USS Cole* bombing information regarding an al-Qaeda meeting in Malaysia that was attended by 9/11 hijackers-to-be Nawaf al-Hazmi, who was already in the United States, and Khallad al-Mihdhar, who had obtained a visa for travel to the United States.[67] Had the walls not existed, the CIA might have been more inclined to pass on the information to the FBI, with a potential consequence of an increase in focus on these two individuals and perhaps some additional opportunities to thwart the 9/11 attacks.

Of course, the CIA is not the only agency involved in gathering foreign intelligence. Thus the "wall" separating foreign from domestic intelligence activities has affected the behavior of other agencies as well. For example, National Security Agency officials are concerned about sharing raw signals intercepts because some of the intercepts contain information about "U.S. persons"[68] that the Agency must protect under "minimize procedures" established by the Attorney General and the Foreign Intelligence Surveillance Court to limit the amount of data it collects on "U.S. persons" as a means of protecting their privacy.

Critical Thinking

Perhaps the greatest challenge that confronts management is stimulating critical thinking. Nearly always, conclusions drawn by analysts express probabilities, not certainties, based on information that is at best incomplete and often subject to deception, camouflage, manipulation, and/or misinterpretation by the target or intermediaries. Thus the analyst must be trained to ask counterintuitive questions: questions that challenge contemporary wisdoms, the views of those around him, and even his own personal biases. Analysts must constantly be asking the question, what "might" the information at hand suggest? and not the question, what "does" the information suggest? It short, the analyst must be challenged by management to have an open mind.

Directly or indirectly pressured by political leaders to confirm their biases, to offer analyses that will support their policy preferences, or to conform to their favored view of the world order, agency level managers sometimes find it difficult to be the "devil's advocate," encouraging analysis to examine existing data from "every possible perspective." And here I deliberately avoid using the term "every reasonable perspective." Great intelligence failures often are the result of such "reasonable" reasoning. Japan would not start a war with the United States it could not hope to win. The Allies will cross the Channel and land at Pas de Calais, everything points to that. Moscow would not put nuclear weapons in Cuba. The Arabs would not attack Israel in 1973 in a war they could not win. All these conclusions and many more are examples of analytical perspective that is conditioned to be "reasonable." However, we know from history that adversaries frequently choose to act counterintuitively, employing secrecy, camouflage, and deception to encourage the opponent to judgmental error.

THE WAY AHEAD

Managing the analytical efforts of the Intelligence Community is a monumental task. Sixteen different entities, fifteen of which are part of other agencies with differing roles and missions, each dedicated to its particular agency's mission, each called to respond to national priorities, but also the specific needs of its own leadership, and each competing with the other for resources and visibility, make managing overall national intelligence efforts a task befitting perhaps only the gods.

Congress and the President have recognized the critical importance of improving overall management within the Intelligence Community. The Intelligence Reform and Terrorism Prevention Act of 2004 (Public Law 108–458) gives the Director of National Intelligence greater authority and responsibility in the overall management of the Intelligence Community than was afforded the antecedent Director of Central Intelligence.

For example, the Intelligence Reform Act has given the Director of National Intelligence authority to "determine the requirements and priorities for, and manage and direct the tasking of, collection, analysis, production, and dissemination of national intelligence by elements of the Intelligence Community."[69] It also has tasked him to, among other things, improve the quality and timeliness of Intelligence Community products through such efforts as the education and training of personnel resources and the widening of their perspective via a broadening of experiences. The latter includes the rotation of personnel through various elements of the Intelligence Community and service in more than one occupational specialty in the course of their careers.[70]

Furthermore, to ensure accuracy in analysis, the Director of National Intelligence is tasked to implement policies and procedures that encourage sound analytical methods and tradecraft and ensure that

- analysis is based on all sources available;
- elements of the Intelligence Community regularly conduct competitive analysis;
- resource allocation for analysis is appropriately proportional to that of collection to maximize analysis of all collected data;
- differences in analytical judgment are fully considered and brought to the attention of policymakers; and
- sufficient relationships are established between collectors and analysts to facilitate greater understanding of the needs of analysts.[71]

These are tall orders. It is, of course, too early to assess how successful the Director of National Intelligence will be in carrying out his new authorities and responsibilities. However, a few preliminary comments are worth mentioning.

First, though he has the authority to set requirements and tasking, they will remain in a continuous state of flux, as the pressure of events alters the requirements and priorities of policymakers. Thus, if he is to be successful in ensuring that the Intelligence Community provides timely and accurate intelligence to policymakers on issues of both short- and long-term importance to the security of the nation, he must not only stay closely attuned to the changing priorities of policymakers based on the pressure of events, but also have a sound understanding of the broader, longer-termed intelligence needs that sometimes may fall from the sight of policymakers as they are confronted with the heat of everyday battle. Moreover, it is equally important that he balance these needs and regularly communicate them to agency managers. This will require a constant dialogue with agency managers, who must then translate Director of National Intelligence tasks and priorities into productive efforts on the part of their analysts.

All this, however, will not change a basic equation that demands greater dialogue between policymaker and analyst. To respond efficiently and effectively to policymaker needs, an analyst must have

- a sense of the consumer's level of knowledge on the issue at hand;
- a feeling for any attitudes, beliefs, perceptions, and misconceptions that might be influencing policymaker thinking;
- an unfiltered understanding of the specific information required; and
- immediate feedback on any intermediate information provided in order to make any "on course" corrections necessary to meet the specifics of policymaker needs.

Second, although the Director of National Intelligence is charged with improving the quality of intelligence through education and training, this will still require removal of the many barriers to education and training that currently exist. Not the least of these, of course, is lack of personnel. It remains to be seen whether the President and Congress are prepared to pay the bill. The Intelligence Reform Act does give the Director of National Intelligence the authority to establish a system of rewards to encourage the rotation of personnel between and among agencies. Only time will tell whether such a system, akin to the joint management policies established by the military in response to the Goldwater-Nichols Department of Defense Reorganization Act of 1989, will be successful.[72]

Third, in the wake of the intelligence failures associated with the attacks of 9/11 and the War in Iraq, much criticism has focused on the lack of the sharing and coordination of intelligence. As a result, access to and the sharing and coordination of intelligence have received a great deal of attention. The Intelligence Reform Act of 2004 gave the Director of National Intelligence "principal authority to ensure maximum availability of and access to intelligence information within the intelligence community." Among other things, the DNI was given authority to

- establish uniform security standards and procedures;
- establish common information technology standards, protocols, and interfaces;
- ensure the development of information technology systems that include multilevel security and intelligence integration capabilities; and
- establish policies and procedures to resolve conflicts between the need to share intelligence and the need to protect intelligence sources and methods.

However, it would be a mistake to believe that by simply fixing those bits, the management problem will be solved.

Again, it will take time to evaluate Director of National Intelligence success in this critical area. So far efforts to improve access, sharing, and cooperation appear to have had mixed results. A March 2006 U.S. Government Accountability Office report noted: "More than 4 years after September 11, the nation still lacks government-wide policies and processes that Congress called for to provide a framework for guiding and integrating the myriad of ongoing efforts to improve the sharing of terrorism-related information critical to protecting our homeland."[73] In regard to the establishment of uniform security standards and procedures, the report noted that federal agencies use "56 different sensitive but unclassified designations (16 of which belong to one agency) to protect sensitive information—from law or drug enforcement information to controlled nuclear information."[74] Among the designators are: For Official Use Only, Sensitive Security Information, Law Enforcement Sensitive/Sensitive, and Limited Distribution Information. The Government Accountability Office report goes on to note:

> There are no governmentwide [*sic*] policies or procedures that describe the basis on which agencies should use most of these sensitive but unclassified designations, explain what the different designations mean across agencies, or ensure that they will

> be used consistently from one agency to another. . . . Finally, most agencies do not have limits on who and how many employees have authority to make designations, nor do they have policies for providing training to employees on making designations or performing periodic reviews.[75]

All of this is in addition to the limitations imposed on access and sharing of intelligence by classified designators and compartments such as SECRET AND TOP SECRET/CODEWORD. It would appear that the Director of National Intelligence faces a daunting task if he/she is to be successful in opening the door to increased access, sharing, and coordination.

Some progress, however, has been made, particularly in breaking down some of the "Walls" that existed between the Intelligence Community and law enforcement community. In October 2001 Congress passed and the President signed the USA PATRIOT Act (Public Law 107–56). Among other things, the law changed the requirement that "the purpose" of a surveillance under the Foreign Intelligence Surveillance Act be to collect foreign intelligence information, to a requirement that collecting such information be "a significant purpose" of a Foreign Intelligence Surveillance Act authorized electronic surveillance or physical search. This change provides some additional latitude to use Foreign Intelligence Surveillance Act authority for information gathering by electronic surveillance or physical searches where the primary purpose may be criminal investigation, as long as a there is a significant foreign intelligence presence.[76] The Act also: (1) removed some of the restrictions on federal government attorneys sharing grand jury information; (2) permits the disclosure, subject to certain limitations, of foreign intelligence, counterintelligence, or foreign intelligence information obtained as a part of a federal criminal investigation to any federal law enforcement, intelligence, protective, immigrations, national defense, or national security official in order to assist that official in carrying out his or her duties; and (3) subject to specific guidelines, requires that the Attorney General or heads of other Federal agencies with law enforcement responsibilities expeditiously disclose foreign intelligence acquired in the course of a criminal investigation to the Director of National Intelligence.[77]

While it is beyond the scope of this discussion to examine in detail the complex provisions of the USA PATRIOT Act, suffice to say it has been a subject of considerable debate in Congress and among the American public. How its provisions will withstand the test of time is, at present, uncertain. Nevertheless, three needs remain. There is the need to balance the advantages to be reaped from the sharing and coordination of intelligence efforts with the need to protect sources and methods. There is the need to ensure that those guilty of a crime, whether it is one of narcotics trafficking or terrorist plotting, are successfully prosecuted. And there is the need to ensure that the constitutionally protected civil liberties of Americans against unwarranted searches and seizures, guaranteed under the Fourth Amendment, are not violated by an unrestrained use of electronic surveillances and physical searches. The first of these is likely to continue to serve as a barrier to the access and sharing of intelligence. The task will be to minimize the compromising of sources and methods while maximizing access to classified or, as the case is at present, unclassified, information. The second, as well as third, "need" also will continue to serve as barriers for fear that information obtained under the Foreign Intelligence Surveillance Act might be disallowed in Court out of concern that the Fourth Amendment has been violated. The result of such an action might then be that the guilty "walk." Under such conditions law enforcement officials might well prefer to eschew materials obtained through surveillance act measures.

Perhaps one of the most difficult tasks will be to harmonize technologies for data storage and retrieval so that multiple agencies have immediate access to information required to protect the nation's security. Aside from the issues associated with secrecy and law enforcement mentioned above, at present there is yet to exist a single technology that fits all. As noted above, the Director of National Intelligence has been tasked by law to develop information technology systems that include multilevel security and intelligence integration capabilities. At present, such systems appear to be far off.

Finally, as we look to the future, a brief mention of the all-important topic of "critical thinking" is surely warranted. Certainly, this is an issue that the Director of National Intelligence and all agencies' managers, mission managers, program managers, and any other manager of intelligence resources should emphasize. However, it should be made a special charge for those tasked with executive or congressional oversight of the Intelligence Community. It should ultimately fall to the oversight offices and committees to demand quality in the intelligence effort and ultimately this can only be achieved through the application of imagination and the application of critical thinking. If the individuals in those offices and committees are more concerned about supporting or undermining a particular set of policies than they are about the depth of analysis and veracity of the data used to support competing claims, then the quality of U.S. intelligence efforts will surely decline and U.S. national security will suffer.

4

Analysis: Torments of Sisyphus

"Quality is not an act. It is a habit."

—Aristotle

Once requirements have been clearly defined, and trained resources have been allocated to an intelligence task, it falls to an intelligence analyst (or team of analysts) to evaluate the information at his or her disposal in order to determine specific patterns that suggest relevant answers to the intelligence needs of policymakers. Analysis invariably involves many unknowns, demands a sharp mind and clear thinking and, in general, an extraordinary understanding of peoples, cultures, issues. It is a complex process and there are few, if any, "slam dunks."

Analysts must first evaluate the sources, then the channels through which the information was passed. Finally, they must evaluate the evidence itself. Along the way they will face innumerable challenges. They must have a sound understanding of the strengths and limitations of both the technical and human collection processes. They often must draw conclusions from a paucity of information. Or on the other hand, they may be forced, nearly always under the pressure of time, to sift through an extraordinary amount of collected information for the relevant. In either case, they must separate the important from background noise and see through any attempts to deceive. They must overcome their own biases. They must beware of the dangers of "groupthink." They must avoid the temptations of wishful thinking or the desire to please superiors. And in all of this, they must think imaginatively and strategically as they confront the daunting complexities of estimating the future. Only then will they be in a position to make sound judgments about a given situation or a given set of factors. Moreover, given the growing global interests of the United States, all of this usually must be accomplished in an environment of personnel scarcity.

PRINCIPAL TASKS

Evaluation of Sources

The first step an analyst must take is to evaluate the sources of the information he or she has received.[1] For example, if the information came from human sources, how many sources were involved? Were the sources in agreement? Did any of the sources have direct access to the information reported? Were they competent or knowledgeable enough to accurately report on the issues? What was their motivation for reporting—did they have a financial or political agenda they might be seeking to advance? Have they been a source of information in the past? If so, has the information they provided in the past been accurate? Are they a likely conduit for disinformation—that is, false information designed to obscure the truth? On such issues, the analyst could consult any number of individuals within the intelligence community or elsewhere in the government, academe, the business community, etc. who may have had contact with the sources.

If the information came from technical means, the analyst must have some understanding of the technical capabilities and limitations of the collecting source and be prepared to make judgments on the quality and accuracy of the information obtained. For example, if the information required came from satellite observation, was the quality of the pictures received adequate to make judgments about what was observed? If the satellite was nongeosynchronous,[2] is it possible that the opponent concealed whatever was to be observed from view as the satellite passed overhead? If the information came from acoustic or other submarine tracking technologies, was that means sufficiently capable to differentiate between say a Russian Delta class submarine and a Typhoon class submarine with its significantly greater capabilities? If the information was a product of conversations garnered through communications intelligence, was the communication speculative or specific? Was the source reporting or kibitzing? Or perhaps, an adversary, knowing full well that his conversations were being monitored by U.S. communications intelligence, was deliberately passing on false information.

Does an increase in the number of signal intercepts from an adversary's military forces indicate an increase in activity in a particular area or along a particular military front? Or perhaps it is an effort to deceive by suggesting activity that doesn't exist (as was done during World War II to convince the Germans that the allied invasion would come at Paz de Calais instead of Normandy). Or is it simply a reflection of increased collection activity on the part of one's own military intelligence community?

Evaluating the Channels

Next the analyst must evaluate the channels though which the information was communicated. Like the old story told at a bar that changes dramatically from one end to the other as it is passed along, information when passed through multiple channels is likely to become distorted and sometimes unrecognizable from the original message. Thus the analyst must determine whether the information at hand has arrived undistorted. Is the information "primary source information?" For example, have intelligence sources recorded the words of a president, prime minister, or senior civilian or military official ordering a specific action; or from secondary sources—for example, an intermediate source or sources reporting on what a primary source has said or written. The more intermediate channels the message has traveled the greater the suspicion that the message may have been distorted and therefore either incomplete, overdrawn, or perhaps totally inaccurate.[3]

Evaluating the Evidence

Finally, the analyst must evaluate the evidence itself. He or she must examine each piece of evidence to ascertain whether worthy judgments can be made about the information as a whole. Such an examination involves a three-step determination. First, how much of the evidence is an indisputable fact. Second, how much is knowable, but either not known or only partially known by the United States. Finally, how much of the evidence is not truly known by anyone and therefore speculative.[4] For example, during the Cold War an analyst or group of analysts might have been given the task to ascertain whether the Soviet Union had the *capability,* using its land- and sea-based intercontinental ballistic missiles and strategic nuclear bombers, to launch a first strike eliminating all or most of U.S. strategic nuclear forces.

It was an indisputable fact that the USSR had large numbers of land- and sea-based intercontinental missiles and long-range bombers armed with nuclear warheads. Beyond that, much of the information available to the analyst more than likely fell into one of the latter two categories. Thus, in responding to the tasking, the analyst was called on to make reasoned judgments on a host of issues. On first inspection, the information available may have indicated that the land-based missiles were accurate enough to be able to deliver a potential knock out blow to U.S. missile silos. But the analyst would have had to dig much further before any reasoned answer could be delivered to a policymaker. Among the questions the analyst might be obliged to ask: how was the information on the accuracy obtained? Was it from an analysis of data transmitted by telemetry to Soviet ground stations that had been intercepted by U.S. signals intelligence capabilities? Or was it from some other source, and if so, how reliable has that source been in the past? Was the information about the accuracy of Soviet missiles the result of data from a single test or multiple confirming tests? Were the tests undertaken under simulated operational conditions or in a highly controlled test environment? Were Soviet Intercontinental Ballistic Missile (ICBM) tests run on an east-west trajectory or a north-south trajectory, which might provide a better measure of the accuracy of a Soviet missile attack on the United States that would traverse the North Pole region? Had Soviet onboard inertial navigation systems solved the problem of the earth's polar magnetic/gravitational anomalies that might well affect the accuracy of their missiles as they traversed the polar regions? Could the arrival of attacking missiles be so timed to avoid the thermal radiation, violent upper atmosphere winds, and debris caused by previously arriving missiles that might either destroy or cause later arriving missiles to be thrown off track? Additionally the analyst(s) would be forced to evaluate Soviet capabilities for detecting and destroying U.S. submarines that carry Sea-Launched Ballistic Missiles, as well as U.S. nuclear bombers before any final evaluation could be made. In short, the analyst not only must understand the problem in detail, from beginning to end, but also understand how much of the information he/she is relying on rests on facts and how much on judgments about information that is knowable as well as not knowable.

Furthermore, if policymakers had asked a subsequent question about whether the USSR might *intend* to launch such an attack, the analyst or group of analysts would be obliged to posit a range of scenarios, and their responses most assuredly would be solely speculative, since the answer to the question might not even be known to Soviet leaders until the moment of decision.

Of course not all tasks assigned to the Intelligence Community are so complex. However, if analysts are to have any hope of responding to policymaker needs with useful intelligence, most tasks they face will require a reasonably detailed knowledge of the issues involved. Furthermore, it is likely that there will always be some part of an issue for which solid information is not available to the analyst—either because it hasn't been collected, hasn't been made available to the analyst, or simply can't be known. Here the analyst must rely entirely on his/her experience and judgment.

Thus, analysts are not mere conduits for raw intelligence. Through their expertise and experience they add value to the intelligence that has been collected. They separate the wheat from chaff. They identify issues that are likely to need timely policymaker attention. They apply their experience and judgment and bring historical, cultural, and contemporary perspectives to information available, not only from other technical, functional, and area/country experts in the Intelligence Community, but also from the vast array of other sources—new media, embassies, military commanders, other government analysts, and academe. All of this when combined with the objectivity of an analyst detached from policy, provides decision makers with a more informed picture of a particular problem than might otherwise be available from the sometimes conflicting and frequently incomplete raw intelligence.

IMPEDIMENTS TO SUCCESS

Analyst–Collector Disconnect

Technology has become a great friend of the analyst. Not only is information from around the world instantly available via the Internet, the global media, and the like, analysts also benefit greatly from data automation within the Intelligence Community. Automated data handling has greatly reduced the time between intelligence collection and its availability to analysts. It has also increased efficiency, since data arrives at the desk of the analyst "often presorted based on keyword searches."[5] But there can be a downside to this automation. With all of the data now available to analysts, they may not take or have time to understand fully the nature of the collection effort, including the scope of the effort, its limitations, and the relative worth of intelligence sources, which sometimes can only come about through greater collector–analyst dialogue.

In their examination of the U.S. failure to correctly determine the nature and extent of Saddam Hussein's chemical weapons capabilities prior to the U.S. invasion of Iraq in 2003, the President's Commission on Weapons of Mass Destruction noted that an important part of the failure could be attributed to the absence of a close connection between analysts and collector. For example, the absence of close dialogue between collectors and analysts may have led analysts to believe that there had been an increase in activity at suspected Iraqi chemical warfare sites when in fact there was none. According to the President's Commission, collectors did not adequately communicate the limitations of imagery collection, specifically noting that analysts did not realize that the observed increase in activity at suspected Iraqi chemical weapons sites may have been the result of increased imagery collection by U.S. satellites rather than any increased activity.[6] Until 2000, imagery collection on Iraq had been focused primarily on supporting military operations associated with the no-fly zones. However, in 2001 and 2002, imagery collection on targets suspected to be associated with Iraqi weapons of mass destruction more than doubled. Apparently not all Intelligence Community analysts were aware of this change, resulting in a failure to distinguish between *actual* increased activity at suspected chemical warfare sites and the *appearance* of increased activity due to increased satellite coverage. "Not coincidentally," the commission concluded, this was "the same time that analysts began to see" new activity they associated with CW [Chemical Warfare] transshipments.[7]

Former CIA analyst and executive Robert M. Clark sees another problem associated with the apparently all too frequent disconnect between collectors and analysts. According to Clark, analysts "too seldom try to stimulate collectors, and thereby they restrict the breadth or focus of what flows to them."[8] For example, the National Security Agency reported some but not all communications intercepted in 1999 and early 2000 involving a suspected terrorist facility in the Middle East linked to al-Qaeda. Included in the information it did not report were communications involving this facility and associated with a participant in a January 2000 meeting in Malaysia, 9/11 hijacker Khalid al-Mihdhar. In explaining this to the joint House-Senate committee inquiry into 9/11, National Security Agency officials noted that those communications fell below the Agency's reporting threshold, a threshold that is subjective and can change daily. Agency officials further emphasized that the threshold

> is a product of several factors including the priority of the intelligence topic . . . , *the level of customer interest in a particular subject, the perceived value of the information* [emphasis added], and the amount of intercept available for analysis and reporting.[9]

In short, collection agencies have considerable discretion in what they pass on. The major concern is that vital but seemingly irrelevant information, perhaps that small piece of information that completes the mosaic, will not get passed on to analysts. Through closer connections between analysts and collectors, analysts will better be able to stimulate collectors and collectors will be better able to gage the level of customer interest in a particular subject, as well as the potential value of a specific bit of information they have collected. On this National Security Agency officials complained that while they deploy many people to customer agencies to understand their needs and help shape their reports, customer agencies rarely reciprocate.[10]

Too Little Information

Often analysts are confronted with too little information. This can be the product of a number of factors, including limited collection capabilities, clever efforts by an adversary to deny or deceive, contradictory information, insufficient sharing of information within the Intelligence Community itself, or lack of activity on the part of the target nation. For example, prior to the U.S. attack on Iraq in 2003, there was little information available on Iraq's nuclear weapons programs. In 1998 the Intelligence Community noted that there was only limited and oftentimes contradictory intelligence reporting on Iraq nuclear weapons efforts, with some human intelligence sources indicating that Iraq had continued with "low-level theoretical research for a weapons program" following the Gulf War of 1991. At the same time, other sources reported "all nuclear-related activity [had been] halted."[11]

Similarly, there was little information available on Iraq's Biological and Chemical Warfare programs or on Iraq's intended use of Unmanned Aerial Vehicles as delivery vehicles for biological or chemical weapons.[12] In such circumstances, analysts, under pressure of time, politics, or other factors, may well be tempted to draw conclusions that go well beyond the evidence at hand. Such was the case in analytical judgments rendered by the Intelligence Community before the Iraq War. Indeed, the Intelligence Community assessed with "high confidence" that Iraq "has" biological weapons and that "all key aspects" of Iraq's offensive biological warfare program "are active and that most elements are larger and more advanced than before the Gulf War."[13]

The problem is often compounded when the little information that is available is too vague to yield *actionable* intelligence. For example, after bin Laden's February 1998 press conference in which he called for attacks against all Americans and announced al-Qaeda was merging with eleven other militant Islamic groups to form the World Islamic Front for Jihad Against Crusaders and Jews, the Intelligence Community began acquiring information that bin Laden's network intended to strike inside the United States. This information was widely available within the Intelligence Community and disseminated to senior policymakers. However, the information lacked specifics, such as where, when, and how such attacks might or would occur. The credibility of sources was sometimes questionable. And there was no corroborating information. Furthermore, information about possible al-Qaeda attacks within the United States was dwarfed by threat information the Intelligence Community received during this period, which pointed toward al-Qaeda attacks against U.S. overseas interests.[14]

Focus on Limited Sources

Too little information often can lead analysts and their supervisors to an overreliance on limited sources or even a single source or type of intelligence, as they attempt to discern a meaningful picture of unfolding events. For example, On January 21, 1968 the North Vietnamese Army attacked the American Marine base at Khe Sanh, South Vietnam. The attack was not unexpected. Toward the end of 1967, North Vietnam had been boasting of great victories to come and several North Vietnamese army divisions had been observed moving into the Khe Sanh region. In response, General William Westmoreland, commander of U.S. military forces in Vietnam, aware of the mistakes made by the French at Dien Bien Phu, reinforced Khe Sanh and had additional reinforcements positioned at Hue.

However, while the battle waged at Khe Sanh, North Vietnam Army and Viet Cong forces, disguised as peasants, workers, refugees, and South Vietnamese soldiers and operating in small groups, were infiltrating major cities and towns throughout South Vietnam. With the world still focused on Khe Sanh, in the early hours of January 31, 1968, the first day of the Vietnamese "Lunar" New Year, over eighty thousand Viet Cong and North Vietnamese troops and commandos launched what became known as the "Tet Offensive," attacking virtually every major town and city in South Vietnam and most of the important American military bases. The attacks came as a near total surprise everywhere.

How could this happen? In late November 1968, CIA analyst Joseph Hovey, reporting from the Agency's Saigon station, correctly predicted the Tet Offensive. Basing his judgments largely on captured enemy documents, he foresaw an attempt by the Viet Cong and their North Vietnamese allies to launch the long-promised "general uprising" aimed at occupying and holding some urban centers in South Vietnam and isolating others. The Directorate of Intelligence at CIA Headquarters in Langley, Virginia, disagreed, contending that Hovey was not privileged to important intelligence. The intelligence which he lacked "was probably Signal Intelligence." Only five percent of the CIA Saigon station personnel were cleared for Signals Intelligence and Langley was focused on information gathered by that method.[15]

Normally a reliable source of information under certain circumstances, Signals Intelligence can give a distorted impression of the disposition of enemy forces. The movement of regular forces usually requires coordination among units, which generates a significant amount of radio traffic. Hence Signals Intelligence was able to provide sound intelligence on North Vietnamese regular forces, preparing for an assault on Khe Sanh but little on irregular forces infiltrating South Vietnamese cities.[16] In Saigon alone, while generating little radio traffic that might draw the attention of Signals Intelligence personnel, the equivalent of about five North Vietnamese Army and Viet Cong battalions infiltrated the city prior to the offensive.[17]

Similarly, in its October 2002 National Intelligence Estimate of Iraq's alleged chemical warfare program, the Intelligence Community, confronted with a "paucity of supporting human and signals intelligence"[18] and the complexity of differentiating chemical warfare production facilities from legitimate chemical infrastructure, concluded that Iraq had reinitiated the production of chemical weapons.[19] This judgment was heavily influenced by a single source, imagery intelligence.[20] It also was a departure from past Intelligence Community judgments. As late as 2001 the Intelligence Community maintained that there was no evidence that Iraq had started large-scale production of chemical weapons. However, imagery began showing trucks transshipping materials to and from ammunition depots, including previous chemical warfare sites. At nearly a dozen of these locations analysts saw a number of "indicators," including trucks regularly associated with chemical weapons shipments in the late 1980s and during the Gulf War, which suggested to them that some of these trucks might be transporting chemical munitions. Since numerous shipments were observed though imagery, analysts wrongly concluded that Iraq had a significant number of chemical weapons and therefore had restarted the production of chemical weapons.[21]

Likewise, in the National Intelligence Estimate produced in the fall of 2002 the Intelligence Community assessed with "high confidence" that Iraq "has" biological weapons and that "all key aspects" of Iraq's offensive biological warfare program "are active and that most elements are larger and more advanced than they were before the Gulf War."[22] Like the Intelligence Community's assessment of Iraq's Chemical Warfare program, this judgment stood in contrast to previous assessments that had concluded that Iraq *could* have biological programs.[23] This new assessment was based primarily on information, largely received from a single human source.[24] The single source was a chemical engineer codenamed "Curveball." Curveball was handled by Germany's Federal Intelligence Service.[25]

However, they could not verify his reporting, considered him a "flake,"[26] and would not permit U.S. agents direct access to him. Lack of access to the source clearly complicated efforts to ascertain the truthfulness of Curveball's reporting. Unfortunately, between January 2000 and September 2001 Department of Defense Human Intelligence personnel disseminated nearly a hundred reports from Curveball regarding mobile biological warfare facilities.[27] By spring 2000 this information was provided to senior policymakers. In December 2000 the Intelligence Community produced a Special Intelligence Report based on Curveball reporting, noting that while it could not confirm that Iraq had produced biological agents, "credible reporting from a single source suggest" that Iraq had done so.[28] Reliance on a single human source of intelligence, on occasion, can be very valuable, especially if that source has direct access to specific information and his or her judgment and performance have proven reliable in the past. Such was the case in the early 1960s with the information provided by Russian Colonel Oleg Penkovsky. For eighteen months he supplied U.S. intelligence with highly valued information, including information that enabled President Kennedy to deal effectively with the Soviet Union during the Cuban missile crisis of October 1962. Unfortunately, Curveball was not a credible source. Questions about his reliability were well known before the United States went to war with Iraq and he had no significant track record of good judgment or accurate reporting. Equally unfortunate, Defense Intelligence Agency human intelligence personnel made no attempt to determine Curveballs' veracity. In the end, unsurprisingly his reporting was found to be unreliable.[29]

Too Much Information

While the Intelligence Community is often confronted with a paucity of information, it is perhaps more likely to be confronted with a plethora. Twentieth-century advances in transportation and communications technologies and in miniaturization, in missile and satellite technologies and the like greatly increased the information available to intelligence analysts. Hence, lack of information has not been the usual problem. For example, though the United States, according to President Nixon, was completely surprised by the simultaneous attacks by Syria and Egypt on October 6, 1973, the Jewish holy day of Yom Kippur, it was not for lack of intelligence. British historian Christopher Andrew has noted,

> . . . the sheer volume of SIGINT came close to swamping the system as analysts were faced with the classic problem of distinguishing the crucial signals pointing to the Egyptian-Syrian attack from the mass of distracting, and sometimes misleading, background noise.[30]

Later, a leaked report of the House select committee on intelligence chaired by Congressman Otis Pike concluded:

> NSA intercepts of Egyptian-Syrian war preparations were so voluminous—an average of hundreds of reports each week—that few analysts had time to digest more than a small portion of them.[31]

The problem has been further exacerbated in the late twentieth century. Information age technologies, especially the computer and the Internet, coupled with the collapse of the Soviet Union, have greatly increased global political, economic, and social activity, while improvements in information gathering, storage, and retrieval technologies have resulted in an exponential increase in the volume of data available to analysts. Today, one of the Intelligence Community's major challenges is to transform the "mountains of heterogeneous, noisy, and incomplete information into actionable intelligence. . . ."[32] To further complicate the task, information about a given issue of interest to policymakers is often "faint, subtle, and transient and imbedded in a myriad of databases maintained by separate agencies." And "[e]ach of these databases contains massive amounts of heterogeneous, incomplete, inaccurate, and even contradictory information, the overwhelming majority of which has no relevance to the task at hand."[33] They may even contain information deliberately planted by an adversary or a mischievous hacker to confuse, deceive, or deflect the attention of others.

For example, the Jeremiah report detailing causes for the Intelligence Community's failure to foresee India's May 11, 1998 nuclear tests noted that the nation's spy satellites typically produce far too much information for overworked and under-trained intelligence analysts to handle.[34] Similarly, as one looks back at the events leading up to the attacks of 9/11, paucity of information is not what comes to mind. Throughout 1999 there were many reports of possible attacks by bin Laden. Among the dozens of reports that flooded in were the threat to blow up the FBI building in Washington, D.C., and a possible threat to an airline flight from Los Angeles or New York.[35] By spring 2001 the level of information on possible terrorist threats and planned attacks increased dramatically. In March 2001 Richard Clarke, then National Security Council counterterrorism coordinator, informed National Security Advisor Condoleezza Rice that he thought there were terrorist cells, including al-Qaeda, operating in the United States. Shortly thereafter, Rice was briefed on the activities of Abu Zubaydah, a senior al-Qaeda figure. In the weeks that followed, then Director of Central Intelligence George Tenet issued warnings that Abu Zubaydah was planning an operation in the near future. By May 2001 the "drumbeat of reporting grew louder," including a report by a "walk-in" to the FBI claiming that there was a plan to launch attacks on London, Boston, and New York. In mid-May there was a phone call to a U.S. embassy that warned of a possible attack by bin Laden supporters on the United States using "high explosives." Later that month was a report that terrorists might hijack an aircraft or storm a U.S. embassy. There were reports of possible attacks in Israel, Yemen, and Italy. By midsummer Saudi Arabia, Bahrain, and Kuwait were added to the list of warnings. In June there was a report that Khalid Sheikh Mohammed (who later confessed to having masterminded the 9/11 attacks) was recruiting people to travel to the United States to meet with colleagues already there in order to conduct terrorist attacks on bin Laden's behalf. Then there was the information that led to the late June advisory that there was a high probability of near-term "spectacular" terrorist attacks resulting in numerous casualties. Other reports warned of imminent attacks by bin Laden. In early July the CIA briefed Attorney General Ashcroft on al-Qaeda, warning that preparations for multiple attacks were in the late stages, if not already complete and that a significant attack was imminent. On August 6, in response to questions raised by President Bush on several occasions to his intelligence briefers as to whether any of these threats pointed to attacks on the United States, an article was inserted into the President's Daily (Intelligence) Brief titled "Bin Laden Determined to Strike in U.S." The article indicated that bin Laden had wanted to conduct terrorist attacks in the United States since 1997, had al-Qaeda members in the United States, was planning to exploit an operative's access to the United States to mount a strike, and that FBI information indicated patterns of suspicious activity in this country consistent with preparations for hijackings or other types of attacks.[36]

What is evident is that prior to the 9/11 attacks there was no dearth of information about the possibility of an attack, though some asked whether all these threats might be a deception. As then Director of Central Intelligence George Tenet later noted, "the system was blinking red."[37] What were missing were the specifics. There were no targets, no timing, or evident method of attack identified in the gathered information. And information that might have led to answers to some of those questions often found itself at the bottom of a pile of information, some of which related to information of more immediate concern to already overworked intelligence staffs, or were imbedded in databases maintained by separate agencies.

One evident example was the case, mentioned in Chapter 3, of the FBI agent in the Phoenix office who sent an "Electronic Communication" to FBI Headquarters expressing his concerns, based on firsthand knowledge, that bin Laden was sending students to the United States for civil aviation-related training and expressing his suspicion that this was an effort to establish a cadre of individuals who might later engage in terrorist activity.[38] The Phoenix agent testified to the joint House-Senate intelligence committee on 9/11 noting:

> I understand that the people back at FBI Headquarters are terribly overworked and understaffed, and they have been for years. . . . I knew that this was going to be at the bottom of the pile . . . because they were dealing with real-time threats, real-time issues trying to render fugitives back to the United States.[39]

The Phoenix agent guessed right. His communication remained at the bottom of the pile and, presumably though in the FBI database, was not made available to other agencies at the time.[40] Nor did outside agencies have easy access to the FBI database.

Denial and Deception

The objective of denial and deception is to protect secrets. Denial is aimed at limiting the availability of information to insure that it does not fall into unwanted hands or to mislead the adversary. Denial comes in many forms. Among its more common forms are classification of materials, encryption, and jamming, all as a means to limit access to information, and camouflage, as a means of hiding information from view.[41] Camouflage is usually used to deceive an adversary by disguising what one does not wish the opponent to know. Army personnel wear battle dress uniforms that are designed to blend in with the background in which they are operating. Military personnel and equipment might be hidden from view by nets. Aircraft that frequently operate at low altitudes or land mobile missiles might be painted to match surrounding terrain in the area of operations. A bombed runway that has been repaired might be disguised to look like it remains cratered and therefore unusable. Chemical or biological warfare facilities might be designed to appear as just another facility for the production of pharmaceuticals or common use chemicals. These are all examples of denial.

Deception, on the other hand, is generally a more proactive effort. It generally involves deliberately attempting to lead an opponent to a false conclusion. Arguably camouflage may be considered by some to be a passive form of deception.[42] However, half-truths, outright lies, false messages, bogus codes, increased communications activity in order to suggest military activity in a particular location, and other forms of disinformation or misinformation are clear efforts to deceive. Both denial and deception play prominent roles in both intelligence collection and analysis. On the one hand, denial limits collectors on what they can report. However, often the absence of information, in and of itself, is information to analysts. On the other hand, deception is useful in providing false or misleading information in hopes that intelligence analysts will interpret it as true.

History is replete with examples of the skillful use of denial and deception. The first recorded example of deception was the Mycenaean Greek use of the "Trojan Horse." Prominent recent examples include Hitler's use of deception to mislead Stalin prior to the German invasion of Russia in 1941; Japanese efforts to disguise preparations for attacks on U.S. military forces on Oahu in 1941; Soviet efforts prior to the Cuban missile crises of 1962; North Vietnamese and Viet Cong deception prior to the Tet offensive in 1968; Soviet deception prior to the invasion of Czechoslovakia in 1968; Arab efforts to conceal preparations for the 1973 war against Israel; and of course, Saddam's counterproductive deceptions that ultimately resulted in the March 2003 war and his downfall.

Perhaps the most celebrated use of deception in the last sixty-plus years was by the Allies in preparation for the invasion of Europe in 1944. As the month of June approached, the German's knew the Allies planned to invade Europe. The problem the Germans confronted was knowing where the Allies would invade. On the ground the Allies, with eight divisions, including three airborne, available for the initial assault, confronted fifty-nine German divisions in occupied France. If the

German's were able to concentrate their forces against an Allied attack, there would be little chance for an Allied success. Ultimately, success depended on convincing the German's that the assault that was to take place at Normandy was only a feint to draw German forces away from their elaborate defenses around Calais, and thus weaken the German ability to defend against the supposed main attack that would come at Pas de Calais, the narrowest point in the English Channel. So convinced, the German's then might limit the forces positioned in Normandy, position the bulk of their forces to confront an impending attack at Calais, and delay the movement of German reserves to Normandy in a counterattack. To deceive the Germans, the Allies concocted an enormous ruse, codenamed "Operation Fortitude."[43] Across the Channel from Calais, they created a nonexistent 50-division force of over one million men, the First U.S. Army Group commanded by General George S. Patton. To add to the ruse the Army Group was replete with nonexistent units, inflatable rubber tanks and trucks, plywood vehicles and guns, false radio transmissions, and dummy landing craft and supported by all-night truck convoys supposedly delivering supplies and munitions and a papier-mache giant oil pumping head. This enormous force was to attack after the attack at Normandy. They also employed captured or defecting German agents to send back false information to German intelligence services and used controlled leaks of information through diplomatic channels.

Deception was greatly aided by "Ultra." Earlier in the War Britain had broken the code used by the Germans on their standard enciphering machine, Enigma. Information obtained, codenamed "Ultra," was used to determine how well the German's were taking the bait. If the Germans had bought on to the ruse, information could be planted that reinforced those beliefs. If there were doubts, additional information could be passed to the Germans to encourage them to believe the attack would come at Pas de Calais.[44]

The grand deception worked. Hitler, convinced that the attack would come at Pas de Calais, positioned his strongest forces in that region. When the Allies landed at Normandy, they were able to secure the beachhead and achieve a strategic advantage.

Intelligence professionals recognize that an opponent's use of denial and deception can be a significant impediment to collection and analysis, and understand well that an opponent's successful use of denial and deception can swing the balance in its favor in peace and war.

Cognitive Bias

Perhaps the most insidious and pernicious impediment to successful analysis is what is often called the "mind-set problem." As with collection, analysis is all too frequently plagued by adverse effects of the personal biases and predispositions held by the analyst. As one former CIA deputy director for intelligence put it, ". . . intelligence is a profession of cognition . . . how we absorb and mentally process information coming to us."[45] Cognition is about how we come to know something. It involves not just the rational and intellectual processes of thinking, reasoning, and remembering, but also, in the first instance, the processes by which we filter the vast amount of information our senses confront in the world around us and how we interpret the filtered information. And those processes are largely shaped by our prior attitudes and beliefs, as well as our physical and psychological needs. They are also influenced by emotions, such as fear, anger, surprise, and acceptance, which have both evolved over thousands of years and are influenced by those attitudes and beliefs we currently hold, both consciously and unconsciously. Thus, for example, it is not surprising that Adolph Hitler chose nighttime torchlight parades and the drumbeat of rhetoric and marching boots to insure that his message was absorbed by those listening. Nor is it surprising that candidates for office in the United States like to have their picture taken with the American flag in the background and use bumper stickers that are in red, white, and blue to advertise their candidacy. For most Americans, the flag and its colors evoke positive emotions that candidates hope will be transferred to them. As noted earlier, cognitive bias is a normal part of human behavior. As such, it can never be completely eliminated from the analytical processes.

Nor perhaps should it. Many psychologists and cognitive scientists see cognitive bias as a distortion of reality. A more compelling case can be argued that cognitive bias is what defines reality. As a product of our past experiences and emotions, our cognitive biases shape the way we see things. Thus cognitive bias can have effects that are positive as well as negative. We develop attitudes and beliefs about phenomena around us based on our experiences. The more experiences we have, the more informed are those attitudes and beliefs. Moreover, emotions have served the human species well: alerting us in time of danger, for example, calming us in times of stress and providing adrenaline when situations dictate. Together these cognitive processes can frequently assist us in quickly interpreting events and screening the relevant from the irrelevant, and thus enable us to quickly focus our attention on what is essential or critical. Indeed, previously formed attitudes and beliefs coupled with emotions are the likely basis for quick and ready insight or what is commonly called "intuition." When time is lacking for investigation and reasoned analysis, intuition can be of great help, especially if it is informed by extensive knowledge of the issues at hand. Thus, the cognitive bias of highly experienced analysts can be of substantial initial assistance as they sort through the mountains of information with which they are confronted.

The truly pernicious side of cognitive bias is related to the insidious way it can undermine our capacity to think beyond our initial interpretations of a given situation. When the President's Commission on Weapons of Mass Destruction, for example, criticized the Intelligence Community for it lack of imagination in its failure to "even consider the possibility that Saddam Hussein would decide to destroy his chemical and biological weapons and to halt work on his nuclear program after the Gulf War,"[46] they were indicting the Intelligence Community for its inability to think "outside the box," so to speak. The Intelligence Community was not able to go beyond its predispositions, its biases, and think imaginatively. When it has been accused of engaging in mirror imaging, what the Intelligence Community was being criticized for was its predisposition to think that others would act in a given situation in the same way the United States would. When those investigating past failures of intelligence contend that the Intelligence Community engaged in "groupthink" or "wishful thinking," they were emphasizing their concern that the Intelligence Community fell back on what was comforting, what was consonant with their psychological needs, avoiding what potentially threatened those needs. In the case of "groupthink," perhaps it was the need to be a part of the group, to not stand out, especially if you might be wrong. Those of us who have spent years in government know well the power of the phrase "get on the team." In the case of "wishful thinking," perhaps it was to avoid the discomfort associated with confronting the cold realities of what might lie ahead should an alternative assessment be indicated. Here the "cold realities" might include the displeasure of superiors eager to please policymakers, or the wrath of policymakers themselves, who believe they "know" the answers, and are simply seeking confirmation before policy implementation.

Well-trained, highly disciplined minds frequently will recognize when bias is playing a role in analysis and can reduce its impact. Aware that, from the very selection of information upon which to focus during their initial analysis, their efforts have been shaped by their predispositions, disciplined analysts will actively seek information that challenges those predispositions. Equally aware that adversaries, through the use of deception and subterfuge, often seek advantage through exploitation of preconceptions, the disciplined analyst will test as many alternative explanations of events that the expansiveness of his or her mind and the extent of his or her contacts with others suggest. Unfortunately not all analysts are so disciplined or highly trained. On this Sherman Kent has commented:

> Some minds when challenged respond with a long-harbored prejudice, some with an instantaneous cliché. Some minds are fertile in the generation of new hypotheses and roam freely and widely among them. Other minds not merely are sterile in this respect but actively resist the new idea.[47]

Certainly, the history of intelligence failures bears witness to Kent's comments. Pearl Harbor in 1941, the 1973 Arab-Israeli War and, more recently, the intelligence analysis leading up to the 2003 U.S. invasion of Iraq are among the more noteworthy examples where analysis fell prey to the darker effects of cognitive bias, where unchallenged predispositions resulted in assumptions about a potential adversary's behavior and a resultant rejection of contrary indicators or an unwillingness or inability to examine alternative hypotheses.

• *Pearl Harbor, 1941*. In the early morning hours of "December 7, 1941—a date that will live in infamy—the United States of America was suddenly and deliberately attacked by naval and air forces of the Empire of Japan."[48] When the final count was over, 2403 Americans lost their lives. Another 1178 were wounded. Five battleships, three destroyers, three cruisers, and 188 aircraft were destroyed. The attack crippled America's Pacific Fleet and left the United States with insufficient military power in the region to retaliate for more than a year. Though there had been indications of an impending Japanese attack somewhere in the Pacific region, the attack on Pearl Harbor came as a total surprise. Our forces had not been placed on heightened alert. No torpedo nets protected the harbor. No scout aircraft were airborne. Antiaircraft weapons were not manned. Most munitions were stored. Army Air Corps aircraft were parked wingtip to wingtip to protect against sabotage not air attack.

Of course, many factors contributed to the inability of American intelligence to foresee such a well-prepared, well-practiced attack. Undoubtedly, as suggested by Roberta Wohlstetter, in her famous 1962 study of intelligence failures preceding the attack, some very significant information was lost in the background noise of communications traffic and signals,[49] Certainly, the absence of a centralized system of intelligence assessment played a role, resulting in the President receiving multiple and frequently differing assessments of the situation.[50] Other factors such as a lack of trained analysts, the underresourcing of the various intelligence providers, the absence of a single analysis of all available evidence, and interservice rivalry played a role.[51] Perhaps if President Roosevelt had shown more interest in Signals Intelligence or if the U.S. Navy had done so and had assigned an adequate number of cryptanalysts to work on breaking the Japanese Naval code (JN25b), which was introduced in 1940, the attack could have been foreseen.[52] And, of course, Japan employed deception. For example, the Japanese task force rendezvoused off of remote northern islands where it was unlikely to be noticed, even by Japanese citizens, Aware that others would notice the absence of Japanese aircraft carriers and other capital ships from the normal port locations, deceptive communications were employed to create the impression that the task force was training off Kyushu, the southernmost of Japan's four main islands.[53]

However, perhaps the single greatest failing was that the United States fell prey to its predispositions. It didn't think the Japanese could or would engage in a direct and deliberate attack on the military forces of the United States. In an article adapted from an award-winning monograph and published in conjunction with the 50th anniversary of the Japanese attack on Pearl Harbor, Harold Ford noted that despite mounting evidence to the contrary,

- there was a predisposition in the Army Command at Pearl Harbor to view the Japanese threat as one that would probably arise primarily from sabotage, not air attack;
- the prevailing belief in top military circles before the attack, with a few notable exceptions, was that the chances of a Japanese air attack on Pearl Harbor were "negligible" and "very remote"; and
- that Pearl Harbor's waters were too shallow to permit the Japanese to launch aerial torpedo attacks; and
- if the United States did not have such a capability; then the Japanese did not."[54]

Such attitudes, undoubtedly, were a reflection of the views held in the United States about the Japanese, which included racial prejudice and cultural arrogance, coupled with limited knowledge and understanding of Japan and the Japanese military, and more than a modicum of mirror imaging. Many thought "the Japanese people lacked inventive powers." "They could imitate but not innovate." "Their arms were no more than copies of Western models. Japan's industry could not turn out a durable product."[55] And finally, since under similar circumstances the United States would not go to war, then Japan, because of her limited industrial and military capability, would never engage in a war against an enemy it could not hope to defeat.

So captive of its cognitive biases, the United States could not bring itself to believe that the "little yellow men," as Churchill sometimes spoke of them and Roosevelt thought of them, were capable of such an astonishing feat of arms.[56] When General Douglas MacArthur first heard of the attack, he insisted that the pilots must have been white mercenaries.[57]

• *Arab–Israel War, 1973.* Following the Israeli victory in the 1967 War with Syria and Egypt, Israeli Defense Minister General Moshe Dayan was asked how the Israeli Defense Forces were able to defeat three armies in six days. What was their secret? His answer: "*Fight Arabs.*" In other words, the Arabs don't have a military culture and therefore they can be easily defeated in combat.[58] Israeli Chief of Staff Haim Bar-Lev, reflecting the same mind-set declared in 1970: "The Arab soldier lacks the characteristics necessary for modern war."[59] The speed with which Israel forces handily dispatched the numerically greater Arab force in what became known as the "Six Days' War" no doubt contributed to the Israeli sense of superiority manifest in the Dayan and Bar-Lev comments.

At approximately 2 PM on October 6, 1973, Egypt and Syria launched a coordinated attack against Israel, which resulted in one of the most intense and devastating conflicts since World War II. The Arab attacks caught the Israelis by surprise. On the eve of the attack, Israeli intelligence reported that war was unlikely. Major General Eliyahu Zeira, chief of Israeli Intelligence, was convinced that Egypt and Syria, which had deployed to the Golan Heights and along the Suez Canal, were only conducting routine training and engaged in saber rattling and would not attack.[60] Indeed, Major General Shmuel Gonen, commander of Southern Command,[61] received an intelligence evaluation two days before the war began that the possibility of war was "the lowest of the low."[62] How could the Israelis, regarded to have one of the world's best intelligence services, have been caught so off-guard?

There were many factors suggesting conflict. Many Arabs continued to feel the humiliation of the disastrous defeat of 1967. Egyptian president Anwar Sadat believed that in order to solve Egypt's political, economic, and military problems it was necessary to restore Egypt's self-confidence and the respect of the world community. To do this it would be necessary to "wipe out the disgrace and humiliation [of 1967]."[63] In 1971 Sadat began seeking arms and ammunition from the Soviet Union. That same year he began to "beat the drums of war." In January

1973 Syria signaled its interest in military action against Israel, entering into negotiations over combined military operations against Israel. In February Egypt and the USSR concluded the largest arms "deal" ever and deliveries of surface-to-air, and surface-to-surface (SCUD) missiles and other munitions and equipment began immediately. Sadat approached Jordan's King Hussein in an effort to bring him into the alliance with Syria.[64] Surely, Israeli intelligence was aware of most, if not all of these efforts. Furthermore, in the month before the attack, Syria began moving forces to the Golan Heights bordering Israel. And, Egypt began calling up its reserves and, on six occasions, maneuvered combat forces up to the Suez Canal in elements as large as divisions.

Yet, a degree of uncertainty remained. Signals throughout this period were mixed. In February 1971 Sadat had launched a "peace initiative."[65] In July 1972, distressed by Soviet delays in the delivery of weapons, Sadat sent packing the 15,000 Soviet military personnel and technicians that were present in Egypt and began making conciliatory gestures toward the West. Moreover, as war approached, Egypt and Syria were extraordinarily adept at deception. In May 1973 the Egyptians, contending that they needed equipment for a fire brigade, purchased powerful, turbine-driven water canon from a West German manufacturer of fire-fighting equipment. The equipment actually would be used to cut through the ramparts on the sides of the Suez Canal so Egyptian forces could cross. Even in mid-September, as the Egyptians and Syrians began to assemble their forces, few Israelis were worried. For the past ten years, except in 1967, the Egyptian Army had held maneuvers every autumn and had moved forces up to the Suez Canal so regularly that there was nothing in the movements on the eve of the attack to necessarily lead to the conclusion that war was imminent.[66] In fact on the morning of the attack Egyptian forces lounged and sunned themselves along the canal.[67] On the Golan, Syria's methodical buildup of forces was seen as a response to recent Israeli air raids into Syria. Claiming concern over the possibility of an Israeli attack, the Syrians deployed their armor in full view of Israeli observation posts in what appeared to be defensive positions—hull down, dug in to resist assault rather than mount one, with medium artillery placed to cover Syrian territory, not Israeli.[68] The Egyptians added to such deceptions through cleverly planted rumors—about poor maintenance of Egyptian weapons systems, that Egyptian forces could not properly operate the Surface-to-Air (antiaircraft) Missiles (SAMs) acquired from the Soviet Union, and there had been a falling-out between Egypt and Syria.[69]

However, it wasn't the uncertainty, the mixed signals, the clever deception on the part of the Egyptians and Syrians so much as Israeli preconceptions, prejudices, and mirror imaging, wishful thinking, that is, cognitive biases, call it "mind-sets" if you will, that led to the Israeli intelligence failure. "Past military successes led to a certain amount of hubris" and an Israeli belief that their inherent superiority would serve as an adequate deterrent to an attack by their Arab neighbors.[70] Indeed, "an attitude of disdain for Arab military capability had etched itself insidiously into the national psyche."[71] Less than two months before the attack, Moshe Dayan reportedly told the Staff College of the Israeli Defense forces, "the balance of forces is so much in our favor that it neutralizes the Arab considerations and motives for immediate renewal of hostilities.[72] Thus, Israeli intelligence was vulnerable to the cleverly devised campaign of deception. Particularly as conflict approached and warning signs increased, the Israelis interpreted Egyptian troop movements as training exercises or saber rattling and were inclined to accept the Syrian explanation for the disposition of its forces in the Golan. Neither Egypt nor Syria would be so foolish to attack such a superior enemy, an enemy they could not defeat. The Israelis refused to contemplate that the Egyptians and Syrians might measure success in ways that differed from their own, that rather than defeating the Israelis, their strategy might have contemplated limited military action followed by political pressure to compel recovery of the occupied territories.[73]

Moreover, the United States reinforced the overall Israeli assessment. Then Secretary of State Henry Kissinger, looking back on the events of October 1973, has commented that our erroneous assumptions about Egyptian and Syrian views of Israeli military superiority resulted in "an intelligence failure" that grew out of "our mindset."[74] On this Christopher Andrew has added:

> The root cause of the [U.S.] intelligence failure . . . was that, at all levels in Washington from the president to junior analysts, the Egyptians and Syrians were not thought capable of the offensive that they launched on October 6.[75]

More to the point, Abraham Robinovich writes:

> The intelligence chiefs believed they knew a deeper truth . . . that rendered irrelevant all the cries of alarm going on around them. Zeira and his chief aides were to demonstrate the ability of even brilliant men to adhere to an *idée fixe* in the face of mountains of contrary evidence. Explaining away every piece of information that conflicted with their thesis, they embraced any wisp that seemed to confirm it.[76]

This was "Cognitive Bias" at its best.

•*Iraq 2002–2003*. In its examination of the intelligence failures preceding the 2003 U.S. attack on Iraq, the President's Commission on Weapons of Mass Destruction concluded "that the Intelligence Community was dead wrong in almost all of its pre-war judgments about Iraq's weapons of mass destruction."[77] In the "Overview of the Report" the commission noted:

> On the brink of war, and in front of the whole world, the United States government asserted that Saddam Hussein had reconstituted his nuclear weapons program, had biological weapons and mobile biological weapon production facilities, and had stockpiled and was producing chemical weapons. All of this was based on the assessments of the U.S. Intelligence Community. And not one bit of it could be confirmed when the war was over.[78]

How could this have occurred? The Intelligence Community's prewar assessments of Iraqi weapons of mass destruction did not occur in a vacuum. Rather they were grounded in the Intelligence Community knowledge about Iraq since before the 1991 Gulf War and dating at least as far back as the Iran–Iraq war of 1980–1988. For example, it was well documented that Iraq had used chemical weapons in its war with Iran: indeed, perhaps with targeting assistance from the CIA.[79] Information also was available that Iraq had imported, under licensing agreements with the United States, potentially "dual use" (i.e., pharmaceutical and/or weapons use) biological agents, including anthrax bacillus and other biological research materials from the United States.[80] Moreover, there was evidence that Iraq had undertaken efforts to develop its nuclear capability since the 1960s. In 1981 Israeli aircraft attacked and crippled the light-water reactor at Osirak to prevent the Iraqis from using the reactor for the creation of nuclear weapons.

Following the 1991 Gulf War, UN inspectors were deployed to Iraq to monitor Iraqi compliance with UN Resolution 687, which confirmed the end of the war and established an inspection regime designed to preclude the future development of Iraqi chemical, biological, and nuclear weapons and missiles with ranges greater than 150 kilometers.[81] Two teams were deployed. The United Nations Special Commission was charged to monitor compliance with the removal and destruction of chemical and biological weapons and missile capabilities. International Atomic Energy Agency personnel had similar responsibilities related to Iraqi nuclear weapons programs. What UN inspectors found out, and the Iraqis later admitted, was that prior to the 1991 war Iraq had been trying to enrich uranium. More significantly, International Atomic Energy Agency's chief inspector David Kay found an Iraqi paper describing their planned nuclear weapons program.[82] Indeed, the U.S. Intelligence Community was surprised to discover the extent of Iraq's nuclear weapons program, which indicated that Iraq had been much closer to developing a nuclear weapon than anyone expected.[83] Indeed, following his defection to Jordan in 1995, one of Hussein's sons-in-law and the Minister of Industry, General Hussein Kamal, reported that he had ordered a crash program to develop a nuclear weapon in August 1990.[84]

Following Kamal's defection, Iraq also admitted that prior to the 1991 war it had a program to develop biological weapons, had produced large quantities of a bulk biological weapons agent, and had actually produced biological weapons.[85] Such an admission was even more troubling in light of the fact that throughout the post-1991 war period not only were there discrepancies between what Iraq was reporting on the number of chemical weapons they had destroyed and what UN Special Commission could actually verify, but UN inspectors were also confronted with increasing Iraqi intransigence.[86] A common practice of the Iraqis was to conceal information or procrastinate on the delivery of information. More significant, however, was the denial to UN inspectors of access to certain sites or delaying entry while vials, diskettes, documents, and the like could be removed or concealed.[87] In July 1998 a group of international biological experts concluded the Iraqi declaration of its biological weapons program was not verifiable.[88] In August 1998 the Revolutionary Command Council and the Ba'ath Party command decided to end cooperation with International Atomic Energy Agency and the UN Special Commission until the UN Security Council lifted sanctions and reorganized and moved the Special Commission to Geneva or Vienna. In December, then chairman of the UN Special Commission Richard Butler submitted a report to the Security Council, concluding:

> Iraq had not in fact provided the full cooperation it promised . . . that the Commission is not able to conduct the substantive disarmament work mandated to it by the Security Council and thus, to give the Council the assurances it requires with respect to Iraq's prohibited weapons programmes.[89]

Finally, in mid-December 1998, in anticipation of Operation Desert Fox bombings by British and American forces in response to Iraq's continued failure to comply with UN Security Council resolutions and its interference with UN inspections, inspectors were withdrawn.[90] They did not return for four years. Freed of the constraining influence of UN inspections, Saddam Hussein would have an opportunity to reconstitute his chemical, biological, and nuclear weapons programs should he chose to do so.

In 1999 "small streams" of intelligence began to appear that suggested that Iraq might be restarting its biological warfare program. Among the key reports were: a foreign source reported that two large companies were involved in the production of nerve gas; a report from a source with "good but historical access" contending that, as of 1998, Iraq was producing mustard and binary chemical agents; and another report from a defector, who contended that he was an expert on VX nerve gas production, claimed Iraq was producing "tons" of nerve agents in mobile laboratories. In September 2002, a liaison service also reported that a senior Iraqi official had indicated that Iraq was producing and stockpiling chemicals weapons and imagery data suggested transshipment activity associated with chemical weapons.[91]

In early 2002 there was a "substantial volume" of "new information" regarding Iraq's biological warfare programs from a source codenamed Curveball. Reports claimed that Iraq had several mobile production facilities and that one of those units had begun production of biological warfare agents. Reports from three additional sources confirmed the existence of mobile facilities.

As for the reconstitution of Iraqi nuclear program, following the overseas seizure of a ship bound for Iraq, the Intelligence Community obtained samples of high-strength tubes made of an aluminum alloy and in March 2001 reported its findings. Some specialists believed the tubes most likely were for centrifuges for enriching the uranium needed for nuclear weapons.[92] In late 2001 and early 2002 the Intelligence Community received three reports from a foreign liaison service that Iraq was seeking to procure uranium ore and yellowcake and that "Niger planned to send several tons" of yellowcake to Iraq. Yellowcake, a uranium concentrate, is an intermediate step in the processing of uranium ore and is used in the preparation of fuel for nuclear reactors. Yellowcake can also be refined to bomb grade material needed in the production of nuclear weapons. One report received from a foreign intelligence service was that in meetings between the Iraq ambassador to the Vatican and Niger officials an agreement was signed for the sale of 500 tons of uranium.[93] In mid-October 2002 a copy of a letter was delivered to the U.S. embassy in Rome written in French, addressed to Saddam Hussein. The letter approved the sale to Iraq of 500 tons a year of pure uranium, which according to nuclear weapons specialists could produce about 10 nuclear weapons a year if properly refined. Mamadou Tandja, president of Niger in 2000, purportedly signed the letter.[94]

Given such a backdrop, it is unsurprising that as the situation began to escalate into a crisis following 9/11, initially one might be predisposed to believe indeed that Saddam Hussein had something to hide and Iraq might well have clandestinely embarked on efforts to reconstitute its chemical, biological, and nuclear weapons programs. However, as war drew closer and policymakers charged the U.S. Intelligence Community to provide them with all the Community knew about Iraq's nuclear, biological, and chemical weapons programs, there was other, often clarifying, sometimes contradictory information available to Intelligence Community analysts, which included the following:

- In addition to reporting that prior to the 1991 war he had ordered a crash program to develop nuclear weapons, General Kamal also reported that *all chemical and biological weapons had been destroyed* on his orders in 1991.[95]
- "The long period of inspections from 1992 to the end of 1998 had yielded much insight into Iraqi weapons programs but *no significant finds of hidden weapons* [emphasis added]." This was even more significant given the techniques and tools developed during this period, not the least of which included environmental sampling that had advanced to a point where "even small particles found in installations or equipment or in the air could yield information about past presence of nuclear, chemical, or biological material."[96]
- Of the earlier "small stream" of reports on Iraq's biological warfare capabilities, none was considered "highly reliable" and only six were considered "moderately reliable." The "substantial volume" of "new information," beginning in 2000 and increasing significantly in 2002, was largely from a single source codenamed "Curveball." Yet *doubts about Curveball's reliability* arose within the CIA's Directorate of Operations as early as May 2000. By early 2002 the foreign intelligence service handling Curveball sent a message to the CIA noting that Curveball's behavior was typical of individuals who they would normally assess as fabricators, and inconsistencies in his reporting have caused them "to have doubts about Curveball's reliability."[97] Of the three other sources that provided reports that seemingly corroborated Curveball's contention that Iraq had developed mobile labs for the production of biological agents, one source, a member of the

Iraqi National Congress had been judged a fabricator in early 2002. The other two also proved problematical.[98]

- The National Ground Intelligence Center, a component of the U.S. Army and recognized as national experts on conventional military systems, largely discounted the notion that the aluminum tubes might be used for rocket bodies rather than for nuclear uses. The Department of Energy, the U.S. government's primary experts on nuclear matters, concluded that although the tubes "could be used to manufacture centrifuge rotors," they were "*not well-suited for centrifuge application*" *and were more likely intended for use in Iraq's 81 millimeter Multiple Rocket Launcher program* [emphasis added]. The International Atomic Energy Agency agreed with this assessment.[99]
- At the request of Vice President Cheney, the CIA sent Ambassador Joseph Wilson to Niger to ascertain whether reports of Iraqi attempts to procure yellowcake could be substantiated. In early March 2002 Ambassador Wilson informed the CIA that he "had found nothing to substantiate the rumors" of Iraq's efforts to purchase yellowcake. In addition, according to Wilson, there were two other similar reports filed, one by American ambassador to Niger Barbro Owens-Kirkpatrick and the other by General Carlton Fulford,[100] who as Deputy Commander of European Command had military responsibility for forty-two countries in Africa, including Niger. The Owens-Kirkpatrick report presumably was what led the State Department Bureau of Intelligence and Research on March 1 to conclude that the Niger sale of uranium to Iraq was unlikely. Moreover, after receiving the documents presented to the U.S. embassy in Rome in October 2002, which seemingly confirmed the Niger sale of "yellowcake" uranium to Iraq, the State Department Bureau of Intelligence and Research alerted the Intelligence Community that it had serious doubts about their authenticity.[101]
- Finally, following their reentry into Iraq on November 17, 2002, UN inspectors, having the best information the United States and other states were willing to provide about possible locations of weapons of mass destruction or their precursors, could find no evidence that Iraq had reconstituted its biological, chemical, or nuclear weapons programs.

Thus the question remains: Why did the Intelligence Community fail so miserably in its assessment of Iraqi weapons of mass destruction programs? How could it have continued to hold fast and so assuredly to the view that Iraq had reconstructed its biological programs, including the use of mobile labs to develop biological agents? How could it have supported the notion that Iraq had reconstructed its nuclear weapons program based on, as the October 2002 National Intelligence Estimate put it, the "compelling evidence" provided by Iraq's aggressive pursuit of high-strength aluminum tubes?[102] How could it have ignored the fact that UN inspectors on the ground in Iraq could find nothing? Why did the Intelligence Community engage in "mirror imaging," assuming that Saddam would act as we would under similar circumstances and only make it difficult for inspectors to verify his compliance with the 1991 agreement to destroy his weapons of mass destruction, if he had something to hide? Why did the Intelligence Community fail to imagine that domestic and regional pressures or other political or psychosocial factors might have prompted Saddam Hussein to destroy his stockpiles of prohibited weapons, yet continue to make it difficult for inspectors to verify that he had done so, or that Saddam might have concluded that uncertainty about whether Iraq had weapons of mass destruction or not might serve as a deterrent to any future attack by the United Sates or others?

Perhaps it was because the Community did not want to make the same error of underestimation it had before the 1991 Gulf War. On this the President's Commission on Weapons of Mass Destruction concluded:

> Th[e] humbling discovery that Iraq had successfully concealed a sophisticated nuclear program from the U.S. Intelligence Community exercised a major influence on the Intelligence Community's assessments throughout the early 1990s and afterwards.[103]

Surely there were other factors also at play. Information was indeed scarce. As it turned out, of course, this was because there were no weapons of mass destruction programs. Perhaps it was the pressure of events. Troops had been deployed to the region. Hot weather was on the way. Decisions had to be made or troops would bake in the desert. Perhaps the political environment played a role. Policymakers don't like the word "maybe." Rather, they prefer a definitive answer, especially if it supports a policy they seek to pursue. On the other hand, operating in an environment in which essential information is often unavailable, analysts can seldom respond definitively. Uncertainty is frequently the coin of the realm. Thus, while analysts feel compelled to communicate uncertainty where it exists so that policymakers will have an unadulterated basis upon which to address policy alternatives, they often feel pressured to provide more definitive answers.

Most assuredly, the failure was driven by a failure within the Intelligence Community, from top leadership levels to analysts, to adequately challenge their own predispositions. Given Iraq's past history of producing chemical and biological weapons and its inability to account for previously declared stockpiles, and given that Iraq had effectively concealed its nuclear program prior to the 1991 Gulf War, analysts operated from the initial premise that it was very likely that Iraq still possessed chemical and biological weapons, was hiding them from inspectors, and continued to seek to rebuild its nuclear weapons program. However, as the President's Commission on Weapons of Mass Destruction noted:

> The analytical flaw was not that this premise was unreasonable (for it was not); rather, it was that the premise hardened into a presumption and analysts began to fit the facts to the theory, rather than the other way around.[104]

The commission went on to note that it "appears that in some instances analysts' presumptions were so firm that they simply *disregarded* [emphasis in original text] evidence that did not support their hypotheses."[105]

In short, as the nation approached war with Iraq, the critical analysis demanded was sidetracked by cognitive biases. Call them assumptions, predispositions, mind-sets, or groupthink, mirror imaging, or lack of imagination—they all are products of cognitive bias.

"Worst Case" Analysis

Though truly a subset of the mind-set problem, worst-case analysis, because it can so insidiously undermine sound analysis, deserves special mention. Richard Betts has written:

> A common reaction to traumatic surprise is the recommendation to cope with ambiguity and ambivalence by acting on the most threatening possible interpretation. If there is *any* evidence of threat, assume it is valid, even if the *apparent* weight of contrary indicators is greater. [emphases in original text][106]

Given Russia's history of invasions by Cumans, Mongols, Swedes, Teutonic Knights, Lithuanians, Crimean Tartars, Poles, French, and Germans—twice in the last century, it is likely Russian Cold War policies were heavily influenced by a desire to not experience any such traumas in the future. Likewise, there is little doubt that in the United States thinking at all levels of government was influenced by the events of December 7, 1941. When addressing issues of Soviet strategic nuclear capabilities or Soviet military capabilities in Europe, from policymaker to analyst there was a singular determination not to be caught by surprise yet again. More recently, the traumatic events of 9/11, proved to have had a lingering effect on the mind-sets of analysts as they engaged in assessments of Iraqi weapons of mass destruction.

The general assumption that it is better to overestimate an adversary's capabilities or intentions than pay the price of underestimating is, in many respects, completely understandable and justifiable. Yet worst-case analysis can have truly pernicious effects. It can be extremely costly and counterproductive. For example, as opponents seek to procure armaments to offset what they perceive as the worst-case trajectory of each other's force structures, armaments costs can spiral upward. Moreover, increases in armaments may threaten to produce a more intensive and/or extensive conflict and thus actually provide for less security rather than more. Increases in arms expenditures also may well result in an increase in mutual suspicions, which in turn feed the next round of worst-case analysis. Worst-case analysis, oft-repeated, also can dull the senses, lulling one side or the other into a false sense of security. Analysts can only "cry wolf" a limited number of times, especially if there are significant costs in responding, before no one listens. Betts notes, for example, between 1971 and 1973 the Egyptians engaged in three exercises similar to those that led to the 1973 Arab-Israeli War. In each case Israel, at great cost, mobilized in response, and nothing happened. As a result, the Israeli Chief of Staff was sharply criticized for the unnecessary cost. Betts also notes that General Westmoreland recalls that U.S. headquarters in Saigon had predicted each year a winter-spring offensive, without any dire results. In ignoring the warnings Westmoreland received prior to the Tet offense in 1968 the inevitable question was: What's new?[107]

Worst-case analysis also can thwart efforts to resolve differences with others through negotiation, with each proposal offered by the opponent interpreted in its worst light, it is likely to be difficult to find solutions that will satisfy all alternative worst-case scenarios. It may even be difficult to get negotiations underway. Worse-case analysis might well suggest to either or both sides that efforts to negotiate are futile, since the other side would only accept a solution that provided it with an advantage. Worst-case analyses can also lead to unwarranted and unwanted conflicts.

Among other things, the tendency to favor worst-case analysis may well have played a role in inviting only tepid efforts to seek alternative hypotheses as explanations for Saddam's unwillingness to cooperate with UN inspectors, who then could clearly establish that Iraq had truly eliminated its biological and chemical weapons and had not attempted to reconstitute any programs involving the acquisition of weapons of mass destruction. As the President's Commission on Weapons of Mass Destruction noted, following the Gulf War of 1991 the Intelligence Community had been traumatized by "the humbling discovery that Iraq had successfully concealed a sophisticated nuclear program."[108] This had a major influence on Intelligence Community assessments of Saddam's biological, chemical, and nuclear programs. Add to that the trauma resulting from its failure to uncover the 9/11 plots and you have the ideal mixture for worst-case analysis, the result of which was an unwarranted and, to many today, unwanted war.

Competence

The issue of "competence" means many things to many people. For example: "His knowledge and experience equipped him with the competence to render an assessment of the situation." Or, "Though he was well-trained and knowledgeable, his assessment reflects an absence of competence." In the first case the judgment of competence was based on the individual's level of knowledge and experience on a given subject. Let us call this Type A competence. In the second case the word "competence" was used to denote his level of skill in applying his knowledge and experience or Type B competence. Intelligence services are frequently confronted with issues associated with Type A competence. Changing threats, personnel turnovers, and lack of personnel to cover the variety of tasks are among the problems that can lead to a failure of Type A competence. Type B competence is usually the result of a failure of the mind to merge knowledge and experience with an understanding of the current situation and its level of seriousness and to engage in the effort required in order to make timely and effective decisions based on the information at hand. Of the two types of competencies, Type B is by far the more problematical. Both types are susceptible to improvement through education and training and the close monitoring and mentoring of supervisors. However, the potential for Type B failure is less easily identifiable and frequently is the unnoticed impediment to effective analysis. For example, if a person has never worked Middle East issues, it is usually obvious to all that there will be a need for some period of education to provide at least a basic level of country, area, and issue competence. On the other hand, Type B competence is more difficult to identify. Unfortunately, often it can only be identified ex post facto. In the intelligence business Type B failures frequently go under the euphemism "failure to exercise good tradecraft" and are often disguised and/or accompanied by other factors that affect one's judgment. Several recent examples stand out as excellent illustrations of this obstacle to successful analysis.

- The Intelligence Community's case in support of the contention that Iraq not only had reconstituted its biological weapons program, but was also producing biological agents in mobile labs largely rested on the reporting of Curveball. Yet, Defense Intelligence Agency personnel did not attempt to validate Curveball's reporting—"a major failure in operational tradecraft."[109]
- The Intelligence Community's judgment about Iraq's nuclear program hinged chiefly on an assessment about Iraq's intended use of high-strength aluminum tubes it was seeking to procure. This error was, in the final analysis, "the result of poor analytical tradecraft—namely, the failure to do proper technical analysis. . . ."[110]
- The Intelligence Community failed to authenticate the documents regarding an alleged agreement for the sale of uranium yellowcake from Niger to Iraq.[111]

Thinking Strategically

Effective analysis requires that analysts think strategically as well as tactically. They must not only be able to identify what are the known facts in a given situation and be able to separate them from their own presumptions and those of others, but also understand the concerns that their country has about the given situation in the context of their country's broader concerns and its short-, medium-, and long-term objectives. But this is just a starting point. Analysts must also have a firm understanding of the tactical and strategic objectives of the other parties involved, as well as their short- to long-term concerns. All this is essential if they are to be able to place the information they receive in its proper perspective and thus provide policymakers with the intelligence required to craft policy alternatives. For Example, Douglas MacEachin noted:

> ... some historical studies have . . . concluded that the more fundamental shortfall that led to the surprise attack on Pearl Harbor was the strategic intelligence produced in the preceding year. [These studies] cite information going back well before the summer of 1941 that revealed that Japanese imperial aspirations in the pacific region were already in conflict with U.S. interests there, and that these were taking Japan on a path that could result in a military confrontation. According to this interpretation, it was the U.S. failure to absorb this strategic risk fully that resulted in military forces' and intelligence resources' unpreparedness, their failure to give priority attention to intercepted communications that suggested that some significant action by Japan was imminent.[112]

Certainly a case can be made that the inability to think strategically was one of the factors that led to the intelligence failures leading up to 9/11. The FBI's Assistant Director for Counterterrorism acknowledged:

> We will never move away from being reactive. We understand that. And that's what people want to talk about most of the time is how's that case going in East Africa, or how's the *USS Cole* investigation going? But if you step back and look at it strategically you need to have people thinking beyond the horizon and that's very difficult for all of us. It's particularly difficult for law enforcement people.[113]

The lack of emphasis on strategic thinking was also evident at the CIA. The former chief of the CIA's Counterterrorist Center testified before the joint House-Senate 9/11 committee:

> We have under-invested in the strategic only because we've had such near-term threats. The trend is always toward the tactical.... The tactical is where lives are saved. And it is not necessarily commonly accepted, but strategic analysis does not . . . get you to saving lives.[114]

There is little doubt that many factors are at play that limit the time and inclination to think strategically. Over-tasking, shortages of personnel, what counts for promotion, and demands of policymakers for current intelligence and its corollary, the prospect of face time with the policy pachyderms, are among the many. Nevertheless, reflecting on the intelligence failures of 9/11, former Director of Central Intelligence George Tenet underscored the importance of strategic thinking:

> [T]he single lesson learned from all of this is the strategic analytical piece of this has to be big and vibrant to give you the chance to be predictive, even when you don't have much information to go on.[115]

Politicized Analysis

Chiseled over the main entrance to CIA headquarters in Langley, Virginia, are the words: "And ye shall know the truth and the truth shall make you free." There is no greater service that analysts within the Intelligence Community can provide the nation's policymakers than objective, thoughtful intelligence, untainted by the personal preferences of supervisors or those of the policymakers themselves. In accomplishing this task it is, of course, paramount that the analyst clearly understand policymaker needs. Understanding those needs requires a dialogue between analysts and their supervisors and policymakers. However, there is a danger in the latter that often threatens the former. Thus, analysts and their supervisors, all the way up to the Director of National Intelligence, should not get so close to policymakers that judgments become "politicized." In short, they should not "become part of the team." It is difficult to measure the magnitude of the politicization problem, though it is likely that the large majority of analysts, as well as their supervisors, are strongly committed to objective analysis. However, on occasion and sometimes with significant adverse consequences, intelligence can and does get politicized.

Politicization of analysis "involves the deliberate distortion of analytical judgments to favor a preferred line of thinking irrespective of evidence."[116] It can occur in several ways. For example, intelligence products can be forced to conform to policymakers' views or to the pressures by management to define and drive certain lines of analysis and substantive viewpoints. It can occur more subtly as a product of efforts on the part of management or policymakers to encourage changes in tone or emphasis or limit the expression of alternative viewpoints made during the normal review or coordinating processes.[117] Or analysts themselves may intentionally skew their views "in order to support the options or policy outcomes preferred by policymakers." Such actions may stem from a variety of motives, including "an effort to be supportive, career interests, or outright pandering."[118] Finally, "analysts have sometimes gone overboard to prove the policymaker wrong."[119] Some years ago, then Deputy Director of Central Intelligence Robert Gates noted: "there is sometimes a strong impulse on the part of intelligence officers to show that a policy or decision is misguided or wrong, to poke an analytical finger in the policy eye."[120]

There is yet another avenue open to the politicization of analysis: that is, the careful manipulation of minds by policymakers through repetitive explanations of events, sometimes reinforced by a compliant press, the consistent discrediting of alternative explanations, and persistent expressions of unadulterated certainty concerning their own conclusions. All of this is intended to affect the development or reinforcing of "conventional wisdoms" about a given situation or series of events, and to shape, at least in part, the body of supposed knowledge available to the public and Intelligence Community analysts and to suppress alternative explanations.

The problem of politicized intelligence predates recorded history. More recently, during the Cold War, concerns that intelligence was politicized were expressed, for example, over reporting of the missile gap of the late 1950s, during the Vietnam War, particularly with regard to reporting on Viet Cong strength, and about the infamous "Team B" findings expressed in the National Intelligence Estimate on Soviet strategic objectives commissioned in 1976.

Following his confirmation as Director of Central Intelligence in 1991, Robert Gates appointed a task force to examine the issue of the politicizing of intelligence. The task force reported that half of those interviewed in the CIA Directorate of Intelligence said, "forcing intelligence to conform to a view higher up the chain of command occurs often enough to be of concern."[121] Indeed, during his confirmation hearings, several intelligence analysts accused Gates himself of politicizing intelligence while serving as Deputy Director of Intelligence under Director William Casey.[122] In 1985 Gates had a meeting with Casey. Casey, not one to divorce himself from politics,[123] expressed the view that the Soviet Union had been behind the 1981 attempt to assassinate Pope John Paul II. Following the meeting, Gates commissioned a paper that was to assemble all the evidence the CIA had that supported the view that the Kremlin was in fact behind the assassination attempt.[124] Nor was former Director of Central Intelligence (1966–1973) Richard Helms, according to some in the CIA, loath to overlay intelligence with politics. Though Helms is reported to have rarely entered the fray until a deadline was looming. "At that point he would often approve one version or another without much by way of explanation, editing out inconvenient information and making other decisions that some saw as arbitrary. Others saw it as cooking the books to [President] Johnson's taste."[125] Later on during his term as Director of Central Intelligence, as the United States was preparing to secretly invade Cambodia and interdict supplies funneled from China through Cambodia to Vietnam, Helms decided not to pass on to the President a CIA report that warned of dangers of invading Cambodia. Helms said he didn't pass the information on because President Nixon and his advisor for national security Henry Kissinger had made up their minds and the report would have just angered them.[126]

Having served as an analyst for nine years at the U.S. Army's Strategic Studies Institute, I became all too familiar with the frequent disparities that existed between analytical products produced by Defense Intelligence Agency and the CIA. More often than not, defense department analysts viewed Soviet strategic, theater nuclear, and conventional capabilities as more capable and more threatening than did CIA analysts. Afforded access to highly classified, even compartmented information, I was charged by the Army to examine some of these same issues. In doing so, I often wondered whether Defense Intelligence Agency analysts were producing truly objective analyses, or as "part of the team," they were reflecting the preferred views of their military and Department of Defense masters. On this Stansfield Turner has commented: "The intelligence agencies in DOD [Department of Defense] are all subject to pressures not to produce intelligence that undercuts policies DOD is pursuing."[127]

Politicization of analysis also can be found outside of government, in organizations that are in theory paid to provide an independent and presumably objective view. While interviewing for a position at a well-known think tank in Washington D.C. in the mid-1970s, it was made clear to me by a senior official at the think tank that the Army was a principal customer and it was "important that our findings met their needs." To this, the senior official added, "on occasion that might mean bending a little, if you know what I mean."

More recently, the issue of politicized intelligence has arisen with regard to Iraq and its weapons of mass destruction programs. The President's Commission on Weapons of Mass Destruction noted: ". . . there is no doubt that analysts operated in an environment shaped by intense policymaker interest in Iraq." And that some analysts were affected by the "conventional wisdom" that Iraq had weapons of mass destruction "and the sense that challenges to it—even refusal to find its confirmation—would not be welcome."[128] A careful reading of the Commission's report might lead one to conclude that while there may not have been direct and overt pressure on the Intelligence Community, a climate had been created that resulted in the politicized intelligence. Since 9/11 there was a growing drumbeat that not only supported but also may well have helped shape the so-called conventional wisdoms about Iraq's weapons of mass destruction—conventional wisdoms that were reiterated and reinforced by a compliant press. The result may have been a subtle, even subconscious, self-inflicted psychological pressure on the part of analysts and their supervisors to conform, which, in turn, may well have led to an altering of tone or emphasis in reporting and a suppression of alternative views.[129]

LOOKING TO THE FUTURE

Like Sisyphus, the tasks that confront intelligence analysts are unending and like Sisyphus each task involves many uphill challenges. Strengthening the relationships between analysts and collectors will require intra- and interagency educational efforts to insure analysts are well informed of the capabilities and limitations of the various collection methods and the complexities collectors face. Collectors will need to have a better understanding not only of the information an analyst needs in order to round out the picture, but also what challenges analysts face as they try to make head or tail of the information they receive. In the past, cross-assignment to other agencies within the Intelligence Community has had some success. But that process has received uneven support. Both education and cross-assignment can help, but both approaches consume the resources of time, energy, and, in the latter case, personnel. In an environment where tasks outstrip resources and are likely to do so for the foreseeable future, transforming the desire for a closer relationship between analysts and collectors into a reality will remain a significant challenge.

As we look to solving the challenges of information, there is little doubt that analysis has benefited greatly from the blossoming of technical capabilities.

Technology has overcome many of the complexities imposed by too little information. However, as threats have shifted away from a few nation-states of security concern to a plethora of international actors, analysis can only benefit from further Intelligence Community investments in human intelligence resources. This will require significant efforts by the Intelligence Community to encourage young people to take up studies in regions and languages of growing security interest. Among other things, it will require advertising and providing attractive career opportunities for those same people. It also will require a well-constructed continuing program of advanced education within the Intelligence Community not only to add depth and currency to an analyst's perspective, but also to provide a means for adapting to changing threats.

However, the oft-forgotten piece in the information puzzle is that many human intelligence sources are not homegrown Americans or émigrés. Rather, they are citizens of other countries, willing to serve the interests of the United States, sometimes at the cost of their own lives. In this sense, the ability of the Intelligence Community to expand its Human Intelligence resource base, and thus reduce its dependency on limited sources, even overcome some efforts by others to deny or deceive, is completely intertwined with the overall success of American foreign policy. Those foreigners who risk their lives by serving the United States do so for a variety of reasons. However, one reason we should not ignore is that some do so because they believe that advancing the interests of the United States is a worthy cause. Thus, America needs to maintain a strong reputation for advancing global interests, not just its own.

The problem of "too much" information is likely to remain. Indeed it is likely to grow. The information age has greatly increased the flow of communications and information. Political, economic, and social globalization have greatly increased the number of those communicating and traveling cross-nationally. Such factors will inevitably add to the information problem. Improvements in data sorting and information sharing can alleviate some of the existing problems by contributing to more efficient, more effective, and timelier analysis. Whether such improvements can keep pace with the increasingly large volumes of information remains to be seen.

The frequently hidden roadblock on the pathway to sound analysis is, of course, cognitive bias—those attitudes, beliefs, and predispositions that we hold, sometimes knowingly and at other times subconsciously, which obscure reality, blind imagination, impede creativity, lead us to seek a haven in comfort of the crowd, and cripple our ability to think "outside of the box." The first step in confronting this challenge is recognizing it not only as an "inherent human frailty,"[130] but also as the point of departure for normal human inquiry. This is a step already taken by the large majority of intelligence professionals. However, in an environment typically characterized by uncertainty in which the analyst is frequently called to render his or her best judgment, it is absolutely essential in follow-on steps that analysts separate what are the known facts from what are hypotheses and cross-examine each and every hypothesis, with a particular emphasis on those derived from their known predispositions and particularly aware of the dangerous role emotions such as fear, anger, hubris, and shame can play.

Education, competitive analysis, brainstorming, and separate teams are among the approaches that can be taken to limit the impact of cognitive bias. Education can be a tool to help analysts better recognize and understand their own attitudes, beliefs, needs, and emotions that filter their perceptions of the external world. It also can help in understanding the outward manifestations of underlying predispositions that color the views of others.

Another approach is to encourage competitive analysis. One of the reasons frequently advocated for maintaining the relative autonomy of the various intelligence agencies has been to encourage and sustain competitive analysis. By encouraging more than one agency to examine issues of national importance, the premise is that "these components would bring their distinct points of view to an issue, increasing the likelihood that all aspects would be considered."[131] Of course the problem today is that with too few resources to address the tasks at hand, the trend has been toward increased specialization among agencies.[132] Furthermore, efforts to further centralize the intelligence processes may improve the sharing of information but run counter to the concept of competitive analysis.

A third method is brainstorming. Brainstorming can be used to enlarge the pool of potentially useful insights. It might include the so-called "brown bag" sessions where analysts present their views to colleagues who may or may not be experts in the specific material under discussion, but are well-versed in the "rules of logic, evidence, and inference."[133] This method is much like that used at professional academic conferences where a paper is presented in hopes that colleagues will challenge the validity of the arguments presented.

Yet another method for limiting the impact of cognitive bias has been to rely on what has become known as the "Team A–Team B" approach. One of the early uses of this approach was in 1976 in the latter days of the Ford administration. Concerned that the CIA had systematically been underestimating Soviet strategic capabilities, the President's Foreign Intelligence Advisory Board first asked Director of Central Intelligence William Colby to establish a "Team B" of outsiders to offer a competitive analysis of the same materials available to the CIA—Team A, so to speak. This approach was finally approved by Colby's successor George H.W. Bush. Team B included team leader Professor Richard Pipes, General John Vogt, Lt. General Daniel Graham, Dr. Thomas Wolfe, and Professor William Van Cleave. The team's advisory panel was composed of Paul Nitze, Ambassadors Foy Kohler and Seymour Weiss, Major General Jasper Welch, and Dr. Paul Wolfowitz. Whether such an approach risks being undermined by fundamental cognitive biases of members of the alternative team remains an open question. Certainly in the 1976 variant, Team B players shared a strong conservative bias in their thinking about Soviet strategic capabilities. Indeed, in a subcommittee report, which examined the 1976 Team A–B episode, members of the Senate Select Committee on Intelligence concluded that Team B "reflected the views of only one segment of the spectrum of opinion." Thus "the outcome of the exercise was predetermined."[134] The team was also accused of falling prey to "worst case" analysis.[135] The subcommittee, however, did note that when properly structured and tasked, such competitive estimates can be helpful and on occasion should be encouraged.[136]

Whatever approach, or combination of the above approaches, is taken to combat cognitive bias, it will not necessarily assist in helping analysts think strategically. Today's education system does not educate people to think strategically. For some, thinking strategically is a self-developed habit of the mind. For others, it is a totally underdeveloped skill. Lawyers learn the rules of evidence and this has made them a valuable commodity in government. But they are not trained to think strategically. Knowledge of the background history and culture of a people and the facts in a given situation is essential, but it is only the starting point and should not be confused with thinking strategically. There are, however, educational tools available to help develop such skills. Some crisis management courses provide techniques that assist in developing the ability to separate facts from assumptions, outline a spectrum of long-term concerns and objectives that might drive the current actions of others, and thus assist analysts in developing the habit of thinking strategically. Certainly, education is a first stop on the agenda in overcoming this impediment to effective analysis. Such education should begin early in an analyst's career and sustained through continuing education.

Finally, while it is difficult to ascertain just how widespread the problem of politicized intelligence really is, the task force appointed by then Director of Central Intelligence Gates following his appointment to examine politicization found that "most analysts and managers remained determined to resist direct or indirect pressures from policy officials for products conforming to their view." The task force also concluded that "concerns about politicization [*sic*] are serious enough to warrant action."[137] Yet it is likely that the problem is more common among political appointees who serve in the Intelligence Community, primarily in supervisory positions, up to and including the Director of National Intelligence and perhaps among some analysts in the Defense Intelligence Agency or on service intelligence staffs. However, the proper relationship between policymakers, and here I include senior Department of Defense and military officials, and the Intelligence Community should be one in which the policymakers "influence which topics intelligence agencies address, but not the conclusions they reach." For its part, the Intelligence Community should limit "its judgments to what is happening or what might happen" in situations under examination.[138]

A great disservice is done to supervisors, policymakers, and the nation, by permitting policy or personal political considerations to skew analyses.

Part III

Dissemination and Use

The final steps of the intelligence cycle involve communicating the information to appropriate policymakers, who then use the information to advance American foreign policy or security interests. It falls to the Intelligence Community, based on the best judgments of intelligence experts, to report to policymakers its conclusions about the information that has been collected and analyzed. This is what is called the "dissemination" phase of the intelligence cycle. Even when current intelligence includes raw data, there is an obligation on the part of the Intelligence Community to make sure that policymakers understand the context and limitations of the data provided. So, ideally, no information provided to policymakers goes to them completely unexplained.

While technically the so-called intelligence cycle ends with the dissemination phase, the success of the overall intelligence effort can not be measured until the intelligence provided by the Intelligence Community is put to use. These last two steps of the U.S. intelligence effort, dissemination and use, are where the "rubber meets the road," and where the final payoff for the elaborate U.S intelligence system is realized. Thus, they are perhaps the most critical in the entire intelligence process.

Chapter 5 will address the means and methods used by the Intelligence Community to communicate intelligence to policymakers and the impediments to the efficient, effective, and timely dissemination of intelligence. Chapter 6 addresses major problems in the use of intelligence.

5

Dissemination

"...a man's judgment cannot be better than the information on which he has based it."

—Arthur H. Sulzberger

MEANS AND METHODS OF DISSEMINATION

Decision makers receive intelligence in a number of ways and via a variety of intelligence products. Sometimes senior intelligence officials personally brief policymakers on significant items of interest. Sometimes intelligence is received in written form. Some intelligence products are passed to policymakers on a regular basis, some periodically, as the situation warrants. Some documents, when passed to senior policymakers, are accompanied by a briefer from the Intelligence Community that is there to answer questions and clarify as may be necessary. Sometimes intelligence is passed in the form of prepared statements and answers to questions during hearings, as is often the case with Congress. Products received by policymakers include intelligence that focuses on current events and issues and estimative intelligence, as well as a wealth of assessments, reports, and memoranda.

Current Intelligence

Intelligence on day-to-day events and developments around the world, or "current intelligence" as it is called, is provided to policymakers daily, sometimes several times a day, especially during crises. For example, each morning the President receives the *President's Daily Brief*, a practice that dates to the Truman administration. It is a written document that is briefed to the President orally by a small cadre of senior Intelligence Community analysts. It usually consists of six to eight relatively short articles or briefs covering a broad array of events of the past day or two or on issues expected to arise within the next few days. Appended to the Brief is the *National Terrorism Brief*, which includes the latest information on terrorist activity and counterterrorist efforts. The President's Daily Brief often contains highly sensitive intelligence about sources and methods or operational information. Its dissemination is limited to a small number of individuals designated by the President. This group, which usually includes the Vice President, the Secretaries of State and Defense, the President's national security advisor, and the chairman of the Joint Chiefs of Staff, also is briefed orally by senior analysts of the Intelligence Community on the contents of the Brief.

Should questions arise during these daily briefings, the Intelligence Community is tasked to provide answers. Responses are then provided to those who receive the President's Daily Brief in what is called the *President's Daily Brief Memorandum*.

The President and his close advisors also receive the *Director's Daily Report*. This document is produced by the FBI and is the basis for regular oral briefings to the President by the Director. It includes information on terrorist threats, counterterrorism operations and other areas of FBI focus, such as investigations of criminal, cyber, and counterintelligence activities.[1]

The Intelligence Community also distributes intelligence to other senior policymakers within the executive branch. For example, *The Senior Executive Intelligence Brief* is disseminated to several hundred senior officials within the executive branch and to those members of congressional committees charged with overseeing the work of the Intelligence Community. It is similar in format and content to the President's Daily Brief. However, in order to protect sources and methods and certain operational data, it usually contains less information. Senior members of the executive branch may also receive the *Senior Executive Memorandum*, a document tailored to inform them of responses to questions raised by the President and his close advisors during the President's Daily Brief, without revealing sources or other sensitive information. The FBI's *Director's Daily Report* also is circulated to other senior officials in government.

Senior decision makers, with subordinate intelligence organizations or agencies, also receive daily briefings from those entities. For example, no matter where on the globe he or she may be, every morning the Secretary of State is provided with a summary of important intelligence. Prepared by the State Department's Bureau of Intelligence and Research the *Secretary's Morning Summary* focuses on intelligence relevant to American foreign policy. The Secretary of Defense receives a similar brief. The *Military Intelligence Digest* is prepared by the Defense Intelligence Agency. Both the *Secretary's Morning Summary* and the *Military Intelligence Digest* are prepared primarily for policymakers within their respective departments but are circulated elsewhere within the executive branch.[2]

As is appropriate and the occasion warrants, the President and other senior decision makers receive intelligence updates throughout the day or week. Updates may include raw intelligence—that is, unevaluated intelligence, or slightly finished intelligence that contains some commentary on the credibility of sources. Updates may be delivered in person by intelligence officials or passed through a secure communications network. They also may be accompanied by *Situation Reports*, which are short reports that comment on current, fast-breaking events.

Senior policymakers, as well as members of Congress, also have access to what are known as *Serial Fliers* and *Sense of the Community Memos*. Serial Fliers are short and concise memorandum style intelligence products that usually focus on a specific topic of current relevance and are generally a few pages in length. Sense of the Community Memos are Intelligence Community-coordinated and National Intelligence Council chairman-approved one-page memoranda that evaluate current or day-to-day events. Current intelligence also is disseminated to senior policymakers and others with a need to know as the information and situation dictate.

Estimative or Long-term Intelligence

In addition to current intelligence, the President and other senior policymakers receive or have access to a number of longer-term intelligence estimates and analyses. Most prominent among those are the National Intelligence Estimates, Intelligence Community Assessments, and Intelligence Community Briefs.

National Intelligence Estimates are the most authoritative assessments of the Intelligence Community of the future course of events on a particular national security issue. However, they only estimate, not predict, the future, assign confidence levels to key judgments and note dissenting opinions should they exist. In these documents, words such as "we judge," "we assess," or "we estimate" are used to convey the notion of an analytical assessment or judgment. Words like "we cannot rule out," "unlikely," "probable," or "almost certainly" are used to convey judgments about the degrees of likelihood of occurrence of a particular event. And, words like "high," "moderate," or "low" are used to express the degree of confidence the Intelligence Community has in its assessment of a particular issue or event, based on the scope and quality of information supporting its judgments. Some analytical judgments are based directly on collected information, others on previous judgments that serve as building blocks. Still others are based on incomplete or at times fragmentary information. National Intelligence Estimates are fully coordinated within the Intelligence Community, reviewed, and approved for dissemination by the National Intelligence Board, which is composed of the Director of National Intelligence and other senior Intelligence Community officials.

Intelligence Community Assessments are research papers, usually 20–30 pages or more in length, that provide a detailed data logic trail on key national security issues. They are coordinated within the Intelligence Community, noting any disagreements in analytical judgments, and disseminated only after the approval of the chairman of the National Intelligence Council. The FBI produces its own *Presidential Intelligence Assessment*, covering topics of particular interest to the President.

Intelligence Community Briefs are six-page, quick turnaround, estimative Intelligence Community-coordinated analytical intelligence products that focus on particular issues. Like the National Intelligence Estimates and Intelligence Community Assessments, Intelligence Community Briefs also note any disagreements that exist among intelligence analysts.

Policymakers also have available to them a range of additional documents such as *Conference Reports*, the *Strategic Perspective Series*, *Research Projects/Papers*, *Leadership Profiles*, and *Situation Reports* to assist them in understanding a particular issue. Moreover, intelligence agencies, such as the State Department Bureau of Intelligence and Research, the Defense Intelligence Agency, and the military service intelligence organizations, prepare an extraordinary array of assessments for their respective departments and organizations.[3]

Other Intelligence Products

Conference Reports are memoranda-for-the-record of conferences sponsored by the National Intelligence Council on various topics. Conferences frequently include Intelligence Community personnel, as well as experts from outside the Community.

Strategic Perspective Series is a CIA product. Each paper in this series usually is from 5 to 25 pages or more in length and focuses on a key strategic issue that often cuts across analytic disciplines or regions. Examples include "Muslims in the EU: Reshaping Islam and Transforming Europe," and "China's Global Strategic Ambitions." Strategic Perspective Series papers include a "Key Findings" or "Summary" section and may include graphics, maps, and other supporting material.

Research Projects/Papers are the primary vehicle used to explore new analytic research areas and to develop the CIA Directorate of Intelligence's corporate knowledge of a given issue. A research project may culminate in a *Serial Flier, Intelligence Assessment,* or a *Strategic Perspective Series* paper or, depending upon the results, may be disseminated only within the Intelligence Community or limited to the CIA's Intelligence Directorate, serving then as a "capital-building" research paper.

Leadership Profiles are generally 1–2 page biographic assessments of foreign leaders. They often are tailored for a particular meeting or event.

Situation Reports are short reports that comment on current, fast-breaking events. Up to two or three situation reports can be issued daily, if warranted.

IMPEDIMENTS TO DISSEMINATION

Among the more salient impediments to the effective dissemination of intelligence are such factors as

- the need to protect sources of intelligence and the methods by which it is garnered;
- limitations on the time available to policymakers to read materials or receive briefings from the Intelligence Community;
- flaws inherent in the dissemination processes;
- absence of policymaker trust or confidence in judgments of the Intelligence Community;
- decision maker frustrations over intelligence that is often ambiguous, incomplete, changing, or perceived to offer only forecasts of gloom and doom; and
- the Intelligence Community's occasional penchant for failing to adequately caveat its findings, thus leading decision makers to conclude that Intelligence Community findings are backed by a greater degree of certainty than the actual intelligence warrants.

Protection of Sources and Methods

In 1950, as the postwar intelligence effort was being shaped, the National Security Council issued Intelligence Directive Number 11. In that directive the National Security Council set forth the policies and procedures for protecting both the sources of intelligence and the methods by which intelligence is acquired. It gave to the Director of Central Intelligence the responsibility for protecting intelligence sources and methods from unauthorized disclosure. It also directed all U.S. entities engaged in intelligence activities to take steps to prevent the unauthorized disclosure of information that might lead to a revelation of sources and methods. It fell to the Director of Central Intelligence to coordinate the policies of those U.S. government entities within the Intelligence Community toward this end. The Directive also noted that the phrase "intelligence sources and methods" includes information ostensibly acquired overtly that requires security protection because of its specific means of procurement or specific place of procurement, the revelation of which would endanger intelligence sources and methods. It also further limited such information to only those whose official duties require such knowledge.[4] The result has been the establishment of a series of classifications and sensitive compartments (see Chapter 3) additionally circumscribed by the "need to know" criterion that restricts the dissemination of intelligence.

Perhaps the most noteworthy historic U.S. example of the effect of classifications and other restrictions on the dissemination of intelligence was the case of Pearl Harbor. The United States had been intercepting Japanese diplomatic transmissions under the codename MAGIC (see Box, also see Chapter 3).

Among Things Known by U.S. Intelligence from MAGIC Intercepts

- Japan was anticipating a break in relations with the United States.
- Japanese offices abroad had been informed that when they receive a weather report with the words "East Wind Rain," they were to destroy all code papers in preparation for war.
- Two weeks prior to the attack the Japanese had been padding the volume of their radio traffic with previously issued or deliberately garbled messages, presumably to thwart U.S. decoding efforts.
- Foreign Minister Togo informed Japanese Ambassador Nomura in Washington that U.S.–Japanese negotiations had to be settled by 29 November, because "after that things are going automatically to happen."
- The message "East Wind Rain" had been transmitted on December 4, 1941.

See Richelson, *A Century of Spies*, 118–119 and Ford, "The Primary Purpose of National Estimating," 69–70.

From MAGIC and other sources the U.S. intelligence agencies also knew that in mid-November the Japanese government had requested its consulate in Honolulu to report at least twice a week on the ships in the Pearl Harbor. They knew as well that Japan had been practicing simulated aerial torpedo bomb attacks against ships in harbor, and that Japanese agents had been reporting on local military installations at Pearl Harbor, Clark Field in the Philippines, and elsewhere. They knew three days before the attack that all Japanese offices abroad were to destroy all coded papers, that Japanese aircraft carriers were out of port and their location was unknown, and that the United States had lost track of Japanese submarines. And they knew that Japan had engaged in a surprise attack with especially lethal effect when it attacked the Russian fleet at Port Arthur in 1904 without a prior declaration of war.[5]

Unfortunately, neither General Walter C. Short, the Army commander in Hawaii, nor Admiral Husband E. Kimmel, the naval commander at Pearl Harbor, were cleared to receive MAGIC. It wasn't until late November that Washington shared MAGIC intercepts with Kimmel. None were shared with Short, though he had a MAGIC-related monitoring station under his command at Fort Shafter. Likewise, Joseph C. Grew, our ambassador to Japan, was not cleared for MAGIC.[6]

One can only speculate that had either or both of our senior military officials in Hawaii been privy to MAGIC on a regular basis, it might have had a dramatic effect on their estimates of Hawaii's vulnerability to Japanese attack. As a minimum, it might have been enough to set alarm bells ringing on November

27, when Washington cabled a warning meant to express a heightened degree of concern.[7]

Similarly had our very able ambassador in Japan been a regular recipient of MAGIC, he might have pieced together events as they were unfolding and provided a measure of warning to Washington. In January 1941 a Peruvian minister had warned him that the minister had learned "from many sources" that in the event of a serious breakdown in U.S.–Japanese relations, Japan "intended to make a surprise attack against Pearl Harbor with all their strength and emphasizing all their equipment."[8]

Today, concerns of intelligence leaks that might reveal sources and methods continue to limit the dissemination of information. Though the President identifies those individuals that will receive the information in his Daily Brief, the appended National Terrorism Brief, and the Presidents Daily Brief Memorandum, the Intelligence Community entities must every day decide who else gets what intelligence and when. Not all individuals who believe they have appropriate clearances and need to know are regular recipients of classified information. This includes members of Congress with intelligence oversight responsibilities, as we shall see in Chapter 8.

Other factors, such as bureaucratic politics and institutional culture and policies, undoubtedly play a role in limiting the dissemination of classified information. For example, in terms of bureaucratic politics, Jennifer Sims has noted:

> Competitive and iterative policy formulation encourages policymakers singly and as a group to limit those who have access to the best information. The decision maker's interest in maximizing influence and control over the decision-making process is entirely compatible with the intelligence manager's interest in limiting access to sources and methods to only a few customers.[9]

An example of how institutional culture and policies can affect the dissemination of intelligence was noted by the joint House–Senate inquiry into 9/11. According to the Committee the CIA considered it the FBI's responsibility to deal with the domestic threat posed by terrorists. As a result, the CIA was not sufficiently focused on advising the State Department on all terrorist operatives who might be traveling to the United States, so the operatives could be placed on the "watchlist" used to screen such persons at ports of entry.[10] Similarly, the joint House–Senate inquiry noted that a perception among agencies that they have "ownership" of the information they acquire also impedes the free flow of information.[11]

However, the need to protect sources and methods frequently provides the principle impetus and underlying rationale for restricting the flow of intelligence. For example, according to the joint House–Senate inquiry, officials in the departments of Treasury, Transportation, and State reported that, although they received threat warnings from the Intelligence Community, they did not always receive information that adds context to the warnings. This lack of context, they contended, prevented them from estimating the value of the threat information and thus taking any necessary preventive action.[12] Such limits on context, more frequently than not, result from concerns over sources and methods. This is perhaps nowhere truer than the frequent failure to disseminate information to state and local authorities.

While state and local officials have been adamant about the need to share intelligence, they have often been left in the dark. For example, former Virginia governor James Gilmore testified that in his four-year term he never received any intelligence or law enforcement information on terrorists. Similarly, the police commissioner for Baltimore testified that he did not receive intelligence information about suspected terrorists living within his jurisdiction, even though some may have been associated with the 9/11 hijackers.[13]

Limitations of Time and Space

It is not by whim that the number of items addressed in the President's Daily Brief or the Senior Executive Intelligence Brief is limited. Senior policymakers have limited time in their daily schedule to focus on intelligence. Thus, it falls to the Intelligence Community to decide what 6–8 or so issues warrant inclusion in such documents. Such judgments are likely to be based on a range of factors such as: What is the likely policymaker interest in the issue? Is the information critical to U.S. security and/or foreign policy concerns? Is it related to a current or ongoing crisis? Does the information represent a significant change from previous data that had been provided? Has the information been specifically requested? In each case, except where information has been specifically requested, the Intelligence Community must make a judgment call. Something that might not seem critical today, may be just the information needed for the policymaker to make decisions to preclude a calamity tomorrow. Yet the time policymakers can devote to intelligence issues and the space available in current intelligence briefs place limits on what is disseminated on a daily basis.

It also is not surprising that an executive summary accompanies the usually future-focused National Intelligence Estimates. Few senior policymakers, whether in the executive branch or in Congress, have the time or will take the time to read through most National Intelligence Estimates. At best, they may read the executive summary. Here again it is up to intelligence officials to determine what information to include. Wording, style, and inference are important, as are the issues to be highlighted and the extent to which concurrence exists within the Intelligence Community. A slight shading of information, failure to emphasize nonconcurrence by an agency with primary responsibility for a particular issue, and omissions can color an executive summary in a way that obscures issues that warrant challenging, reduces the probability that decision makers will feel a need to read beyond the summary, and thus can lead policymakers to decisions unwarranted by available facts. Even the Director of National Intelligence can have an effect on the inferences drawn from estimates. During the Reagan administration,

Director of Central Intelligence, as the position was then called, William Casey is reported to have argued, fought, yelled, and grumped with analysts in person or on paper and wordsmithed documents. In the end, if he didn't agree with an estimate, "it was not unusual for him to attach a letter to the President saying, 'This is the estimate, but I disagree.'"[14]

Available time and policymaker interest also can result in the inability of intelligence officials to disseminate information or to get policymakers to focus on an issue they deem important. Such was more than likely the case in January 2001 when Richard Clarke, then serving as the first National Coordinator for Security, Infrastructure Protection, and Counterterrorism, tried to get the George W. Bush administration to focus on the growing threat of al-Qaeda. He approached then Assistant to the President for National Security Condoleezza Rice in an effort to get her and the new President to accord terrorism a high priority. Within days he submitted his recommendations in a memorandum to Rice, urging a "Principals Committee" or cabinet-level meeting to review what Clarke considered the imminent al-Qaeda threat. Clarke reports that Rice told him that though the Principals Committee had been the first venue for terrorism policy discussions during the Clinton administration, the Bush administration would not address the issue until it had been "framed" by the Deputies (i.e. deputies to those on the Principals Committee). No Deputies Committee meeting on terrorism occurred until April. Although the Principals Committee met frequently on other subjects, such as the Middle East peace process, Russia, and the Persian Gulf, no Principals Committee meeting on terrorism was held until September 4, 2001, seven days before the devastating attacks.[15]

Flaws Inherent in the Dissemination of Intelligence Products

The very formats used to disseminate intelligence may, on occasion, mislead policymakers. On examining the evidence that led to the Iraq war, the President's Commission on Weapons of Mass Destruction noted deficiencies in the dissemination of intelligence. For example, after reviewing a number of articles that appeared in the Daily Briefs received by the President and other senior officials relating to Iraq's weapons of mass destruction, the Commission concluded that there were flaws inherent in the format of some current intelligence documents. Such documents contain a series of short "articles" often based on current intelligence reporting. However, their brevity leaves little room for doubts or nuance. Their attention-grabbing "headlines" leave no room at all. The daily drumbeat of repetition, left the impression of many corroborating reports where in fact there were few sources, sometimes only one. And they were more alarmist than the National Intelligence Estimate on Iraq.[16]

Moreover, in some instances, although intelligence suggesting the existence of Iraqi weapons programs was conveyed to policymakers via the *Daily Briefs*, subsequent information casting doubt upon the validity of the earlier reports was not.[17]

The Commission also noted that the National Intelligence Estimate process has its flaws. Its length tends to encourage policymakers to rely on the less cautionary worded Key Judgments. Furthermore, most agencies believe that the language of consensus may obscure situations in which the dissenting agency has more expertise than the majority view.[18] Furthermore, the very format of the document, in terms of what is addressed and how, can have an impact on the utility to the policymakers of the document's conclusions. In its critique of the National Intelligence Estimates produced by Teams A and B in the mid-1970s,[19] a subcommittee of the Senate Select Committee on Intelligence faulted the narrow format that had been chosen for the Estimate. According to the subcommittee, while the strategic weapons balance was the principal subject of both the Team A and B Estimates, the documents were dominated by military hardware questions and defined "strategic power" quite narrowly.

> . . . the NIE [National Intelligence Estimate] did not address the question of how Soviet strategic weapons development fits into important larger concerns (the entire panoply) of Soviet domestic, military, diplomatic, economic, and cultural efforts.[20]

Indeed according to the subcommittee, by design neither document placed U.S.–Soviet strategic matters within the "wider framework of other dynamic world forces, many of which are essentially creatures of neither U.S. nor Soviet initiative or control." As a consequence, the subcommittee concluded: ". . . the NIE's discussion of Soviet objectives was too brief to be useful."[21]

Absence of Trust or Confidence

The President and other senior executive branch officials know that sometimes the views among some intelligence analysts differ from their own. But they often believe that those differences are driven by policy biases that exist within the Intelligence Community, particularly the CIA. On such occasions they frequently are suspicious that analysts are using intelligence to sabotage selected administration policies. Thus, policymakers are sometimes predisposed to downgrade or disregard analyst views. It might be facile to conclude that this is just a case of policymakers simply rejecting intelligence that does not conform to their favored view. However, former Deputy Director of Intelligence Robert M. Gates conceded that, on occasion, policymaker concerns are warranted. For example, Gates noted:

> When Secretary of State Alexander Haig asserted that the Soviets were behind international terrorism, intelligence analysts initially set out, not to address the issue in all of its aspects, but rather to prove the secretary wrong—to prove that the Soviets do not orchestrate all international terrorism. But in doing so they went too far themselves and failed in early drafts to describe extensive and well-documented indirect Soviet support for terrorist groups and their sponsors.[22]

When intelligence analyses that differ from their own views are widely circulated among members of Congress and made available to the public, policymakers become doubly suspicious, believing that some within the Intelligence Community are engaging in a malicious effort to undermine administration policies by providing information that could be used by critics of its policies.[23] Such concerns frequently have resulted in high classifications and tight controls on intelligence documents, including limiting, delaying, or denying information to Congress.

Analyses and Forecasts Often Based on Incomplete, Ambiguous, and Changing Information

Policymakers labor under the enormous pressures of a never-ending string of issues demanding resolution. When they turn to a specific issue and seek information in order to take a specific action, generally they seek definitive answers and they usually want them now not later. On the other hand, the intelligence processes are seldom given to provide definitive answers, the final story so to speak. Rather intelligence more often than not is, at best, capable of providing a series of time-constrained snapshots. What may seem true today, even be true today, may change tomorrow as more information comes available for analysis. Thus, analysts, in attempting to provide as accurate an assessment of a given issue as is humanly possible, are engaged in a never-ending search for information that either confirms or challenges the more generally held views. At any given time the information available may be incomplete, ambiguous, or worse—it might be wrong. Hence, analysts are often forced to revise, update, or correct information previously provided to policymakers as new information becomes available. This can be a source of unending frustration for policymakers attempting to set a policy course and devise an accompanying strategy. When they find that they have made decisions based on Intelligence Community assessments only to see them change or find they are wrong, they are unlikely to think fondly of the Intelligence Community or soon be willing to make decisions based on assessments provided by intelligence officials in the future.[24]

In the 1970s, when the United States and the Soviet Union were engaged in negotiations to limit conventional forces and equipment in Europe, CIA assessments of Warsaw Pact forces changed on several occasions. This was frustrating for policymakers, who had made decisions and developed negotiating strategies based on earlier assessments only to see those assessments change over time. Likewise, the constantly changing and frequently differing estimates of Viet Cong strength coming from the Intelligence Community during the Vietnam War were a continuing source of stress between decision makers and intelligence personnel.

Similarly, in his State of the Union address to the nation on January 10, 2007, President Bush called for an increase in the number of U.S. military forces in

Iraq to counter growing terrorist attacks—the so-called "troop surge." However, changing intelligence assessments on the threat posed by al-Qaeda, on the success of ongoing efforts to reduce violence in Iraq, and on prospects for the future complicated President Bush's efforts to develop a consensus among the American people and in Congress.

The "Gloom and Doom" Syndrome

The willingness of policymakers to take seriously information provided to them is often troubled by what some policymakers see as the "gloom and doom" syndrome. While serving as deputy director of the Central Intelligence Agency, Robert M. Gates noted:

> . . . a special criticism by policymakers is that the CIA is too frequently a voice of gloom and doom. For policymakers who must try to find solutions to intractable problems or a way out of a no-win situation—for example, the various conflicts in the Middle East—the CIA's forebodings and pointing out of perils and dangers are of little help and may be highly irritating.[25]

Equally troubling to policymakers can be a tendency among analysts to overly qualify their findings—a problem more prevalent among analysts drawn from the academic community who have only a few years of experience in the Intelligence Community. Such overly qualified findings can lead to analyses that thoroughly obscure an analyst's best estimate of a situation and significantly complicate, rather than assist, in overcoming a policymaker's dilemma in devising a strategy to deal with a given situation.

Providing Certainty Where Facts Only Indicate Uncertainty

The task of communicating intelligence to decision makers involves a great deal of judgment and a high degree of emotional detachment and honesty on the part of the Intelligence Community. Assumptions must be made explicit. The quality and freshness of the information must be revealed. Limitations in collection and analysis must be outlined. Conclusions must be well supported and well reasoned. Intelligence officials also must detail just how speculative or firm their judgments are and include significant dissenting views. Unfortunately this is not always the case. The President's Commission on Weapons of Mass Destruction in its investigation of pre-Iraq War intelligence concluded that the President's Daily Brief likely conveyed a greater sense of certainty about analytical judgments than was warranted.[26]

Moreover, commenting on the October 2002 National Intelligence Estimate on Iraq and other prewar intelligence assessments, the Commission noted:

> In many instances, we found finished intelligence that was loosely reasoned, ill supported, and poorly communicated. Perhaps most worrisome, we found too many analytic products that obscured how little the Intelligence Community actually *knew* about an issue and how much their conclusions rested on inference and assumptions . . . analysts must be willing to admit what they don't know. . . .[27]

Put simply, the Commission concluded, ". . . pre-war intelligence assessments failed to articulate the thinness of the intelligence upon which critical judgments about Iraq's weapons programs hinged."[28] Rather than clearly conveying the level of uncertainty that existed in several critical judgments, a sense of certainty prevailed.

For example, the October 2002 National Intelligence Estimate judged with moderate confidence that "Baghdad ha[d] reconstituted its nuclear weapons program." By this the Intelligence Community meant that Iraq was in the "process of restoring [its] uranium enrichment capability."[29] Much of this judgment rested on the question of whether Iraq was attempting to acquire aluminum tubes for use in centrifuges designed for the production of nuclear weapons grade materials.[30] The Estimate indicated that Iraq was attempting to acquire aluminum tubes and that according to sensitive reporting, Saddam Hussein was "personally interested in the procurement of aluminum tubes," of which one of the likely uses might be part of an effort to reconstitute Iraq's nuclear weapons program. However, the "sensitive reporting" was a single report from a foreign intelligence service that supposedly reported that Saddam was "closely following" the purchase. The report could not be confirmed and remained in dispute. CIA officials even disputed whether it was the report from the foreign intelligence service that contended that Saddam was closely following the aluminum tube purchase or another CIA official.[31] Nevertheless, the National Intelligence Estimate did not reflect the level of uncertainty associated with the aluminum tube issue.

Moreover, the Estimate also identified other evidence to support its conclusion about Iraq's nuclear weapons program, including Iraqi attempts to procure the so-called dual-use items such as magnets and balancing machines that could be used in centrifuges for the production of nuclear weapons materials. According to the President's Commission, this evidence, like the information on the aluminum tubes, "was based on thin streams of reporting." Thus the Commission concluded that the Intelligence Community failed to communicate the paucity of information supporting its findings and failed to reflect the level of uncertainty associated with its judgments.[32]

Similarly, the October 2002 National Intelligence Estimate assessed with "high confidence" that Iraq had biological weapons. However, U.S. intelligence officials knew little about Iraq's biological weapons program prior to the 2003 war. Though in 1995, after the United Nations Special Commission on Iraq (which had been tasked to monitor compliance with removal and destruction of such weapons following the 1991 war) presented evidence that the Iraqis were continuing to import biological warfare-related materials, Iraq did admit it had produced and weaponized biological agents prior to the 1991 Gulf War. U.S intelligence also knew there were serious concerns about the reliability of the reporting received from "Curveball," the human intelligence source providing the vast majority of information on Iraq's current biological weapons program. Yet such concerns and the level of uncertainty associated with Iraq's efforts to rebuild their biological warfare capabilities were not clearly conveyed in the Estimate. Rather, as the President's Commission concluded, our analysts allowed "reasonable suspicions about Iraqi BW [Biological Warfare] activity to turn into near certainty."[33] On the other hand, the Commission went on to note that policymakers must be prepared to accept uncertainties and qualifications in intelligence judgments and not expect greater precision than the evaluated data permits.[34]

In its October 2002 National Intelligence Estimate the Intelligence Community also concluded with "high confidence" that Iraq had renewed production of chemical warfare agents. Though it was careful to caution that it had little specific information on the composition, location, or size of the Iraqi stockpile of chemical warfare agents, it estimated that Iraq had somewhere between 100 and 500 metric tons—a significant jump from the10- to 100-metric ton estimate earlier in the same year. These judgments relied primarily on imagery and some leaps of imagination (see Chapter 4). It also relied on small streams of reports from human sources, none of which were considered "highly reliable" and only six deemed "moderately reliable."[35] Once again, much of the evidence lacked the credibility necessary for the level of certainty assigned by the Intelligence Community in its National Intelligence Estimate.

In terms of communicating certainty when only uncertainty is warranted, no greater disservice was done to the nation than in the days before the 2003 American invasion of Iraq when, in answer to President Bush's question about how confident he was that Saddam Hussein possessed weapons of mass destruction, then Director of Central Intelligence George Tenet responded: "Don't worry, it's a slam-dunk case."

Looking to the Future

While it is beyond the scope of this effort to examine alternatives to improving the dissemination and use of intelligence, much can be done. Among the initial steps that can be taken, intelligence officials can avoid the iterative inclusion of questionable single source reporting in such documents as the President's Daily Brief and the Senior Executive Intelligence Brief.

Second, the intelligence officials can ensure that policymakers are immediately privileged to any subsequent information that casts doubt on earlier information that was provided to them. Briefers accompanying such updated analyses can be helpful in bringing perspective to competing and contrasting information.

Third, the Intelligence Community can avoid transmitting a greater degree of certainty than is warranted. This problem, of course, is not new. Early in the

Cold War, as Atomic Energy Commission chairman David Lilienthal watched CIA analysts assemble estimates of Soviet progress toward acquiring atomic weapons, he found a complete "lack of integrity." "Meager stuff" was written up in a way that obscured their lack of information and level of uncertainty.[36] As an enduring problem, transmitting a perception of certainty where the nature of the information available only warrants uncertainty has some pernicious effects. It provides policymakers with misleading impressions that can lead to significant policy failures. Moreover, once discovered it undermines policymaker confidence in the very intelligence system upon which the security of the nation depends. This is a serious problem that must be addressed. You can only cry wolf with certainty so many times, before your cries are completely ignored. Once the integrity of the system is restored, policymakers may well be receptive to changes in the intelligence they receive.

Furthermore, to the extent that the Intelligence Community, including the Director of National Intelligence, can influence the situation and as the situation warrants, National Intelligence Estimates should be constructed to address specific issues within the broader framework of other dynamic forces at work that might affect the situation, such as global as well as country-specific political, economic, social, cultural, and military factors that might bear on the situation under consideration. An inclusion of such information would provide policymakers with a more robust understanding upon which to base policy decisions. This also will likely help limit policymaker inclinations to make worst-case assumptions on foreign policy and security-related matters.

6

Using Intelligence

"It is sometimes more difficult to make effective use of good intelligence than to collect it in the first place."

—Christopher Andrew

We now leave the carefully structured world of intelligence collection, analysis, and dissemination and enter into a much less structured world when we talk about the use of intelligence. How senior policymakers use intelligence depends largely on the policymakers themselves, their background, knowledge of the subject matter, previous experiences with the intelligence processes, understanding of the strengths and weaknesses of collection methods, and so on. As a result, many are avid users and readers and aggressively seek the views and analyses of the Intelligence Community. Some, from the President on down, dedicate considerable time to discussing substantive issues with intelligence briefers and specialists. Some policymakers directly task the Intelligence Community and offer their reactions to the information they are provided.[1] On the other hand, some policymakers are less engaged, in general or on specific issues. Some are primarily interested in current intelligence. Others, taking a more strategic view, seek a balance of current and longer-term intelligence. Some focus primarily on the "facts," others pay closer attention to Intelligence Community analyses and estimates.

President Truman, despite having served as a U.S. senator for ten years and briefly as Vice President before President Roosevelt's death, was largely ignorant of intelligence matters on assuming the duties of President in April 1945. Though the architect of the post-World War II intelligence system, Truman was primarily interested in current intelligence and preferred facts to analysis. In contrast, President Eisenhower had a deep appreciation for intelligence. Having actually employed it to military advantage in World War II, he understood the vagaries and limitations of data and estimates. Moreover, his wartime experiences helped him develop a broad, long-term view of world affairs and he wanted intelligence to match that outlook.[2] President Kennedy had been badly burned by the CIA's wishful thinking rather than solid analysis that Cubans would rally to the Bay of Pigs insurgents. Nevertheless, he was a strong supporter of John McCone, who replaced Allen Dulles as Director of Central Intelligence after the Bay of Pigs fiasco and remained fascinated by the romance and excitement of secrecy, espionage, and covert action.[3] He also revived, upgraded, and met frequently with the board of consultants on intelligence formed by President Eisenhower, renaming it the President's Foreign Intelligence Advisory Board.[4]

President Johnson is reported to have treated intelligence with disdain, while President Nixon had an abiding distrust of the CIA. Both sought intelligence that confirmed either what they already believed or would support their policies. Neither sought truly independent analyses from the Intelligence Community. Nixon also considered the President's Daily Brief too opinionated. With his background in world affairs and with Henry Kissinger at his side, first as national security adviser and later as Secretary of State, acting much like Truman, Nixon just wanted the facts from which he could draw his own conclusions.[5] As a result, he paid little or no attention to the Daily Brief, while relying on a daily compilation of information prepared by Kissinger.[6]

President Ford took an entirely different approach to intelligence than his two immediate predecessors. He saw the CIA as a think tank where the President could get independent judgments.[7] President Carter had a strong interest in the organization of the Intelligence Community as well as its output. Like Ford, he sought an intelligence apparatus that would provide independent judgments. No one was to direct analysts as to the conclusions they should reach.[8]

President Reagan was the polar opposite of his Vice President George H.W. Bush, who followed him as President. President Reagan apparently didn't care much for the "ins and outs of intelligence." He had no previous experience as an intelligence consumer. He was not a voracious reader. He did not pay much attention to the President's Daily Brief.[9] On the other hand, his successor Bush had an extraordinary degree of experience in foreign affairs and had served as Director of Central Intelligence. Even as Vice President he was an avid consumer of intelligence. As President, the President's Daily Brief was Bush's first order of business. Rather than have the Director of Central Intelligence conduct the Brief, he preferred working-level officers. This would give him and others who were at the Brief a chance to talk directly with those who were possibly the most knowledgeable on the subject. Following the Brief, he often had the briefers stay as he made calls to world leaders, so they could supplement his knowledge on the topic at hand if necessary.[10] Bush used and respected the intelligence processes, kept the Director of Central Intelligence close, and used the information those processes provided.

President Bill Clinton, initially with little foreign policy experience, had an interesting relationship with the Intelligence Community. He was an avid reader of intelligence. According to former Director of Central Intelligence Stansfield Turner, Clinton read and retained every piece of information with which he came in contact. However, though he started every day with the intelligence report, he did not want to be briefed by intelligence officials. He kept his Director of Central Intelligence James Woolsey at arms length. And with the end of the Cold War and Congress demanding that there be a peace dividend, he found himself less concerned with the intelligence establishment than with fulfilling his campaign promise to cut $7.5 billion or about a quarter of the intelligence budget.[11]

Like Clinton, President George W. Bush came to office with little experience in international affairs and not much appreciation for the intelligence processes, their strengths, weaknesses, or limitations. He retained George Tenet as Director of Central Intelligence despite his long association with Democrats. However, he quickly appointed the former national security adviser to President Ford and Bush senior Brent Scowcroft to head a commission to review the state of U.S. intelligence. The President largely ignored the recommendations of the commission.[12] The 9/11 attack, the wars in Afghanistan and Iraq, and the challenges of dealing with terrorism must surely have transformed him into an avid consumer of intelligence.

OBSTACLES TO THE EFFECTIVE USE OF INTELLIGENCE

Time and Institutional Memory

Time remains public enemy number one. The time available for policymakers to focus critically on the intelligence they receive, to digest its implications, to probe for additional information, and to mull over the consequences of multiple policy options in response is greatly limited. As a result, regardless of the amount or quality of intelligence provided to senior policymakers on a particular problem, pressing issues may eclipse the use of that intelligence in the formulation of policy. For example, on October 18, 1990 *National Intelligence Estimate* 15–90 was issued on Yugoslavia. In an unusually bold manner the Estimate forecast the inevitable breakup of Yugoslavia. It characterized the Yugoslavia envisioned by Josip Tito as a failed state and estimated that Yugoslavia would "cease to function as a federal state within one year" and would probably dissolve within two." The breakup would likely be accompanied by intractable and bitter large-scale ethnic violence and unrest, which could lead to conflict that might spill over into adjacent regions.[13] Former Vice Chair of the National Intelligence Council and staff member of the National Security Council Gregory Treverton has written:

> This estimate was no weasel-worded least common denominator. The footnotes that registered dissenting opinions all sought to paint the outcome as gloomier than the basic text, not less so.[14]

Treverton further noted that the document had no effect. Senior members of the Bush foreign policy team were preoccupied with other issues.[15] The Soviet empire was collapsing. Freely elected governments were emerging all over central Europe. Iraq had invaded Kuwait a few months earlier and the United States was in the process of deploying seven Army and two Marine Corps divisions, six Carrier and two Amphibious Battle Groups, fifteen Air Force Tactical Fighter Wings, one Marine Corps Air Wings, and all supporting equipment and supplies to the region. The forty-five-year division of Germany had ended two weeks earlier. Within a month, thirty-four NATO and Warsaw Pact countries would sign a treaty limiting Conventional Forces in Europe. The Bush administration was preparing for a UN Security Council meeting to take place in November, which would authorize member states to use force if Iraq didn't withdraw from Kuwait by January 5, 1991. In three months the United States along with its UN allies would be at war with Iraq.

Against this backdrop, it was understandable that policymakers may have been too preoccupied to pay much attention to the Estimate. As Treverton notes, "It was news they didn't want to hear. Hoping that Yugoslavia might somehow stay together was *convenient*." Besides, Deputy Secretary of State Lawrence Eagleburger and National Security Advisor General Brent Scowcroft had both served in Yugoslavia and had seen it work. However, there were those knowledgeable individuals who believed that only by diverting Slovenia's drive for independence and encouraging it to settle for a loose Yugoslavia federation could disaster be avoided.[16]

In retrospect it is facile to speculate as to whether greater attention by senior policymakers to the warnings provided by the Estimate might have led to more dynamic efforts by Washington to encourage federation rather than independence and thus have spared the peoples of the region the carnage of the conflict that ensued. Indeed, the Estimate was pessimistic on this issue. However, what is certain is that time for thoughtful consideration of the full ramifications of the Estimate and a subsequent search for promising solutions was not at hand.

Lack of time also forces senior policymakers, particularly the President, his White House Team, and cabinet members to rely on the judgments of those around them—their deputies, undersecretaries, and particularly assistant and deputy assistant secretaries. Regrettably, turnover in such positions is frequently high. Today, for example, it is reported that the average tenure for the most senior Department of Defense officials—the Secretary of Defense, Deputy Secretary, and military department secretaries—ranges between eleven and twenty months.[17] Other estimates place the most common tenure for assistant secretaries and other senior officials in government at eighteen to twenty-four months.[18] Worse yet, since political appointees, whose appointments must be confirmed by the Senate, fill almost all those vacancies slow selection and confirmation processes frequently accompany the high turnover. According to one report, an incoming presidential administration will routinely tolerate 50 to 60 percent vacancy rates in Senate-confirmed positions in the first year, easing to 20 to 30 percent vacancy rates thereafter.[19]

Such an environment has several pernicious effects that limit the effective use of intelligence. Institutional memory is degraded with each departure, including institutional memory of previous intelligence findings and their nuances that were dictated by the circumstances at the time. While the immediate vacuum may be filled by a subordinate with longer-term tenure, the temporary replacement, by virtue of his or her previous subordinate position, is often neither to have been privileged to the same broad range of information as the departing senior official, nor to have been afforded the same opportunity to develop the departing official's broad perspective. As a result, presidents pressed for time are forced to rely on advisers who often lack institutional memory of the history and context of intelligence findings and analyses and thus are less able to provide valuable advice.

Preoccupation with Current Intelligence

Under the pressure of events, policymaker preoccupation with current intelligence limits is understandable if not acceptable. It is only natural that policymakers are inclined to spend available time attempting to understand intelligence related to issues of immediate importance in terms of current or pending crises. This is not a new problem. As then Deputy Director Gates noted over twenty years ago, one of CIA's greatest concerns is that policymakers have been either unwilling or unable to spend much time on longer-range issues. Despite CIA efforts, Gates further lamented, policymakers simply fail "to devote time to intelligence issues other than those directly related to a crisis."[20]

Nothing much has changed over the past twenty years. Indeed, if anything the problem has been exacerbated by the general inexperience in foreign and security policies of presidents (few come to office with the wealth of experience in those matters as had Richard Nixon or George H.W. Bush). Moreover, the short tenure of other senior policymakers has frequently further exacerbated the problem. Rapidly trying to grasp the significance of events, sometimes with little background on the issues at hand, presidents and other senior decision makers find little time to worry about the future. Unfortunately, this failure to focus on intelligence that addresses longer-term issues frequently precludes decision makers from making adjustments to current policies that would help circumscribe, if not prevent, future crises. Thus the use of intelligence for long-term preventive purposes remains largely a prayer rather than a reality and this failure is ultimately very costly to the country.

Worst-case Assumptions

Decision makers, like analysts, prefer to err on the side of safety. Risk taking is not a desired feature when the nation's security is at stake. Charged with the security of the nation, policymakers are more likely to see the glass half empty than half full. Thus, intelligence that suggests threats to U.S. foreign policy goals or danger to U.S. security interests is likely to be given more attention and weighted more heavily in policymaker deliberations than counterbalancing information that suggests the contrary. Such an emphasis on the worst of possible cases distorts the information received from the Intelligence Community and thus can significantly limit the effective use of intelligence in the development of policy options. While indeed this approach can lead to decisions that protect the nation's interests should such a worst-case develop, it can also lead to a significant waste of resources, exacerbate or even create a crisis, and close policy doors that might otherwise have been open.

During the Cold War, U.S. and Soviet policymakers frequently made worst-case assumptions about each other's nuclear capabilities and intentions. The result was a spiraling arms race that led to less not more security for each party. Among examples of policies forged on "worst case" assumptions is the Reagan administration's response to the Soviet strategic threat in the early 1980s. During the Carter administration Ronald Reagan had been a member of the Committee for the Present Danger and had accepted the worst-case analysis that was common to many on the Committee. Some members of the Committee made their way on to 1976 National Intelligence Estimate Team B mentioned above. Several Team B members joined the Reagan administration in 1981. Though the Team B estimate had been adjudged flawed by a subcommittee of the Senate Select Committee on Intelligence as well as others,[21] President Reagan was predisposed to Team B views. Among the arguments made by Team B and their supporters were—

- Soviet leaders rejected the concept of mutual deterrence.
- Soviet leaders rejected the western view that nuclear war was unthinkable and subscribed to the view that war, even nuclear war, was simply politics by other means.
- Thus the Soviets were engaged in a drive for dominance based on an unparalleled military buildup. They seek victory, not deterrence; superiority, not sufficiency in weapons; and offensive action, not retaliation.[22]

Perhaps more significantly in terms of worst-case conclusions, it was argued in an oft-posited scenario that the Soviet Union could fight and win a nuclear war. The scenario went like this. First the USSR, using missiles launched from submarines stationed off the U.S. east coast, would explode a few nuclear weapons above the continental United States. Because of the short flight time of these missiles, the United States would be unable to react before the exploding weapons created an electromagnetic pulse that would cripple communications and thus preclude U.S. authorities from launching a retaliatory strike. Subsequent attacks on U.S. nuclear retaliatory forces— intercontinental ballistic missile sites, bomber bases, and nuclear submarine bases and their ocean patrol areas—would then be initiated. Given Soviet air defenses, some limited antimissile defenses, and Soviet civil defenses, the United States would have an insufficient number of surviving retaliatory forces capable of responding. Under such circumstances the Soviet Union would have escalation dominance and the American president would surely seek political accommodation rather than continuing the war. In short, the Soviets would have achieved victory. In response to such thinking, Reagan acted on such worst-case assumptions and initiated what many considered a costly, wasteful, and unnecessary massive military buildup.

The problem with this popular worst-case scenario was that there was a huge gap between theory and political and operational realities. One had to believe that in pursuit of "victory" however defined, Soviet leaders would be willing to risk all in one cosmic throw of the dice. Moreover, they would have to assume that their forces actually had the capability to conduct such an attack (highly unlikely at the time), that everything worked perfectly, and that the United States would not react out of anger and indeed use its few remaining forces to destroy Soviet cites, including Moscow.

Biases and Predispositions

Policymakers are no more disease-resistant to the deleterious effects of cognitive bias than are collectors and analysts. In fact they may be less immune. Training and the constant challenging of views that takes place among colleagues and between competing intelligence agencies serve as self-correcting mechanisms within the Intelligence Community, often limiting the impact of biases and personal predispositions among collectors and analysts. Senior policymakers enjoy few such benefits. Indeed, elected officials often are forced to develop strong-minded views and find ways to defend those views publicly by whatever means available. After all, neither the American public nor the press is culturally prepared to accept the leadership of someone who changes positions on an issue—a so-called flip-flopper.

In such an environment, it is easy to develop resolute beliefs, attitudes, and predispositions, which ultimately limit one's ability to comprehend, absorb, and react to information that runs counter to those beliefs. In the case of the President, this can be a serious impediment to the effective use of intelligence and this impediment often extends beyond the President. Those who chose to hitch their star to an individual who ultimately succeeds in becoming President often come to share the same biases and predispositions. Moreover, convinced of the correctness of their views, presidents often surround themselves with political appointees who also share their personal biases and predispositions. Indeed, sometimes the selection process for senior political appointees is so thoroughly dominated by rigor in the pursuit of ideological homogeneity that the process itself gets bogged down, with doubly pernicious effects. The President is not only denied competing views but, with the delay in filling vacant positions, he is also denied advice that might raise important questions, even if the individual shared similar predispositions. Such an environment of mutual reinforcing beliefs is detrimental to the effective use of intelligence.

History is replete with examples where policymakers let predispositions interfere with the effective use of intelligence. Among the examples one might cite where policymakers fell victim to their own personal bias and predispositions are America's inability to foresee India's 1998 nuclear tests, Stalin's unwillingness in 1941 to accept the intelligence indicating that Germany would attack Russia, and the British defeat in Singapore in 1942.

- *Indian Nuclear Testing, 1998*. In May 1998, to the surprise of U.S. officials, India conducted two sets of nuclear tests.

Background

Jawaharlal Nehru, the first prime minister of independent India, had often pledged that India's interest in nuclear technology was for purposes that were purely peaceful. Since Nehru genuinely abhorred nuclear weapons, he was generally taken at his word.[23] However, with two hostile neighbors—China and Pakistan, Nehru in 1958 openly signaled India's willingness to use such technology for deterrent purposes, noting that India had the capability to build an atomic bomb in three to four years.[24] In the United States the Intelligence Community knew that pressure to develop nuclear weapons as a deterrent was increasing with the growing awareness of China's atomic weapons efforts. A September 1961 National Intelligence Estimate concluded that India was improving its overall capabilities in the nuclear field, possibly in anticipation of a future requirement to develop an operational capability.[25] In October 1962 war broke out between India and China over a disputed region of the Himalayan border. India lost. In May 1964 Nehru died. On October 16 the same year China conducted its first nuclear test. Eight days later the chairman of India's Atomic Energy Commission, Homi Bhabha, in a broadcast on All-India Radio declared "atomic weapons give a State possessing them in adequate numbers a deterrent power against attack from a much stronger State."[26]

Neither Prime Minister Lal Bahadur Shastri, who acceded to the position following Nehru's death, nor Indira Gandhi, who succeeded Shastri following his death from a heart attack, were eager to produce nuclear weapons. However, Indian scientists continued their work and in early September 1971, Gandhi gave the go-ahead to ready a nuclear device for testing. During this period, the U.S. policymakers, as well as the Intelligence Community, were well aware that political and prestige factors as well as India's need to be able to deter Chinese aggression or neutralize any Chinese efforts at nuclear blackmail might impel India toward developing atomic weapons. At 8:05 AM on May 18, 1974, India tested its first nuclear device—a fission device claimed to have been of the explosive power of between 12 and 15 kilotons,[27] roughly equivalent to the atomic bomb dropped on Hiroshima in 1945.

For the next twenty-four years India continued to develop its nuclear capabilities. On three occasions they came close to conducting further nuclear tests. Each time U.S. officials dissuaded them. In 1977, warned by U.S. intelligence that then Prime Minister Morarji Desai had authorized Indian scientists to refine a design of an atomic device, President Carter sent an envoy to meet with Desai. As a result, Desai pledged, "I will never develop a bomb."[28] In 1981, following intelligence reports indicating that Pakistan's nuclear weapons program was moving ahead, Indira Gandhi, who had returned to be prime minister the year before, gave scientists her initial approval to test two nuclear devices. When U.S. spy satellites detected test preparations and U.S. officials confronted the Indian government, Gandhi backed down.[29] Once again, in 1995 the analysis of imagery data obtained from U.S. intelligence satellites suggested India was preparing to undertake nuclear tests. U.S. diplomatic efforts including a call to then Prime Minister Narasihma Rao by President Bill Clinton convinced Rao to forego testing.

In March 1998 India's right-wing Hindu nationalist party, the Bharatiya Janata Party (Indian People's Party) came to power.[30] It had long called for nuclear testing and the introduction of nuclear weapons into India's arsenal. In keeping with its previous position on nuclear weapons, in the run-up to the election, the Party promised to reevaluate India's nuclear policy and "exercise the option to induct nuclear weapons."[31] Once in office, the new Indian government carried through with its promise with two sets of tests on May 11 and 13, 1998.

Why American Officials Were Caught by Surprise

U.S. intelligence had long tracked India's nuclear efforts. Since its first nuclear device was tested in 1974, India had often been on the brink of testing. The Party that came to power in 1998 had often called for nuclear testing and the development of a nuclear arsenal. The Indian public was increasingly in favor of nuclear testing. China already had a well-developed nuclear arsenal. Pakistan, India's arch enemy, was known to be capable of producing nuclear weapons. All of this was known to U.S. policymakers.

Immediately following the 1998 Indian nuclear tests, then Director of Central Intelligence George Tenet initiated an investigation. Admiral David Jeremiah, former vice chairman of the Joint Chiefs of Staff, was called upon to lead the investigation. Admiral Jeremiah's final report remains classified. However, portions of the report were leaked to the press. As might have been anticipated, the report indicated that a host of factors played a role in America's inability to foresee India's nuclear tests. There were failures of imagination, failures of information gathering, and failures of analysis. There was faulty leadership and training in the Intelligence Community. The CIA had too few spies in India. U.S spy satellites produced more information than could be analyzed by overworked and undertrained analysts. But, what really stands out from the report is that not just intelligence officials, but senior American policymakers had an "underlying mindset"[32] that India would not test nuclear weapons. Commenting on this, Gordon Oehler, a former director of the CIA's Nonproliferation Center, said senior Clinton administration officials sometimes disregarded the views from within the

Intelligence Community that did not fit their "preconceived view of what the world ought to look like."[33]

- *Operation Barbarossa, 1941*. Operation Barbarossa was the codename for the German invasion of the Soviet Union. On June 22, 1941, more than three million German troops crossed the Soviet frontier, launching an offensive from the Baltics to the Black Sea. Despite numerous indications of an impending attack, the offensive caught the Russians by surprise, trapping their forward divisions that were subsequently destroyed.[34]

Background

There had been a number of indicators of potentially hostile German military action, among which were:

- Starting in August 1940 the Germans began redeploying their troops eastward. In less than four months the number of German divisions facing the Soviet Union grew from 5 to 34. By the end of February the number was about 70, by May it was 87, and on the eve of the attack stood at 123.
- Soviet authorities detected a significant increase in German spies in the months leading up to the war. Many of these spies were probing Soviet border defenses and assessing the state of affairs inside the country. In the period from April to June 1941 the number of German spies detected was 25 to 35 times higher than in the corresponding period a year earlier.
- Following a secret order in October 1940, the Germans engaged in extensive aerial reconnaissance of Soviet territory.
- German deserters warned the Russians of an impending attack.
- Seven days after Hitler signed the directive authorizing the attack an accurate summary of the document was forwarded anonymously to the Soviet military attaché in Berlin.
- On June 9, 1941, the German embassy in Moscow received instructions to secure its secret documents and authorized the inconspicuous departure of women and children. The Soviets learned about these instructions two days later.
- Finally, warnings of impending attack came from a number of nations, including the United States and Great Britain.

Why The Soviet Union Was Caught by Surprise

Of course there were numerous factors. There was a wealth of information, signals, warnings, and intelligence reports available to the Soviets. Some were credible. Some were not. Some cast doubt on others. Thus there was a degree of uncertainty characteristic of mixed signals in an environment of plenty. Also the

Germans engaged in significant efforts to deceive the Soviets, offering alternative rationales for the eastward deployment of its forces.[35] Indeed, in two secret letters to Stalin, Hitler informed the Soviet leader that the troops are being deployed eastward to protect them from British bombing and to conceal preparations for the invasion of Britain. Hitler wrote "on my honor as a head of state" Germany would not attack the Soviet Union.[36]

However, the principal reason why Russia was caught by surprise was that Stalin simply refused to believe that Germany would attack. Rather he held to the notion that the British were trying to start a German-Soviet war. He held this belief so strongly that he "consistently rejected raw intelligence from his best intelligence officers that suggested Hitler might be planning to attack,"[37] blindly accepted Hitler's explanation, and considered German deserters who warned of impending attack provocateurs and ordered them to be shot.[38] In short, Stalin was trapped by his own preconceptions into ignoring the multitude of indicators of attack.

- *Singapore 1942*. Considered by Winston Churchill to be the "greatest disaster ever to befall British arms,"[39] Singapore fell to the Japanese in February 1942. An island at the southern tip of the four-hundred-mile-long Malay Peninsula, it was the principal British military base in the Far East. The base had been established to protect Britain's economic empire in that region. Considered an impregnable fortress, the Gibraltar of Eastern Asia, Singapore was a strategically vital part of the British Empire.

Background

The Japanese attack on Singapore came almost at the same time as their attack on Pearl Harbor. In their initial efforts they attacked poorly defended British airfields throughout the Malay Peninsula. By December 9 the Japanese had destroyed nearly all of Britain's frontline aircraft. On December 8, 1941, in order to disrupt the landing of Japanese forces on the Malay Peninsula north of Singapore, the British dispatched the modern battleship *HMS Prince of Wales* and the battle cruiser *HMS Repulse* and other supporting naval forces from Singapore. On December 10, as they were making their way north they were repeatedly attacked by Japanese torpedo bombers. Fighting without protective air cover, both British warships were sunk. The British could neither disrupt the landing of Japanese forces nor provide air support for their army, as it fought the Japanese advancing down the peninsula. Of even greater surprise was the swift Japanese advance southward.

On February 15, 1942, Singapore fell to the Japanese. Though estimates of Japanese and British forces vary, by one account "some 130,000 well-equipped British, Australian, and Indian officers and soldiers, with ample battle stocks, capitulated to just 35,000 hungry, exhausted Japanese frontline troops, almost out of ammunition and at their last gasp."[40]

What the British Knew Before the Battle

- Since the turn of the century Imperial Japan was a rising maritime power.
- Japan surprised the world by defeating the Russians in the Russo-Japanese War of 1904–1905. In doing so Japan had demonstrated to the world that they could apply western technology, discipline, strategy, and tactics effectively in war.
- By the 1920s and 1930s Japanese militarism was on the rise.
- For continued economic development and prosperity, Japan needed resources that were readily available in Asia, such as coal, tin, iron, and rubber.
- Japan conquered Manchuria in 1931.
- Japan invaded China in 1937, quickly dispatched Chinese forces and seized Nanjing, the capital of the Nationalist forces under Chiang Kai-shek.
- Having been decisively defeated in the north by Soviet and Mongolian forces in August 1939 at Khakhin Gol, known by many as the battle of Nomonhan, Japan turned its attention southward toward French Indo-China and Thailand, which lie directly north of Malaya.
- In September 1940 Japan aligned with Nazi Germany and Fascist Italy.
- Japan was blatantly spying on British military installations and exercises.
- By June 1941, under the guise of mediating between belligerents, Japan established a formidable military presence in French Indo-China.
- Later that same year Japanese air forces moved to bases in southern Indo-China that were well within range of Malaya.
- During the last several months of 1941, Japanese pilots were openly conducting reconnaissance flights over British airfields and military installations.
- On December 4, 1941, a drunk Japanese civilian spilled the beans, including sketches, about the planned simultaneous attacks on Pearl Harbor and Malaya to a Royal Air Force serviceman in civilian clothing in Cambodia. The following day the serviceman reported the information to British intelligence.

* See Colonel John Hughes-Wilson, *Military Intelligence Blunders* (New York: Carroll and Graf, 1999), 103–120.

Why the British Were Soundly Defeated

Most certainly, there were a number of factors that contributed to the British defeat. Adequate funds were never made available to ensure that the island bastion was truly defensible. British prime minister Winston Churchill believed that Japanese would never attempt a siege of Singapore with a hostile, superior American fleet in the Pacific.[41] The Japanese attacked with fighters that had been battle-hardened fighting the Chinese, while many of the defenders had never fired a shot in combat. The Japanese had light tanks and their infantry used bicycles for mobility. British forces had no tanks and were completely surprised by the clever use of bicycles. Allied air forces were ill trained. Allied aircraft were poorly built, ill equipped, and had too few spare parts. The American-built Brewster F2A "Buffalo" fighter plane was no match for the frequently demeaned Japanese Zero. There were the oft-criticized strategy and tactics employed by British army lieutenant general Arthur E. Percival in commanding the defense. He had stretched his forces across the entire 70-mile coastline of the Island. There was the infamous British captain Patrick Heenan, who provided invaluable intelligence to the Japanese. British intelligence efforts were fragmented, poorly coordinated, and lacked local human resources for collection. The British had confidently predicted an attack would come from the sea. It was inconceivable to the British that the Japanese would attack the Island, as they did, through the jungles and mangrove swamps of the Malay Peninsula north of Singapore.[42]

However, the single most significant factor that resulted in the British defeat can be summed up by the term "cognitive dissonance." The British simply refused to believe that tiny men from Asia could defeat a superior white force. Many genuinely believed the Japanese were physically small, had poor vision, and were incapable of fighting in the dark or operating sophisticated machinery. One naval expert wrote, "Every observer concurs . . . that the Japanese are daring but incompetent aviators . . . they have as a race defects in the tubes of their inner ear, just as they are myopic. This gives them a defective sense of balance." Moreover, they "could not fire rifles because they could not close one eye at a time" and "would flee at the first sight of a white soldier."[43] Perhaps remarks made by Air Chief Marshall Sir Robert Brooke-Popham, then British commander-in-chief of the Far East, on visiting Hong Kong in 1940 best summed up British disdain for the Japanese fighting man.

> I had a good look at them [the Japanese guards on the frontier] close up across the barbed wire, of various subhuman species dressed in dirty grey uniforms. . . . If they represent the average of the Japanese army . . . I cannot believe that they would form an effective fighting force.[44]

Thus, despite all of the information at hand about Japan and the military capabilities of its fighting forces, which had been amply demonstrated by battlefield successes, the British were blindsided into complacency by their own predispositions.

Politicizing Intelligence

Admittedly, there is but a fine line between policymakers who, commanded by their own predispositions, interpret intelligence in accordance with their predispositions and those who knowingly skew intelligence to conform to their preferred policies. Perhaps the difference can be illustrated by a brief example. If in 1942 British policymakers truly believed the Japanese were incapable of forming an effective fighting force and therefore further fortifying Singapore in

1941 was unnecessary, they would have been acting on their predispositions. On the other hand, if British policymakers knew the Japanese were a dangerous and effective fighting force, but chose to ignore that information because it didn't accord with their preferred policy of avoiding expenditures, they would have been politicizing intelligence. Policymaker politicization of intelligence involves attempts to influence the findings of the Intelligence Community, the deliberate disregard of Intelligence Community findings, or selective use (often referred to as "cherry-picking) of intelligence—all to suit policy preferences.

Unfortunately this is an all too common occurrence. Among the cases involving some form of politicization of intelligence that one might mention are the U.S. intervention in the Dominican Republic in 1965, the 1969 SS-9 Controversy, Chinese sanctions in the 1990s, and the 2003 Iraq War.

- *Dominican Republic Intervention, 1965.* In the middle of the Cold War, President Lyndon Johnson, concerned about events in Vietnam and the spread of communism in the Western hemisphere, sent U.S. military forces into the Dominican Republic ostensibly "to protect" Americans and others from the violence associated with an attempted coup which had the support of communist elements in that country.

Background

In May 1961, longtime Dominican dictator Rafael Trujillo was assassinated. Following a period of turmoil, Juan Bosch was elected president in the first free elections in thirty-eight years. Bosch took office in February 1963. He was an anti-communist, leftist reformer who had won by a convincing 2 to 1 majority. During his short tenure, he initiated sweeping economic, social, and political reforms, encouraging labor and peasant movements, sponsoring agrarian reform, nationalizing some industries, rooting out corruption in government, and promulgating a new constitution that advanced civil liberties.

Though the United States supported Bosch with extensive economic, technical, and military assistance, it was leery of further growth of communism in the region. Bosch respected the rights of communists to speak and assemble freely. Conservatives in the United States were concerned that Bosch was allowing communists to infiltrate the country. One reporter for the *Miami News* claims "Communist penetration of the Dominican Republic is progressing with incredible speed and efficiency."[45] Indeed, the U.S. ambassador Bartow Marin, concerned over events in the Dominican Republic, accused Bosch of being soft on Castro communists.[46] Bosch's policies had antagonized the Catholic hierarchy, the military, and the upper classes in the Dominican Republic as well as U.S. officials. Even former supporters on the Dominican political Left were dismayed as Bosch reforms foundered.

After just seven months in office, military leaders who considered him too leftist ousted him in a coup. A civilian triumvirate replaced Bosch. The triumvirate soon became a two-man triumvirate, dominated by appointed President Donald Reid Cabral. Reid's appointment was greeted with enthusiasm in Washington and lavish economic and military assistance followed. However, Reid, though well-intentioned, was as incapable of solving the country's economic and political problems as Bosch had been and succeeded in alienating labor, business, consumers, and many professional groups, as well as senior military leaders. Thus the country remained in turmoil as conspiracy, intrigue, and incessant plotting reigned.

On April 24, 1965, a group of military officers rebelled and attempted to restore Bosch to the presidency. The attempted coup had the support of the far left pro-Moscow, pro-Maoist, and pro-Castro communists who called for Bosch's return, as well as from many moderates including those from Bosch's left-of-center *Partido Revolucionario Dominicano* and a number of colonels, junior officers, and enlisted men within the Dominican Army, Air Force, and the Navy's elite frogman unit.[47] Within a couple of days the pro-Bosch rebels, known as "Constitutionalists" for their determination to restore the constitutionally elected president appeared to be gaining the upper hand. They had captured the National Palace and government radio and television stations in the capital and arrested Reid Cabral. Fighting had spread to the streets. Unruly, armed gangs engaged in arbitrary violence. The streets of the capital city Santo Domingo had become increasingly dangerous, and the American embassy advised U.S citizens to prepare for evacuation. The U.S. embassy attempted to mediate the crisis. However, it was greatly concerned that communists had come to dominate the rebel movement. The battle in Santo Domingo seesawed for two days and with rebel successes on April 27–28, concerns among U.S. embassy personnel escalated. With the Loyalists now dejected and the US embassy concerned that the Dominican Republic would fall to the communists, Ambassador W. Tapley Bennett recommended that Washington send in the Marines.

Johnson Sends in U.S. Military Forces

President Johnson, threatened by adverse developments in Vietnam, and fearing a second communist-oriented country in the region, ordered the U.S. Marines and Army paratroopers into the Dominican Republic "to give protection to hundreds of American" and other nationals.[48] On the evening of April 28, 400 marines were airlifted into Santo Domingo from the USS Boxer sitting offshore. Subsequent contingents of marines and airborne forces followed. Bosch was denied his return to power, and in 1966 new elections were held.

In making his decision, Johnson had not consulted with the CIA. As the crisis unfolded, he immediately suspected Cuba had a hand in the revolt. After making his decision, he turned to his newly appointed Director of Central Intelligence Admiral William F. "Red" Raborn and demanded Raborn provide evidence to justify it. Jack Valenti, a close advisor to the President, noted that Johnson wrote in a presidential memorandum:

> Show indisputable evidence that Castro-types are in charge. This cannot be just a statement. Raborn must have pictures, names, a full dossier.[49]

Raborn apparently was not the only individual required by Johnson to provide intelligence to support his policies. To support his claims that U.S. intervention was necessary, Johnson had claimed that there were "headless bodies lying around the streets of Santo Domingo." When intervention critics challenged his claims, he called Ambassador Bennett personally and told him, "For God's sake, see if you can find some headless bodies."[50] Intelligence had been politicized.

- *SS-9 Controversy, 1969.* The Nixon White House acted in a similar manner in the spring of 1969. In the late 1960s a debate raged over the future of U.S. defenses against an attack by Soviet nuclear forces. In 1966, the Soviet Union deployed a new version of the SS-9 intercontinental ballistic missile. Supported by claims made by his secretary of defense that the Kremlin was seeking a first-strike capability, President Nixon called for the deployment of the "Safeguard" ballistic missile defense system.

Background

In the mid-1960s Secretary of Defense Robert McNamara refused to spend funds appropriated by Congress for an antiballistic missile system. He believed such a system would be destabilizing and unworkable.[51] However, Soviet deployment of the "Galosh" ballistic missile defense system around Moscow in late 1967 had an impact on both defense and political calculations. U.S. defense specialists began to wonder what the Soviets were up to and, with the elections around the corner, President Johnson could ill afford to have a democratic administration accused of failing to protect the American people from a Soviet attack. So in September 1967 Johnson approved the "Sentinel" system to protect American cities.

Richard Nixon had come to office in January 1969 arguing for improvements in U.S. defense posture. Voters had proven unenthusiastic about the "Sentinel" system, contending that it transformed U.S. cities into targets. On March 14 Nixon declared his intent to deploy the "Safeguard" ballistic missile defense system to defend U.S. Intercontinental Ballistic Missile sites against a Soviet attack. This would assure that any attack on the United States would be met by a punishing nuclear retaliatory strike.

However, Nixon's advocacy of Safeguard soon ran into immediate opposition. To cut costs and speed deployment, components of the Sentinel system were incorporated into the new system. Experts contended that Sentinel components weren't up to the job. Moreover, eminent scientists opposed the system, arguing that its radar and command and control centers were vulnerable. Its computer system was insufficient to the task. It could not discriminate between decoys, debris, and incoming Soviet warheads and the Soviets could easily overwhelm the system by building additional intercontinental ballistic missiles more cheaply than the United States could build extra antiballistic missiles. As a result, Congress was not fully convinced of the value of Safeguard.

Then Came the Bombshell

In testimony before Congress on March 16, 1969, Secretary of Defense Melvin Laird accused the Soviet Union of seeking a "first-strike capability"—the ability to deliver such a devastating blow to U.S. defenses and strategic nuclear forces that the United States would be unable to launch a significant counterattack against the USSR. Laird added for emphasis, "There is no question about it."[52] As evidence, he cited Soviet construction and deployment of a new version of the SS-9 an extremely large missile with the ability to deliver a 12,000-pound payload over intercontinental distances. In fact it was a giant compared to the U.S. "Minuteman" intercontinental ballistic missile that could only loft a payload about one-tenth that of the SS-9.

Laird contended that the new version had an accuracy of six-tenths of a mile or better and could carry a MIRV (Multiple Independently Targetable Reentry Vehicle) warhead. This meant that the SS-9 could deliver several nuclear weapons, each of which could be independently aimed to attack a different target. If this were the case, theoretically a single Soviet missile could now attack and destroy several U.S. missiles in their silos, significantly increasing the potential for a successful Soviet first-strike against U.S. strategic missile forces. Laird thus concluded that the emerging SS-9 threat could only be countered by deployment of the Safeguard antimissile defense system.

In late summer of 1968, the Soviets had tested an SS-9 with three 5-megaton warheads. Given the accuracy of the SS-9, U.S. defense officials believed that 5 megatons was sufficient to represent a dangerous threat to the survival of a U.S. missile in its silo. The problem, however, was that the Intelligence Community had reached a consensus. That consensus was spelled out in a National Intelligence Estimate produced in the fall of 1968, which concluded that the latest version of the SS-9 did not have independently targetable warheads. Rather it had three warheads that when released detonated in a triangular pattern.

Laird, however, was receiving intelligence not just from CIA but also from the Department of State Bureau of Intelligence and Research and from agencies under his control, such as the Defense Intelligence Agency, which is manned mostly by military officers and was often suspected of inflating estimates of Soviet capabilities. The Defense Department's Director of Defense Research and Engineering John S. Foster also influenced Laird.[53]

When the dispute over the SS-9 broke out, both the White House and the Pentagon attempted to minimize the appearance of disagreement. President Nixon contended: "Ever since the decision to deploy the ABM [Anti-Ballistic Missile System] system called Sentinel in 1967, the intelligence estimates indicate that the Soviet capability, with regard to their SS-9s, their nuclear missiles, [is] sixty percent higher than we thought then." Laird insisted that nothing he said contradicted the views of the Intelligence Community.[54] However, it was clear that the administration was not happy with the C IA estimate.

Yet there was another problem. Laird had engaged in selective declassification of information to bolster the administration's case for the Safeguard system. Laird was cherry-picking intelligence for political purposes. J. William Fulbright, Senate Foreign Relations chairman was furious about Laird's selective declassification and accused him of indulging in the "technique of fear" in order to sell Safeguard.[55] Moreover, privately, the CIA was pressured to suppress or change its estimate of SS-9 capabilities. According to John W. Huizenga, then deputy director of the Office of National Estimates, "There's no doubt that the White House was determined there should be an intelligence finding that the Soviets were engaged in MIRV testing."[56] When an update of the October 1968 Estimate was completed in the summer of 1969, it restated the view that the USSR was not seeking a first-strike capability. Secretary of Defense Melvin Laird immediately demanded that the statement be withdrawn. Much to the chagrin of those who prepared the Estimate and other CIA analysts, Director of Central Intelligence Richard Helms complied.[57] Intelligence had been politicized.

- *Chinese Sanctions, 1990s*. Following the end of the Cold War, the United States became increasingly concerned about the proliferation of weapons of mass destruction, including the proliferation of technologies associated with their production and delivery. Among the nations of concern was China. China had long been accused of transferring such technologies to other countries (see Box).[58]

To encourage China to alter its behavior, Congress passed the Nonproliferation Act of 1990, which gave the U.S. authority to impose sanctions on China. As one nuclear arms control specialist speaking about the effect of the sanctions law on missile technology put it:

> Our sanctions laws, as written by Congress, are based on a simple idea. A foreign company cannot import American missile technology with one hand and proliferate missile technology with the other. If a Chinese company decides to sell Pakistan or Iran a nuclear-capable missile or the means to make one, that company has to forget about importing any missile-related American technology.[59]

In response to the Nonproliferation Act, in June 1991, the administration of George H. W. Bush imposed sanctions on China for exporting M-11 short-range ballistic missile technology to Pakistan and planning to export M-9 short-range ballistic missile technology to Syria. Sanctions were to last two years. China responded by giving verbal and then written assurances that it would abide by the Missile Technology Control Regime.[60] Sanctions were lifted in March 1992, less than a year later. In August 1993, the Clinton administration applied sanctions to

Among China's Dangerous Exports[a]

- Early to mid-1980s
  - Supplies Pakistan with nuclear bomb design and its fuel.
  - Secretly agrees to supply a nuclear research reactor to Algeria.
  - Sells heavy water to Argentina and India.
  - Supplies 60 tons of enriched uranium to South Africa.
- Mid- to late 1980s
  - Agrees to sell Pakistan tritium gas to boost the yield of nuclear fission bombs.
  - Contacts Syria to sell M-9 nuclear-capable missiles.
  - Trains Iranian nuclear technicians in China.
  - Sells CSS-2 medium range, nuclear-capable missiles to Saudi Arabia.
  - Sells enriched uranium to Argentina.
- 1990s
  - Sells "illegal chemicals" to produce missile fuel and agrees to sell lithium hydride, useful for nerve gas, missiles, and nuclear weapons to Iraq.
  - Secretly delivers more than 30 M-11 short-range missiles to Pakistan. Trains Pakistani nuclear technicians in China.
  - Delivers poison gas ingredients and sells virtually complete chemical weapons factories, including precursor chemicals and glass-lined vessels to Iran.
  - Agrees to supply Syria's first nuclear reactor and train nuclear technicians.

[a] See "Dangerous Exports Table," in Testimony of Gary Milhollin Before the Senate Committee on Foreign Relations, June 11, 1998 at www.wisconsinproject.org/pubs/testimonies/1998/6-11.html

China for two years for its sale of M-11 missile equipment to Pakistan. China responded by calling the sanctions groundless and threatening to withdraw its agreement to abide by the Missile Technology Control Regime. The impasse was broken in October 1994 when the United States and China agreed on a joint statement on missile proliferation, which included a Chinese agreement to ban all exports of Regime-class missiles. The United States once again lifted its sanctions.

Background

Of course, imposing sanctions on China was a politically charged issue throughout the 1990s. Relations between the United States and China had deteriorated since the Tiananmen Square massacre in 1989. Human rights issues were never far from the surface. Relations, always somewhat tenuous over Taiwan, had been further strained when President George H. W. Bush announced in September 1992 his intent to sell Taiwan F-16 fighter aircraft. Moreover, China held the United States responsible for losing its 1993 bid to host the 2000 Olympic games.

Nevertheless, China was becoming an important economic partner. U.S. firms were eager to do business with China. From 1990 to 1995 U.S. trade with China had nearly tripled, with an expectation of similar if not greater growth in the future. In 1993 and again in 1996 Clinton had approved waivers that allowed American companies to launch satellites on Chinese missiles. It was good for American businesses and it was good for U.S.–China relations. Following President Clinton's reelection in 1996, his advisers contended that among his top priorities was repairing relations with China.[61] In February 1997 Clinton approved a waiver to permit Loral Space and Communications and Hughes Electronics to launch satellites in China.

Congress, now in the hands of the Republicans, was becoming increasingly skeptical of Clinton's unwillingness to confront the Chinese on the issue of proliferation of technologies associated with the production and delivery of weapons of mass destruction. Since 1994 reports on Chinese missile exports and other activities in violation of the Missile Technology Control Regime continued to be received in Washington. Reports included the Chinese sale of missile-related guidance and control equipment to Iran and Chinese assistance in helping Pakistan build a plant to produce M-11 missiles.[62] In the autumn of 1996, the Intelligence Community revealed that China had transferred *missiles* [emphasis added] to Pakistan.[63] Meanwhile, in June, Congressman Curt Weldon, obviously privileged to that information before it was more broadly revealed, accused the Clinton administration of willfully disregarding "clear and convincing evidence of proliferant behavior to avoid having to consider imposing legally-mandated sanctions on countries that violate nonproliferation norms." He went on to note:

> Nowhere is this dangerous pattern clearer than in its handling of the evidence associated with China's transfer of M-11 missiles to Pakistan. In the M-11 case, Administration officials either pretend that the missiles in Pakistan simply don't exist, or they argue that, well, just maybe, they haven't become "operational." In fact, the missiles are there—our intelligence community has affirmed this beyond reasonable doubt—and, for the purposes of U.S. law it is irrelevant whether the missiles have become "operational."[64]

U.S. law requires that sanctions be imposed on countries that export equipment or technology restricted by Missile Technology Control Regime guidelines. Though Clinton had imposed limited sanctions on China in 1992 for selling missile parts and had frequently contended that it did not have sufficient proof to impose stricter sanctions, the Intelligence Community had now revealed that missiles not parts had been delivered to Pakistan. Under U.S. law this would have called for far greater sanctions than were imposed, perhaps including the end of all satellite exports. It was increasingly evident that Clinton was not implementing the law as Congress had intended.

The Controversy Reaches a Peak

In mid-1998, former head of the CIA's Nonproliferation Center Gordon Oehler testified at an open Senate Foreign Relations Committee hearing on June 11 that the Clinton administration ignored compelling evidence that China had supplied M-11 nuclear-capable missiles to Pakistan. He told Committee members that Clinton administration officials used almost any measure to skirt intelligence assessments that corroborated reports that China had sold 34 M-11 missiles to Pakistan, which, under U.S. law, would have required mandatory economic sanctions against China. According to Oehler, there was no question in his mind that China transferred thirty-four complete M-11 missiles. Yet, according to Oehler, the administration demanded incontrovertible satellite images and pictures of the transferred missiles. U.S. spy satellites identifying M-11 canisters being delivered to the Pakistani Sargodha air base were not sufficient.[65]

Chairman of the Committee Jesse Helms further noted that political appointees on the National Security Council had altered the language of a 1995 arms control report in order to muddle the widely held belief that China had transferred missiles as well as missile technology to Pakistan. "The NSC [National Security Council] knew full well that it could not let the original text of the . . . report go to Congress unchanged," Helms said. "Sanctioning China for such a violation would mean, among other things, the immediate termination of important licenses held by Hughes and Loral [which allowed for the launching of commercial U.S. satellites from China]."[66]

Early that year in April the President himself acknowledged that he had avoided complying with the laws. While speaking to a group of visitors he lamented that he found sanctions legislation so inflexible that he was forced to penalize other nations for behavior that falls short of our expectations. He went on to say that such an environment creates pressure to "fudge the facts."[67] And indeed the facts had been fudged. The Clinton administration previously maintained that they had not determined that Pakistan had received M-11 missiles from China. Officials sometimes argued that there was a transfer of only missile parts, not full missiles. The extent of the fudging was clearly revealed the following year by the National Intelligence Council. In 1999 the Council issued an unequivocal finding that Beijing had transferred thirty-four complete nuclear-capable M-11 missiles to Pakistan in 1991 and 1992.[68]

In sum, the Clinton administration knew that China had shipped M-11 missiles to Pakistan in the early 1990s. Confirming intelligence had been collected, correctly analyzed, and disseminated. However, for political purposes policymakers chose to ignore Intelligence Community analyses, claiming it lacked proof, and thus they failed to faithfully execute the laws of the nation as required under the Constitution.

- *Iraq War, 2003.* On March 19, 2003, at 10:16 PM, EST (5:16 AM on March 20 in Iraq) President George W. Bush in a televised address from the

White House announced: "My fellow citizens. At this hour, American and coalition forces are in the early stages of military operations to disarm Iraq, to free its people and to defend the world from grave danger." So began America's war with Iraq.

Background

Bush's rationale for war had been advanced often by him and members of his administration. Saddam Hussein had stockpiles of weapons of mass destruction, had used them before, and might be prepared to use them again. Furthermore Saddam had ties to terrorists, had cooperated with al-Qaeda, and might provide weapons of mass destruction to terrorists like those who attacked the U.S. on September 11, 2001. The following are among the many examples that can be cited:

- On October 7, 2002, at the Cincinnati Museum Center in Union Terminal Bush stated,

> [The Iraqi Regime] possesses and produces chemical and biological weapons. It is seeking nuclear weapons. It has given shelter and support to terrorism, and practices terror against its own people. . . .
>
> We also must never forget the most vivid events of recent history. On September the 11th, 2001, America felt its vulnerability. . . .
>
> Saddam Hussein is a threat to peace . . . the Iraqi dictator must not be permitted to threaten America and the world with horrible poisons and diseases and gases and atomic weapons. . . .
>
> Iraq's weapons of mass destruction are controlled by a murderous tyrant who has already used chemical weapons to kill thousands of people. . . .
>
> We know that the regime has produced thousands of tons of chemical agents, including mustard gas, sarin nerve gas, VX nerve gas. Saddam Hussein also has experience in using chemical weapons.
>
> We know that Iraq and al Qaeda have had high-level contacts that go back a decade. . . . We've learned that Iraq has trained al Qaeda members in bomb-making and poisons and deadly gases. . . .
>
> Iraq could decide on any given day to provide a biological or chemical weapon to a terrorist group or individual terrorists. Alliance with terrorists could allow the Iraqi regime to attack America without leaving any fingerprints. . . .
>
> The evidence indicates that Iraq is reconstituting its nuclear weapons program. . . . Satellite photographs reveal that Iraq is rebuilding facilities at sites that have been part of its nuclear program in the past. Iraq has attempted to purchase high-strength aluminum tubes and other equipment needed for gas centrifuges, which are used to enrich uranium for nuclear weapons. . . .
>
> If the Iraqi regime is able to produce, buy, or steal an amount of highly enriched uranium a little larger than a single softball, it could have a nuclear weapon in less than a year. . . .
>
> Knowing these realities, America must not ignore the threat gathering against us. Facing clear evidence of peril, we cannot wait for the final proof—the smoking gun—that could come in the form of a mushroom cloud.[69]

- Vice President Cheney, in a consistent drumbeat, reiterated the same themes. "There is no doubt that Saddam Hussein now has weapons of mass destruction." "We believe he has, in fact, reconstituted nuclear weapons." "We know he has a long-standing relationship with various terrorist groups, including the al-Qaeda organization." On August 7, 2002, he told an audience in California, "What we know now, from various sources, is that [Saddam Hussein] continues to pursue nuclear weapons."[70] About three weeks later, speaking at the Veterans of Foreign Wars 103rd Convention on August 26, Cheney asserted:

> The Iraqi regime has in fact been very busy enhancing its capabilities in the field of chemical and biological agents. And they continue to pursue the nuclear program they began so many years ago. These are not weapons for the purpose of defending Iraq; these are offensive weapons for the purpose of inflicting death on a massive scale, developed so that Saddam can hold the threat over the head of anyone he chooses, in his own region or beyond.[71]

- On September 8, 2002, Condoleezzai Rice, then national security advisor to the president, responded to questions by talk show host Wolf Blitzer on Sunday television. Speaking about the high-strength aluminum tubes that had purportedly been purchased by Saddam for use in his nuclear weapons program, she said the tubes "are really only suited for nuclear weapons programs, centrifuge programs." [Centrifuges are used to separate weapons-grade uranium from natural uranium]. She went on to say:

> We do know that he is actively pursuing a nuclear weapon . . . we know that he has stored the biological weapons. . . . We know that he has used chemical weapons. And we know that he has looked for ways to weaponize those and deliver them.
>
> There is certainly evidence that al Qaeda people have been in Iraq. There is certainly evidence that Saddam Hussein cavorts with terrorists.

Perhaps responding to a comment made by Chief U.N. inspector Hans Blix before the U.N. Security Council that no "smoking gun" had been found since U.N. inspectors resumed their hunt in Iraq for weapons of mass destruction in November, Rice acknowledged that "there will always be some uncertainty" about how close Iraq may be to producing a nuclear weapon, but said, "We don't want the smoking gun to be a mushroom cloud."[72]

The Reality

The problem with all of these pronouncements was that they were wrong. When American forces and inspectors entered Iraq they found nothing—no active arsenal of chemical weapons, only a few old warheads empty of chemical agents, no biological weapons or mobile laboratories designed to manufacture biological weapons, no nuclear weapons. After the conflict was over, top U.S weapons inspector David Kay and his Iraq Survey Team were assigned the task of locating and identifying Iraqi weapons of mass destruction. They found none. Testifying before the Senate Armed Services Committee in January 2004, Kay admitted that with regard to Iraq's possession of weapons of mass destruction, "we were all wrong."[73]

How could the Bush administration have been so wrong? Had the U.S. Intelligence Community completely dropped the ball? Were policymakers totally captive of their personal biases? Certainly the Intelligence Community must bear its share of responsibility for the failures noted in reports such as the *President's Commission on Weapons of Mass Destruction*. Moreover, there is little doubt that many policymakers in the Bush administration were predisposed to believe that Iraq had such weapons. After all, Saddam Hussein had previously used chemical weapons against his own people and against the Iranians in the 1980–1988 Iran-Iraq War. Following the 1991 Gulf War, the United States had discovered that, before the war, Iraq had weaponized such biological agents as anthrax, botulinum toxin, and aflatoxin and deployed some of its bombs and warheads armed to locations throughout Iraq.[74] At that time, the United States also learned that Iraq had been pursuing a wide range of technologies for uranium enrichment, had successfully concealed a sophisticated nuclear program, and had been much closer to producing a nuclear weapon than virtually anyone suspected.[75]

Nevertheless, ample evidence suggests that the Bush administration's policy agenda was the critical determining factor in the decision for war in 2003. Prior to his election as President, George W. Bush had very little experience with or understanding of international issues. His father had introduced him to Condoleezza Rice in 1998. Subsequently, Rice teamed up with Paul Wolfowitz (soon to be deputy secretary of defense) and George W. Bush's education in international affairs began. Over the next year and a half, others joined the effort, most of whom were from a small neoconservative community[76] and many of whom were involved in a "think tank" effort called the "Project for a New American Century." These neoconservatives shared similar views on a number of issues. They saw the world community in a permanent struggle between the forces of good and the forces of evil. They believed appeasement must be avoided and if it is to be avoided you need to have a powerful military capable of defeating any foe, constantly anticipate new threats, and be willing to use military power to preempt those threats. They were suspicious of dialogue, even with allies and friends. They loathed dealing through institutions, such as the United Nations. They preferred unilateral efforts, which they saw as justified, lest by subjecting its will to the wishes of other countries or international institutions, the United States would actually permit its power to be limited.[77]

They also contended that the United States had unfinished business in Iraq. They believed that Saddam Hussein needed to be removed from power. He had attempted to assassinate former President George H.W. Bush, had successfully evaded U.N. weapons inspectors and was secretly engaged in developing weapons of mass destruction, was having a serious destabilizing effect on the entire Middle

East, and was engaging in a global campaign of terrorism against the United States. Thus they concluded that the United States should commit ground forces as needed to hasten Saddam's removal.[78]

President Bush met with the principals of the National Security Council on January 30, 2001, just ten days after his inauguration. Joining the President in the situation room downstairs from the Oval Office were Vice President Dick Cheney, Secretary of State Colin Powell, Secretary of Defense Donald Rumsfeld, Treasury Secretary Paul O'Neill, Chairman of the Joint Chiefs of Staff General Hugh Shelton, Director of Central Intelligence George Tenet, National Security Advisor Condoleezza Rice, and the President's Chief of Staff Andrew Card. The meeting had been called to address "Mideast Policy." In the waning months of his presidency, Clinton had engaged in a dramatic effort to reach a lasting settlement between the Palestinians and the Israelis, only to see it collapse at the last minute as Palestinian leaders Yasir Arafat pulled away from the agreement.

According to O'Neill, after a few opening remarks about the Arab-Israeli situation, Bush indicated that it was time for the United States to leave the combatants to work out the situation on their own. Following some comments by Powell expressing reservations about such a policy, Bush turned to Condi Rice, in what appeared to several at the meeting as a scripted exchange, and asked: "What's on the agenda?" Rice responded: "How Iraq is destabilizing the region, Mr. President," further noting that Iraq might be the key to reshaping the region.[79] At the end of the hour-long meeting, Bush had assignments for everyone. Powell was to focus on a new sanctions regime. Rumsfeld and Shelton were to examine military options, including rebuilding the 1991 Gulf War military coalition, "how it might look" to use U.S ground forces in the north and south of Iraq, and how military forces could support groups inside the country who could help challenge Saddam Hussein. Tenet would focus on improving intelligence on Iraq and O'Neill was tasked to examine how to financially squeeze Iraq.[80]

As O'Neill walked back to Treasury he thought to himself, "Getting Hussein was now the administration's focus, that much was clear." Ten days into the new administration and the issue was about Iraq.[81] According to O'Neill, by February 2001 administration talk was already mostly about logistics, not about *why* the United States should attack Iraq, but the *how* and how *quickly*. Rumsfeld was focused on how an incident might cause escalated tension—like shooting down an American fighter plane by Iraqi antiaircraft batteries—and what U.S. responses to such an event might be.[82]

The drumbeat for action against Iraq continued throughout the spring and summer of 2001. However, the sought-after event as catalyst for action against Saddam came on September 11. America had been attacked. Nearly 3,000 innocent Americans lost their lives. On the morning of September 12, President Bush, speaking from the cabinet room, told the nation that the attacks were "an act of war... in a monumental struggle between good and evil."[83] At a National Security Council meeting that same day, the issue was that this meant war against al-Qaeda and its Afghanistan Taliban regime host. Rumsfeld, however, raised the question of Iraq. His Pentagon team had been working for months on a plan to overthrow Saddam Hussein. However, he recognized that the nation was focused on al-Qaeda and opposed striking Iraq at this point.[84] Over the weekend Bush hosted meetings at Camp David, Maryland, among a subset of his senior officials to deal with the coming war against al-Qaeda. As the Saturday meeting developed, just before lunch Deputy Secretary of Defense Paul Wolfowitz turned the focus to Iraq. Afghanistan could be messy, with U.S. troops bogging down in the country's remote mountains. On the other hand, Iraq was an anti-American regime waiting to be toppled. According to Secretary of Treasury Paul O'Neill, the thrust of Wolfowitz' remarks was "If you want to do something, Mr. President, Iraq is doable." The meeting was adjourned for lunch.[85]

On September 20 in an address to a joint session of Congress President Bush issued an ultimatum to the Taliban demanding, among other things, that they hand over al-Qaeda leaders located in Afghanistan to the United States. The Taliban failed to comply with the ultimatum and on October 7 the war in Afghanistan against al-Qaeda and the Taliban began. However, the issue of regime change in Iraq had not died. By January 2002, with the Taliban largely defeated on the battlefield and with al-Qaeda and Taliban officials in retreat into tribal areas in Pakistan, Rumsfeld and Wolfowitz were pointing to the ease with which the Taliban had fallen as evidence of how doable Iraq would be.[86] Once again Iraq had become the focus of interest. On January 29, 2002, in his State of the Union address to the nation, Bush labeled North Korea, Iran, and Iraq and their terrorist allies an "axis of evil."

On June 1 President Bush delivered the graduation address at the United States Military Academy at West Point in which he outlined a policy of preemptive attack.

> We cannot defend America and our friends by hoping for the best. We cannot put our faith in the word of tyrants, who solemnly sign non-proliferation treaties, and then systemically break them. If we wait for threats to fully materialize, we will have waited too long. . . . We must take the battle to the enemy, disrupt his plans, and confront the worst threats before they emerge.[87]

Given the increasing commentary from administration officials calling for action against Iraq, this was a not-so-veiled threat directed at Iraq.

On July 23, 2002, Richard Dearlove, head of the British secret intelligence service MI6, having just returned from consultations in Washington along with other senior British officials, informed Prime Minister Tony Blair that President Bush wanted to topple Saddam Hussein by military action and warned that in Washington intelligence was "being fixed around the policy." According to Dearlove, in what became known as the Downing Street Memo, "The case was thin. . . . Saddam was not threatening his neighbours and his WMD [weapons of mass destruction] capability was less than that of Libya, North Korea or Iran."[88]

By August the press was reporting that Bush had made ousting Iraqi president Saddam Hussein one of his top priorities.[89] Cheney was declaring that the

"the risks of inaction are greater than the risks of action."[90] That same month the *Washington Post* reported leaked allegations from anonymous administration officials that al-Qaeda members, including "names you'd recognize," had found refuge in Iraq.[91] As U.N. weapons inspectors were preparing for a return to Iraq, Cheney, signaling his preference for preemptive intervention rather than a return of inspectors, said, "A return of inspectors would provide no assurance whatsoever of his [Saddam Hussein's] compliance with U.N. resolutions."[92] In September the President released the 2002 National Security Strategy supporting the concept of preemptive intervention. Then came the late 2002 onslaught of statements aimed at convincing the American people of the necessity of going to war against Iraq.

On November 8, the U.N. Security Council passed Resolution 1441. Iraq would be given a last chance to comply with previous Security Council resolutions requiring it to submit updated declarations of everything it had produced in the way of programs, weapons, missiles, precursors related to weapons of mass destruction. The President, in his State of the Union address, strongly reiterated his contention that Saddam Hussein had for the past twelve years pursued chemical, biological, and nuclear weapons, had materials to produce as much as 500 tons of sarin, mustard, and VX nerve agents capable of killing untold thousands and upward of 30,000 munitions capable of delivering chemical agents. Saddam also had several mobile biological weapons labs and materials sufficient to produce more than 38,000 liters of botulinum toxin and an advanced nuclear weapons development program. Moreover Saddam aids and protects terrorists, including members of al-Qaeda.[93] By February 2003 Colin Powell was detailing the President's case for war to the U.N.

Thirteen days before American forces attacked Iraq, President Bush reiterated his case against Iraq at a National Press Conference in the East Wing of the White House:

> He [Saddam Hussein] possesses weapons of terror. He provides funding and training and safe haven to terrorists—terrorists who would willingly use weapons of mass destruction against America and other peace-loving countries. Saddam Hussein and his weapons are a direct threat to this country, to our people, and to all free people.
>
> If the world fails to confront the threat posed by the Iraqi regime, refusing to use force, even as a last resort, free nations would assume immense and unacceptable risks. The attacks of September the 11th, 2001 showed what the enemies of America did with four airplanes. We will not wait to see what terrorists or terrorist states could do with weapons of mass destruction.[94]

Three days before the war began Bush addressed the Nation from White House Cross Hall.

> Intelligence gathered by this and other governments leaves no doubt that the Iraq regime continues to possess and conceal some of the most lethal weapons ever devised. This regime has already used weapons of mass destruction against Iraq's neighbors and against Iraq's people.

> The regime has a history of reckless aggression in the Middle East. It has a deep hatred of America and our friends. And it has aided, trained and harbored terrorists, including operatives of al Qaeda.[95]

With these statements Bush capped more than a year's commentary that had attempted to link Iraq to al-Qaeda and suggested that the United States was in imminent danger of attack from Iraq's weapons of mass destruction.

The Intelligence Community had long contended Iraq was not working with al-Qaeda. Nevertheless, senior members of the Bush administration continued to insist that there was a clear relationship between Saddam Hussein and al-Qaeda. The Department of Defense's role in this charade was later recognized as "inappropriate" in a report by the Department's own Acting Inspector General.[96] The principal case that Iraq was further developing both biological and chemical weapons capabilities was known to be based on thin evidence. General Kamal, one of Hussein's sons-in-law and the Minister of Industry, had reported after defecting in 1995 that *all chemical and biological weapons had been destroyed* on his orders in 1991.[97] Subsequent evidence supporting the contention that Iraq had continued to develop biological and chemical weapons was based primarily on either a single, known to be unreliable, source, as was the case with biological weapons, or a single collection means, as was the case with chemical weapons. Such thin evidence was further supported by information provided by the Iraqi National Congress, which had long advocating the overthrow of Saddam and thus had a vested interest in providing the administration with whatever information that would hasten that day.

Concerning Iraq's nuclear weapons programs, the Administration's case and concerns were primarily based on two highly publicized pieces of intelligence—Iraq was seeking uranium [yellowcake] and had procured aluminum tubes that could be used in centrifuges used to produce weapons grade uranium. Yet, as we have seen in Chapter 4, as early as March 2002 Ambassador Wilson as well as the U.S. ambassador to Niger and the Deputy Commander of European Command, who had responsibility for overseeing U.S. security interests in Africa, could find nothing to substantiate rumors that Iraq had sought yellowcake from Niger. As a result both the State Department and the CIA had concluded that the Niger uranium reports were almost certainly not true.[98] Despite this evidence, President Bush pressed his case to the American people for war with Iraq during his January 28, 2003, State of the Union address by disingenuously noting, "The British government has learned that Saddam Hussein recently sought significant quantities of uranium from Africa," without a mention that U.S. intelligence had already discounted this report. Reaffirming what American intelligence already knew, on Mar 7, 2003, just days before the war, Dr. Mohamed El Baradei told the U.N. Security Council that the documents related to the purported sale of uranium from Iraq to Niger were not authentic.[99]

As for the aluminum tubes, as noted earlier, the U.S. Intelligence Community was divided over the utility of the use of the tubes as centrifuge rotors, with the Department of Energy and a lead agency on such issues contending that the tubes "were not well-suited for centrifuge application" and were more likely intended for use in Iraq's 81-millimeter Multiple Rocket Launcher program." U.N. International Atomic Energy Agency officials agreed, concluding after extensive investigations that the much publicized aluminum tubes Iraq had attempted to import were not likely to have been related to the manufacture of centrifuges for the enrichment of uranium.[100]

In addition to the information available to it from the U.S. Intelligence Community, the Bush administration had been provided with regular updates on what the U.N. weapons inspectors had found in Iraq since their return in September 2002. The bottom line is that following months of efforts in which Iraqis increasingly cooperated with U.N inspectors and with all the information that the United States and other nations could provide, U.N. weapons inspectors could find no chemical, biological, or nuclear weapons. On February 14, 2003, Hans Blix reported to the U.N. Security Council that the United Nations Monitoring and Inspection Commission in Iraq had not found any prohibited items at any of the sites suggested by intelligence agencies. Similarly El Baradei reported that the International Atomic Energy Agency had found no evidence of ongoing nuclear or nuclear-related activities in Iraq.[101] And all of this in an environment, according to Blix, in which, confronted by strong military pressure as the United States and others deployed or were preparing to deploy forces to the region, the Iraqis became increasingly "almost frantic in submitting material, seeking evidence and finding persons we could interview." There had been no denials of access to facilities, no cat-and-mouse play.[102]

Had the Bush administration not set and adhered to a policy of regime change in Iraq from the first days of assuming the reigns of power in Washington, had it rather sought to avoid war while assuring the world that Iraq was contained, there was ample intelligence to suggest a more careful examination of policy options. While the definitive history on this sad chapter of American history has yet to be written, existing evidence clearly points to the fact that policy trumped intelligence. Intelligence had been "cherry-picked" to support the political objective of regime change in Iraq.

LOOKING TOWARD THE FUTURE

Addressing the impediments that confront the use of intelligence is likely to be among the greater challenges to improving the value of intelligence to our foreign and security policies. The time available for senior policymakers to focus on intelligence issues will remain limited. While reducing the turnover of senior policymakers would add to institutional memory and thus reduce the time necessary to understand the context of the intelligence provided, no easy answers to this problem are readily available. Similarly, cognitive bias will continue to plague the use of intelligence. Policymakers will hear better what is consonant with their current beliefs and will be more likely to act on intelligence that reinforces those beliefs. At best and at the risk of undermining relationships with policymakers, intelligence officials in their presentation of intelligence to policymakers can ensure that policymakers clearly are aware of information that may challenge their predispositions. Perhaps at once the easiest and most difficult problem to confront is that of the politicizing of intelligence. Congress has the constitutionally established role to serve as a check on presidential power in the field of foreign policy. The second line of defense is the so-called fourth estate, the press. Both Congress and the press have the power to coerce, cajole, and ultimately demand that executive branch policies are the product of a complete uncovering of the facts, not a cherry-picking to support preferred policies. The bad news is that both failed the American people badly as war approached in March of 2003. Why you ask? We can all hope it was one of those momentary lapses that even nations devoted to global common good can make. However, I fear that Herman Göring might have been right when, following World War II, he was interrogated in Nuremburg by the German-speaking American intelligence officer and psychologist Gustave Gilbert. In a discussion on why states go to war Göring is reported to have said:

> Why, of course, the people don't want war. Why would some poor slob on a farm want to risk his life in a war when the best that he can get out of it is to come back to his farm in one piece? Naturally, the common people don't want war; neither in Russia, nor in England, nor in America, nor for that matter in Germany. That is understood. But, after all, it is the leaders of the country who determine the policy and it is always a simple matter to drag the people along, whether it is a democracy, or a fascist dictatorship, or a parliament, or a communist dictatorship.

Gilbert, unconvinced of Göring's arguments, when it came to democratic governments and particularly the United States remarked:

> There is one difference. In a democracy the people have some say in the matter through their elected representatives, and in the United States only the Congress can declare wars.

Göring is reported to have replied:

> Voice or no voice, the people can always be brought to the bidding of the leaders. That is easy. All you have to do is tell them they are being attacked, and denounce the pacifists for lack of patriotism exposing the country to danger. It works the same in any country.[103]

Part IV

Oversight

In a democracy, there are few functions of government as critical to the survival of both democratic governance and the nation itself as an intelligence system that operates without infringing on the basic rights of its citizens, remains within the law in its foreign operations so as not to adversely affect the long-term security of the nation, and is efficient and effective in collecting, analyzing, disseminating, and using information that is essential to the security as well as economic and social well-being of the nation. It is the task of those charged with reviewing, monitoring, and supervising, or in common parlance "overseeing," the intelligence efforts to ensure that all three criteria are met.

For much of its earlier history, U.S. intelligence matters were left to the president and his advisors. Indeed, though George Washington was acutely aware of the value of good intelligence, few presidents that followed showed Washington's level of interest. Indeed there were no formal national-level intelligence services until the 1880s. Nor were their any formal mechanisms for intelligence oversight. It took two world wars to change attitudes toward the gathering of intelligence.

Oversight mechanisms as they exist today find their roots in post-World War II efforts of President Truman and key members in Congress. Chastened by American experiences leading up to and during World War II and with the Cold War looming, President Truman set in motion efforts to reorganize U.S. intelligence efforts. As a consequence, Congress passed the National Security Act of 1947 "to provide for the establishment of integrated policies and procedures for the departments, agencies, and functions of the Government relating to national security . . . ." Among other things, the Act established the Central Intelligence Agency, the position of Director of Central Intelligence, and formal provisions for the supervising and evaluating of America's intelligence efforts. Later amended, the Act made explicit the requirement of the executive branch to keep congressional intelligence committees "fully and currently informed of the intelligence activities of the United States." Thus the principle of both executive and legislative branch oversight was established in law.

Chapter 7 outlines executive branch efforts to ensure that U.S. intelligence efforts do not infringe on citizens' rights, operate within the law, and are efficient and effective in providing the United States with timely and accurate information upon which to formulate foreign and national security policies. Chapter 8 examines congressional efforts to oversee Intelligence Community activities.

7

Executive Branch Oversight

"The eye sees only what the mind is prepared to comprehend."
—Henri Bergson

Efforts to gather intelligence essential to the security and foreign polices of the United States are as old as the republic. George Washington, having nearly been killed during the French and Indian War for lack of good intelligence about a numerically inferior and outgunned force of hostile Indians and their French allies at the Battle of Monongahela (1755), was acutely aware of the value of sound intelligence to success in battle. Indeed, when he took command of the Continental Army in 1775, gathering intelligence on British forces and movements and on British spies seeking the same information about American forces became one of Washington's principal objectives. However, the Continental Army had no organized intelligence service. Washington directed the intelligence efforts and did his own analyses.

Later that same year the Continental Congress created the Committee of Secret Correspondence to correspond with friends and ascertain the disposition of foreign powers toward the Americans. Following the war, on the recommendation of President Washington in his first State of the Union address in 1790, Congress set up a Contingency Fund of Foreign Intercourse. The fund, better known as the Secret Service Fund, was used for a variety of purposes, some unrelated to intelligence. However, as the Senate later acknowledged, it was "for spies."[1]

Despite the fact that intelligence played a key role in the American victory during the Revolutionary War, few American presidents showed much enthusiasm for intelligence over the next hundred years. Self-sufficient and seeking to avoid involvement in European Wars, the United States had less need for foreign intelligence than did the great powers of Europe.[2] Intelligence briefly regained prominence during the Civil War, as the Union and Confederacy established spy networks and railed against the press for providing intelligence to the other side. Though the Union side employed code breakers to decode Confederate messages and the Departments of the Navy, War, and State each maintained an intelligence service and the Confederates established the Signal and Secret Service Bureau with the primary purpose of obtaining northern newspapers, it wasn't until the 1880s, when the Office of Naval Intelligence and the Army's Military Intelligence Division were established, that the United States established a formal national level foreign intelligence service.[3] Up until that time, foreign intelligence that was gathered was largely dictated by the temperament, preferences, and experiences of the President and his advisors, undertaken mostly on an ad hoc basis, and devoted almost exclusively to the support of military operations.

Intelligence enjoyed another brief boost under President Theodore Roosevelt. The Roosevelt administration was perhaps the most active of earlier American administrations in the use of intelligence for foreign policy purposes. Also during his administration the Justice Department's Bureau of Investigation, the forerunner of the FBI, was established.[4] However, while the Bureau of Investigations continued to grow,[5] by the time World War I began, budget reductions and bureaucratic reorganization had resulted in a dramatic reduction in U.S. foreign intelligence capabilities. Moreover, oversight of U.S. intelligence efforts was close to nonexistent. Throughout the nineteenth and early part of the twentieth century Congress was generally content to leave intelligence matters to the President and his advisors.[6] Whatever oversight that did exist was undertaken by congressional committees responsible for authorizing or appropriating the budget for the department or agency concerned and by the President, his advisors, and the departments and agencies charged with acquiring and analyzing intelligence.

It took two world wars to lure America from its complacency over intelligence and it took the Cold War to propel U.S. intelligence efforts from their former feeble and fragmented status to the most sophisticated, technologically advanced intelligence system in the world. Today's intelligence system and oversight mechanisms find their roots primarily in President Truman's immediate post-World War II interest in reorganizing U.S. intelligence efforts and the consequent passage by Congress of the National Security Act of 1947. That legislation established a National Security Council, provided for a Secretary of Defense and the National Military Establishment (NME), pronounced "enemy," and soon redesignated the Department of Defense. The legislation also created the Central Intelligence Agency and the position of Director of Central Intelligence as its head.[7]

That National Security Act of 1947 ushered in a new era of oversight. The Director of Central Intelligence was to have access to all intelligence related to national security and had the responsibility, among other things, for the "correlation, *evaluation* [emphasis added], and dissemination" of all such intelligence. This included intelligence obtained by other departments and agencies of government.

The Director's responsibilities were further clarified by subsequent amendment to the National Security Act that explicitly designated him as head not only of the CIA but also as head of the United States Intelligence Community.[8] Responsibilities of the Director as head of the Intelligence Community included promoting and *evaluating* [emphasis added] the utility of national intelligence to consumers within government. As head of the CIA, the Director was to "ensure that the most effective use is made of [Agency] resources."[9]

The Act also mandated that the other departments and agencies of government with intelligence responsibilities, "*evaluate* [emphasis added], correlate, and disseminate" collected intelligence. Hence, from inception, the U.S. post-War intelligence apparatus was to be subjected to a continual monitoring of the overall quality of the intelligence effort and quality of the information collected, not only by the Director of Central Intelligence, but also by all executive branch entities with intelligence responsibilities.

Today, within the executive branch there is an elaborate system of intelligence oversight. That system evolved over time as a result of concerns over intelligence failures and abuses. First came the National Security Council, followed by the creation of the President's Foreign Intelligence Advisory Board, both in response to World War II intelligence failures. Then came the President's Intelligence Oversight Board and the presidential mandate that Inspectors General and General Councils of executive branch departments and agencies with intelligence responsibilities exercise oversight over their respective intelligence activities, as well as a role for the Attorney General of the United States.

Finally the Office of Management and Budget was given limited oversight authority. These presidentially directed efforts were in addition to the normal supervisory responsibilities of executive branch department and agency managers, who had as part of their everyday tasks the requirement to ensure the quality of effort and legality of U.S. intelligence efforts.

Executive Branch
Entities Exercising Intelligence Oversight

National Security Council
President's Foreign Intelligence Advisory Board
Intelligence Oversight Board
Departmental-level intelligence oversight offices
Inspectors General, with assistance from General Councils
U.S. Attorney General
Office of Management and Budget

With the exception of the office of the U.S. Attorney General, which dates to 1789, and the Office of Management and Budget, which traces its history to the Bureau of the Budget established within the Department of the Treasury by the Budget and Accounting Act of 1921, this elaborate system of oversight was primarily a response to the need for intelligence in the post–World War II period and Intelligence Community abuses of the 1960s and 1970s.

NATIONAL SECURITY COUNCIL

Established by the National Security Act of 1947, the National Security Council advises the President on domestic, foreign, and military policies relating to national security. It also assists the President in ensuring that all aspects of domestic, foreign, and military policies related to national security function in an integrated manner. It is the highest executive branch entity that provides "review of, guidance for, and direction to the conduct of all foreign intelligence and counterintelligence activities."[10] The so-called statutory members of the National Security Council (i.e., established by law) are the President, Vice President, Secretary of State, and Secretary of Defense. In addition, the Chairman of the Joint Chiefs of Staff is the statutory military advisor to the Council, while the Director of National Intelligence serves as the statutory intelligence advisor. Other members of the Council are Secretary of the Treasury and the assistant to the President for National Security Affairs (commonly known as the National Security Advisor). President George W. Bush also invites to Council meetings the Counsel to the President, the Assistant to the President for Economic Policy, and his Chief of Staff. Other members of the President's cabinet and senior officials may be invited to attend when appropriate.

The National Security Council meets at the direction of the President. In his absence, the President may direct the Vice President to preside. The National Security Advisor, at the direction of and in consultation with the President and other attendees at Council meetings, sets the agenda, ensures that necessary supporting papers are prepared, and records the Council actions and resulting presidential decisions.[11]

A professional and administrative staff supports the Council. The staff receives its direction from the President through the National Security Advisor. It is organized into geographic, country, functional, and support offices and includes offices that focus on, African, European, Asian, Western Hemisphere, Legal, or Legislative affairs, Russia, Iraq, Afghanistan, International Trade, Energy and Environment, Defense Policy and Strategy, Democracy, Human Rights and International Organizations, Combating Terrorism, Intelligence Programs and Reform, and Administration.[12] Its office of Intelligence Programs and Reforms advises the President and National Security Advisor on intelligence issues relevant to U.S. foreign and defense policies. Among these issues are intelligence priorities, imagery policy, counterintelligence and security, budget, congressional liaison, encryption and other intelligence activities. The office also works with the Intelligence Community to ensure that the President's requirements for intelligence on a broad range of foreign and national security issues are met. In providing this support, the office of Intelligence Programs works with other Council entities to ensure that both intelligence and policy interests are represented objectively in Council and interagency processes.[13] Other offices within the Council also play a role in helping to define and inform the Intelligence Community of presidential and National Security Council intelligence needs and priorities.

One of the Council's early intelligence oversight efforts came in January 1948, less than a year after the CIA was created. Council Executive Secretary Sidney Souers asked three private citizens to undertake a comprehensive examination of the CIA's "structure, administration, activities, and interagency relations." Allen Dulles, William Jackson and Matthias Correa, three New York lawyers with experience in intelligence, submitted a highly critical report in January 1949. The report concluded that the CIA was not coordinating intelligence activities in the Government; that the correlation and evaluation functions were not well organized; that other members of the fledgling Intelligence Community were not fully included in the estimates process; and that the Director of Central Intelligence lacked sufficient day-to-day contact with the work of CIA. The report recommended that the Director of Central Intelligence exert "forthright leadership," and actively use existing coordination bodies, such as the Intelligence Advisory Committee, which brought together leaders of the military and civilian intelligence agencies. The report also urged that the final coordination of intelligence estimates be done through the Intelligence Advisory Committee in order to establish the estimates as "the most authoritative statement[s] available to policymakers."[14]

PRESIDENT'S FOREIGN INTELLIGENCE ADVISORY BOARD

The President's Foreign Intelligence Advisory Board advises the President on the quality and adequacy of intelligence collection, analysis, and estimates, and on the quality and adequacy of counterintelligence and other intelligence activities. The Board currently has sixteen members selected by the President from among trustworthy and distinguished citizens outside of government, based on their achievements, experience, and independence. Board members serve without compensation. The Board has a full-time staff, headed by an Executive Director, appointed by the President. Should there be a need, the President may authorize the use of consultants. In theory, if not always in practice, the Board provides the President with an independent, nonpartisan, and unbiased source of advice on the effectiveness of the Intelligence Community on meeting the nation's intelligence needs.

Board members meet regularly with and are briefed by senior members of the Intelligence Community. Through these meetings and briefings, as well as visits to intelligence gathering facilities at home and abroad, they seek to identify deficiencies in the collection, analysis, and reporting of intelligence, eliminate unnecessary duplication, and ensure that the "technology employed represents the product of the best minds and technical capabilities available" and that intelligence efforts are responsive to the nation's needs.[15]

The history of the President's Foreign Intelligence Advisory Board dates back to 1956 when President Eisenhower created an independent board to advise him on the effectiveness of U.S. foreign intelligence efforts. At that time the board was called the President's Board of Consultants on Foreign Intelligence Activities. President Kennedy gave the Board its current name. Following the intelligence failures leading up to the unsuccessful Bay of Pigs invasion and the Cuban missile crisis, Kennedy directed the Board to assess the quality of intelligence efforts that led to those two events.[16]

Since its founding the Board has served all presidents except President Carter. Carter "abolished the board because he did not consider its reviews any more rigorous than similar evaluations conducted by the National Security Council, Senate Intelligence Committee, or the Intelligence Community itself."[17] President Reagan reinstated the Board,[18] appointing twenty-one members to it. He later reduced it to about fifteen, believing that it had become too unwieldy. President George H. W. Bush was leery of the Board. While serving as Director of Central Intelligence during the Ford administration he had been concerned that a group of outsiders with direct access to the President were in a position to second-guess his decisions as Director of Central Intelligence. While he retained the Board during his Presidency, he reduced its membership to six and called on it infrequently. President William Clinton merged the Intelligence Oversight Board (mentioned below) with the President Foreign Intelligence Advisory Board. This changed little, since it was common practice for the same individuals to serve on both Boards. He also called on the Board to analyze security threats to Department of Energy nuclear laboratories. The resultant analysis strongly suggested that the Chinese may have acquired information stolen by spies at American laboratories in order to further develop their nuclear weapons capabilities. In October 2001, President George W. Bush chose a Board of sixteen members and named Brent Scowcroft, retired Air Force General and former National Security Advisor under Presidents Ford and George H.W. Bush, as chairman.[19] Scowcroft, who had cautioned against a too rapid movement toward war with Iraq, was dropped as chairman of the Board and in October 2005 Bush named Stephen Friedman, dean of Pace University School of Law and former commissioner of the U.S. Securities and Exchange Commission, as chairman.

Over the years the Board has included individuals with broad experience and from a wide spectrum of professional fields.[20] Interestingly, few of the individuals who have served on the Board have had prior intelligence experience. Nevertheless, they brought the advantage of a fresh look at issues that may have been long buried or ignored by those too close to the forest to see the trees.

The Board has had an influence on such things as the composition and structure of the Intelligence Community, the development of major intelligence systems, and the degree of collection and analytical emphasis that is given to substantive areas.[21] The Board also has been involved in the examination of a wide variety of issues relevant to the intelligence processes. For example, it has examined the extent to which the government should be involved in political, psychological, propaganda, and paramilitary activities. It has investigated CIA involvement with Guatemalan military officials who committed human rights abuses, as well as U.S. intelligence failures such as those prior to the Bay of Pigs invasion and in Somalia. It has analyzed the procedures and practices to protect classified information and investigated activities at U.S. foreign missions. The Board also has identified mistaken estimates of Soviet military strength, as well as the Department of Energy's lax security procedures at its nuclear energy facilities. It challenged the charge that China had stolen nuclear weapons secrets from the United States, revealed mistakes made by the CIA and FBI in handling subversion, and investigated Bush administration claims that Iraq had attempted to import "yellowcake" from Niger.[22]

INTELLIGENCE OVERSIGHT BOARD

When the President's Foreign Intelligence Advisory Board was established it was originally concerned with the *quality* and *adequacy* of intelligence efforts. Up until President Ford, presidents had no official advisor on the *legality* of activities undertaken by the Intelligence Community. Following on concerns over illegal as well as questionable practices of U.S. intelligence agencies revealed in the early to mid-1970s, in 1976 President Gerald Ford established the President's Intelligence Oversight Board.

In January1970 Christopher Pyle revealed that while serving in the U.S. Army in the 1960s, he discovered that Army intelligence had 1,500 Army operatives "spying" on the American people. Army intelligence had spied on public demonstrations of more than twenty people all over the United States, had gathered information on civil rights activists, conscientious objectors, members of the Unitarian Church, and other individuals and groups. Concerned about an evolving police state, upon leaving the Army Pyle wrote a long article on the "Army's vast and growing spy operations."[23] The article, which won a Polk Award in 1971 for the *Washington Monthly*, began, "For the past four years, the U.S. Army has been closely watching civilian political activity within the United States." The article prompted hearings by Senator Sam Ervin, which Pyle helped organize.[24] Similar revelations over the next few years resulted in increased concern over U.S. intelligence activities. Though Richard Helms, who served as Director of Central Intelligence from 1966 to 1972, had repeatedly denied CIA wrongdoing, his story began to unravel during the Watergate hearings. On April 15, 1973 John Dean told federal prosecutors that the CIA had assisted in a burglary of Dr. Lewis Fielding's office, engineered by Watergate defendant E. Howard Hunt. Surprised by the revelation, James Schlesinger, who had taken over as Director of Central Intelligence from Richard Helms in December 1972, issued a directive to every CIA employee to come forward with anything the CIA might have done that exceeded the limits of the Agency's charter. On May 21, a twenty-six-page summary report titled "Potential Flap Activities" was forwarded to William Colby, who had succeeded Schlesinger as Director of Central Intelligence earlier that month. The 693-page final report, issued somewhat later, quickly acquired the name "The Family Jewels." It included information on the CIA's infiltration of American radical groups, the CIA's role in President Nixon's surveillance of the American anti-Viet Nam war activists, mail interception, the bugging of American journalists thought to have informants in the CIA, and contacts with the Watergate burglary team. In a special annex the report also summarized the inspector general's 1967 report on CIA involvement in assassination plots against Dominican Republic dictator Rafael Trujillo, President Ngo Dình Diem of South Vietnam, and First Secretary of the Cuban Communist Party Fidel Castro.[25]

Colby tried to deal with the issue of CIA abuse quietly. He cleaned house internally and briefed the chairmen of the four House and Senate Committees with oversight authority, convincing them to let lie what was past, that the CIA would not engage in those sorts of activities in the future, and any revelation of the report in the highly charged Watergate environment would wreck the Agency.[26]

However, the cat could not be kept in the bag. In December the following year Seymour Hersh wrote a lengthy article that appeared on the front page of the *New York Times*. The article "Huge C.I.A. Operation Reported in U.S. Against Antiwar Forces, Other Dissidents in Nixon Years" turned smoldering congressional and public interest into a firestorm of concern.

In response to the wide array of allegations of impropriety on the part of the intelligence agencies, President Gerald Ford, who had assumed the presidency following Nixon's resignation in August 1974, formed the "U.S. President's Commission on CIA Activities within the United States." Vice President Nelson Rockefeller headed the Commission, more generally known as the Rockefeller Commission. The Commission report, issued in June 1975 and considered by some a "whitewash,"[27] examined certain CIA abuses. However, Congress, no longer content to leave such matters solely in executive branch hands, formed its own committees to look into the matter. As a result the Rockefeller Commission Report was quickly eclipsed by Church and Pike Committee efforts.

On January 27, 1975, the U.S. Senate established Senate Select Committee to Study Governmental Operations with Respect to Intelligence Activities, more generally known as the Church Committee after its chairman, Senator Frank Church. Among the issues the Committee examined were the attempted assassination of such foreign leaders as Patrice Lumumba of the Congo and Presidents Trujillo of the Dominican Republic, Diem of South Vietnam, and Castro of Cuba, covert attempts to subvert foreign governments, and spying on U.S. citizens in violation of the law. The Committee took testimony from hundreds of people, collected huge volumes of files from the CIA, FBI, National Security Agency, and many other federal agencies, and published fourteen reports in 1975 and 1976. At the time, the reports were the most extensive review of U.S. intelligence activities ever released to the public.

Shortly after the Church Committee was formed, the House of Representatives created the Select Committee on Intelligence, chaired by Representative Otis Pike.[28] While the Church Committee focused on the more sensational issues that had been raised about Intelligence Community behavior, the Pike Committee focused primarily on the CIA's effectiveness and its cost to the taxpayers.[29] At its first hearing, from its first witness the committee was surprised to find out that the Comptroller General of the General Accounting Office had no idea how much money the CIA spent or whether its management of money was effective or wasteful because his agency had no access to CIA budgetary information.[30]

The final report was never published. However, unauthorized versions of the draft report were leaked to the press and a complete copy of the draft document was published in England.[31] Among the committee's findings the committee concluded that there was insufficient executive and legislative branch oversight of the CIA and that an all "too cozy, almost inbred" relationship had developed between the President's Office of Management and Budget and the intelligence budget makers.[32]

Responding to the findings of the various investigations of Intelligence Community activities, President Ford issued Executive Order 11905. Section 6 of the Order established the Intelligence Oversight Board. The Board was composed of three members from outside of the government, appointed by the President based on their ability, knowledge, and diversity of background and experience and who serve without compensation. Among other things, the board was to

- receive and consider reports by the Inspectors General and General Counsels of the Intelligence Community concerning activities that raise questions of legality or propriety;
- periodically review the practices and procedures of the Inspectors General and General Councils of the Intelligence Community designed to discover and report to the Oversight Board activities that raise questions of legality or propriety; and
- report in a timely manner to the Attorney General and the President any activities that raise serious questions about legality or propriety.

Section 6 also charged the Inspectors General and General Councils with the task of reporting to the Oversight Board any activities that come to their attention that raised questions of legality or propriety, as well as their findings on such issues. It tasked the heads of intelligence agencies and departments to insure that Inspectors General and General Counsels of their agencies have access to any information necessary to perform their duties as outlined in the executive order, to report periodically to the Oversight Board any activities that might raise questions about legality or propriety, and to instruct their employees to cooperate fully with the Board. It also assigned the Attorney General the role of receiving and considering reports of the Board and reporting to the President, not less than quarterly, on activities of the Intelligence Community, if any, that might raise questions of legality.

This was clearly an attempt to preclude future activities of the kind raised by investigations during the 1960s and early 1970s about Intelligence Community violations of the rights of U.S. citizens and about violations of the law in its foreign operations. It did little in terms of overseeing the efficiency, effectiveness, or quality of output of the Intelligence Community. That task remained within the broad responsibilities of the President's Foreign Intelligence Advisory Board.

The Oversight Board has remained a permanent fixture of the executive branch oversight apparatus since its creation. Though President Carter abolished the Foreign Intelligence Advisory Board, he retained the Oversight Board. As noted above, in 1993 President Clinton made the Intelligence Oversight Board a standing committee of the President's Foreign Intelligence Advisory Board. President G. W. Bush failed to appoint anyone to the Intelligence Oversight Board until May 2003, when he expanded the Board from three to five members.[33] Today it continues in its role of providing independent advice to the President on the legality and propriety of intelligence activities that the Intelligence Oversight Board believes are in violation of the Constitution[34] or laws of the United States or are contrary to executive orders or presidential directives. However, the effectiveness of the Board largely depends on the cooperation it receives from executive branch departments and agencies. For example, when accounts of physical abuse and torture conducted by American military personnel on Iraqi prisoners at the Abu Ghraib prison surfaced in the spring of 2004, Lieutenant General (USAF retired) Brent Scowcroft then head of the Intelligence Oversight Board immediately sought information on the events from the Department of Defense. Though the Department of Defense Assistant to the Secretary for Intelligence Oversight did brief the Board on what he knew, which was limited at the time, efforts to obtain additional information from the Secretary of Defense were less than successful.

Though much of the activity of the Intelligence Oversight Board remains confidential, some examples of its efforts do surface from time to time. For example, in March 1995 President Clinton directed the Board to conduct a government-wide review of any and all aspects of the allegations surrounding the 1990 mysterious death of Michael DeVine and the 1992 disappearance of Efrain Bamaca Valasquez in Guatemala. In 1996 the Board examined the role of the U.S. Army School of the Americas in abetting illegal methods used by militaries in Latin America when dealing with those who oppose their governments. From 2002 to 2004 at least thirteen cases, with a minimum of 287 potential violations involving alleged illegal FBI surveillance of U.S. residents, were referred to it.[35] And, as mentioned above, the Intelligence Oversight Board did get involved in Abu Ghraib investigations.

DEPARTMENTAL AND AGENCY OVERSIGHT

Perhaps the most common form of oversight occurs at the departmental or agency level and below. Departments or agencies with intelligence responsibilities maintain an internal office tasked to insure that the department or agency is conducting its intelligence activities according to the law. Most often these offices are located within the respective agency's office of the Inspector General and/or in Inspector General offices located within subcomponents. Typically, the Inspectors General are appointed by and report to their respective department/agency heads.[36] A prominent exception is the Inspector General of the CIA, who is appointed by the President and is subject to Senate confirmation. Inspectors General work in close conjunction with the General Councils in their agencies, who provide the necessary legal support attendant to any investigation into wrongdoing. Indeed some Inspector General offices include an Inspector General for Intelligence.

Within the Department of Defense, however, intelligence oversight predates the establishment of a department-level Inspector General, which didn't occur until 1992. Driven by concerns raised in the 1960s and 1970s, the Secretary of Defense responded to President Ford's Executive Order 11905 by directing the establishment within the Office of the Secretary, of an Inspector General for Intelligence,[37] who would be responsible for the independent oversight of all Defense Department intelligence activities. To further emphasize the importance of effective oversight of intelligence, oversight offices were subsequently established in every Defense Department component with intelligence responsibilities, usually as a separately identifiable entity under the subordinate agency's Inspector General.

Following the creation of the DOD-level Inspector General in November 1992, the Inspector General for Intelligence was redesignated the Assistant to the Secretary of Defense—Intelligence Oversight. Until mid-2007, the Assistant to the Secretary for Intelligence Oversight served as principal staff assistant and advisor to the Secretary and Deputy Secretary of Defense for oversight of all intelligence, counterintelligence, and intelligence-related activities within the Department. The Bush administration, in what gives the appearance of a downgrading of the importance of the office, has directed the placement of the Defense Department's intelligence oversight function within the office of the Department's Inspector General. Moreover, as of this writing the total number of personnel within the Intelligence Oversight office has dropped from the previous eleven to about seven, including purely administrative personnel. Nevertheless, the Intelligence Oversight office remains tasked to ensure that all intelligence activities undertaken by Defense Department entities are conducted in compliance with Federal law, executive orders, presidential directives, and Department of Defense directives, regulations, and policies. This includes intelligence, counterintelligence, and intelligence-related activities undertaken by the Joint Staff, Combatant Commanders, Military Services, Defense Intelligence Agency, National Security Agency, National reconnaissance Office, and the National Geospatial-Intelligence Agency. To accomplish this task the DOD intelligence oversight office is responsible for the management and direction of the DOD intelligence oversight program.

Responsibilities of the Department of Defense Intelligence Oversight Office

- Develop departmental intelligence oversight policies and, in conjunction with the Department's General Counsel, issue oversight guidance to Defense Department components.
- Ensure that all Department entities adequately train their personnel to understand the rules and constraints that govern intelligence operations.
- Review clandestine intelligence activities undertaken by Department entities to ensure they are in compliance with the law.
- Direct Defense Department components to investigate allegations of illegal or improper activities; review, in consultation with the Department's General Counsel, all allegations and findings; and further investigate those allegations when appropriate.
- Maintain a worldwide inspection program of Defense Department intelligence activities, ranging from intelligence staffs at strategic headquarters to tactical intelligence in the field. Inspections include all intelligence disciplines engaged in by Defense Department entities, as well as counterintelligence activities.
- Verify that personnel are trained in and comply with presidential and department oversight directives and are familiar with their obligation to report questionable or improper intelligence activities.
- Conduct an annual financial audit of all funds generated by Defense Department intelligence commercial activities.
- Maintain liaison with agencies of the Intelligence Community and Federal law enforcement organizations at both the national- and field-level locations.

In pursuing its responsibilities, the Defense Department office of Intelligence Oversight receives a quarterly report from each of the services identifying any violations of laws or procedures by their intelligence components and any corrective action taken. Though those incidents reported are usually of a technical nature involving an honest mistake, if an incident is deemed to warrant further examination, the Intelligence Oversight office then steps in and conducts an extensive investigation. The Intelligence Oversight office also conducts on-site inspections in the United States and at U.S. facilities abroad, not only in response to possible wrongdoing, but also to verify that intelligence personnel are adequately informed of the constraints of law and policy, particularly in regard to intelligence collection.

Like the Defense Department subordinate units, the office of Intelligence Oversight must report at least quarterly through the Department's Inspector General to the Secretary of Defense and then through Secretary of Defense to the Intelligence Oversight Board. This report is coordinated with the Department's

General Counsel and describes significant Department intelligence oversight activities. It also includes intelligence oversight submissions from the Joint Staff, combatant commanders, and the eight intelligence organizations under the direction of the Secretary of Defense.[38]

In addition to the above, the office of Intelligence Oversight has developed and maintained "outreach" programs in intelligence oversight with representatives of foreign governments, international organizations, educational institutions, and others. Such programs heighten the level of awareness of Department efforts to ensure that past transgressions are not repeated and to encourage foreign governments to develop or strengthen, as appropriate, their own intelligence oversight programs.

Still, the Defense Department's intelligence oversight process has its limitations. It depends for much of its work on the reporting of individuals, usually through their respective Inspectors General. If those reports are not forthcoming, then breaches of procedure or of law may occur and go unchecked. The oversight process also depends on Defense Department entities with intelligence operations keeping their Inspector General and, in turn, the Department's office of Intelligence Oversight informed of their activities. Unfortunately, this is not always the case. For example, though the Assistant to the Secretary for Intelligence Oversight is cleared for information pertaining to every intelligence program within the Defense Department, during the early Bush years he was not made aware of some of the National Security Agency's intelligence activities. Such a determination to keep the Intelligence Oversight office in the dark is unlikely to have come from the Agency itself, but rather from senior Defense Department leadership, perhaps even from Secretary Rumsfeld.

In addition to the office of Intelligence Oversight, the Defense Department has an Undersecretary for Intelligence. This individual and his office are charged with making sure the Department is receiving the right kind of intelligence

Other agencies and departments have initiated similar programs. The Secretary of Energy, for example, has designated the Director, Office of Intelligence as responsible for management oversight of all Department of Energy intelligence activities. This includes providing the President's Intelligence Oversight Board with all information necessary to ensure that intelligence activities associated with the Department's efforts to analyze foreign nuclear weapons programs, the proliferation of nuclear weapons, and energy-related intelligence issues are conducted in a legal and proper manner. The Energy Secretary also has tasked the Department's Inspector General to report to the President's Intelligence Oversight Board activities that he/she has reason to believe may be unlawful or contrary to executive orders or presidential directives.[39]

DEPARTMENT OF JUSTICE AND OFFICE OF MANAGEMENT AND BUDGET

In addition to oversight provided at the agency or departmental level, two other executive branch bodies provide a degree of oversight of Intelligence

Community actions. The Department of Justice's Office of Intelligence Policy and Review reviews court-ordered procedures designed to protect the privacy rights of "U.S. persons."[40] This office files semiannual reports with Congress on electronic surveillance conducted under the Foreign Intelligence Surveillance Act. It also sets legal standards for surveillance activities. The Office of Management and Budget reviews Intelligence Community budgets in light of presidential policies and priorities, clears proposed testimony by Intelligence Community officials, and approves draft intelligence legislation for submission to Congress.

CONCLUDING COMMENTS

There can be little doubt that efforts by the executive branch to make sure that U.S. intelligence efforts are in full compliance with the law have come a long way since the 1960s and 1970s. At every level there are programs designed to reduce, if not preclude, the Intelligence Community from infringing on the basic rights of "U.S. persons." Do abuses still occur? Of course they do and for a variety of reasons. Situations may not always be perfectly clear-cut. In such situations, intelligence personnel are frequently confronted with balancing the need to protect the general welfare (i.e., nation's security) against the need to protect individual constitutional and statutory rights. Education and training play a role. Under the pressure of circumstances, intelligence personnel may not always receive all the training necessary to fully understand how this situation or that situation relates to presidential directives, executive orders, or departmental directives, policies, and regulations. Changing laws and differing interpretations of the meaning of laws also can lead to confusion among intelligence personnel as to just what constitutes legal activity in the Intelligence Community. Among the more recent events that might be cited in this regard are:

- The Patriot Act, passed with minimal debate forty-five days after 9/11, among other things, increased the ability of law enforcement agencies to search telephone and e-mail communications and medical, financial, and other records; eased restrictions on foreign intelligence gathering within the United States.
- The introduction of the term "unlawful combatants" when dealing with captured individuals.
- The extremely narrow interpretation of Article 3 of the Third Geneva Convention precluding "outrages upon personal dignity, in particular humiliating and degrading treatment" and a presidential determination in January 2002 that United States was not bound by prohibitions against torture in the Geneva Conventions in detaining al-Qaeda and Taliban members.
- Secretary of Defense Donald Rumsfeld's approval of interrogation techniques that were seen by many as a violation of international law and norms, and

- The August 1, 2002, Justice Department memo drafted by its Office of Legal Counsel, which argued that "moderate" torture, as long as it doesn't cause organ failure or death, is permissible in efforts to extract information.

In such an environment, it sometimes is difficult, even for the best-intentioned intelligence personnel, to understand clearly what is lawful and appropriate, especially when the security and well-being of his or her nation is at stake.

A more glaring weakness in executive branch oversight processes is the absence of institutional means and mechanisms for insuring the efficiency, effectiveness, and especially the quality of the intelligence effort and product. At the highest levels only the President's Foreign Intelligence Advisory Board is specifically chartered to identify deficiencies in the collection, analysis, and reporting of intelligence. While one might suppose that the National Security Council also plays a role, it would appear that this is largely dependent on the individual players and their penchant for asking the critical questions. Beyond that, no clearly identifiable institutional mechanisms are in place elsewhere in the executive branch to oversee the quality and effectiveness of the intelligence effort, save perhaps the efforts by bureau, branch, or division managers within specific departments and agencies of the Intelligence Community.

Interestingly, though the National Security Act of 1947 charges executive branch departments and agencies to "evaluate" intelligence affecting national security, which even to the casual observer would include an evaluation of the quality of the overall effort as well as the quality of the intelligence collected, nowhere does that legislation specifically mention the word "quality." The Act mandates that intelligence be timely, that it be objective and independent of political considerations, and that departments and agencies should eliminate waste and duplication of effort in their intelligence activities. It empowers the Director of National Intelligence to evaluate the utility of national intelligence to consumers, while similarly tasking the Director of the CIA to evaluate intelligence related to national security. But it does not further amplify the meaning the word "evaluate." Perhaps this absence of a specific requirement to ensure the quality of intelligence has, at least in part, resulted in an absence of the institutional mechanisms necessary to do so. It would appear from recent failures that the time for such mechanisms has arrived.

8

The Struggle for Congressional Oversight

> "Wise and effective legislation cannot proceed in the absence of information respecting conditions to be affected or changed."
>
> —Pike Committee Report

When the delegates met in Philadelphia in 1787 they drafted a Constitution that divided governmental power among three branches of government—legislative, executive, and judicial. Each branch was to have its own powers and each was to have powers that held in "check" the powers of the others. Justice Louis Brandeis (1856–1941) concisely summed up the purpose of this distribution of powers.

> The doctrine of the separation of powers was adopted by the convention of 1787 not to promote efficiency but to preclude the exercise of arbitrary power. The purpose was not to avoid friction, but, by means of the inevitable friction incident to the distribution of the governmental powers among three departments, to save the people from autocracy.[1]

Thus, the U.S. Constitution established three "relatively" independent branches of government, each with its own powers and prerogatives and each with powers and prerogatives that "check and balance" the powers of the other two branches. For example, Congress has the power to pass or repeal a law, but the President can veto it. Even if both houses of Congress and the President agree on a law, the judicial branch can declare it to be unconstitutional. The President serves as commander in chief of the military services, can appoint ambassadors and other high-level officials, make treaties and, in general, is granted supervision over the conduct of military and foreign policy. But Congress holds the purse strings. Presidential appointments and treaties require the concurrence of the Senate. But only Congress can declare war. Moreover, Article 1, Section 8 of the Constitution not only specifically enumerates such powers of Congress, but also adds:

> The Congress shall have the power. . . .To make all laws which shall be necessary and proper for the carrying into execution the foregoing powers, and all other powers vested by this Constitution in the government of the United States, or in any department or officer thereof.

This clause expanded and protected the enumerated powers by guaranteeing that Congress would have the powers "implied" by those that had been specifically granted in order to undertake its responsibilities as the first branch of government.

Following the intelligence failures leading up to the 9/11 attacks and events leading up to the 2003 Iraq War, there has been a renewed discussion of congressional oversight of the Intelligence Community. Congressional oversight of the U.S. intelligence apparatus operates within the same Constitutional frame of reference described by Justice Brandeis and largely to the same purposes. It serves as a check on the exercise of arbitrary power by the executive branch and thus to preclude arbitrary decisions from being made concerning U.S. intelligence efforts that might infringe on the rights of the people, be contrary to law, or be adverse to the general welfare of Americans.

The so-called implied powers, "necessary and proper" for Congress to carry out those powers it is specifically granted, established the conditions necessary for Congress to undertake its responsibilities in the area of intelligence oversight. Courts have generally interpreted Congress' implied powers to include the power of Congress to require reports from the executive branch on the various issues subject to legislation.[2] Though intelligence agencies operate within the executive branch, they are funded by congressional legislation. Thus the Courts have provided the legal foundation for intrusive investigations by Congress of the Intelligence Community. Hence, in theory, Congress has the authority to require the Intelligence Community to report on its activities. In practice, congressional authority has been limited by at least six major factors—the diffuse nature of congressional oversight, secrecy, workload, congressional self-restraint, the uncritical acceptance of information provided by the Intelligence Community, and politics.

This chapter will review the history of congressional oversight of U.S. intelligence activities, examine the structure and functions of the congressional oversight committees, and identify major impediments to congressional efforts to oversee the Intelligence Community.

A BRIEF HISTORY OF CONGRESSIONAL OVERSIGHT

Historically, intelligence activities have been undertaken on an ad hoc basis by departments or agencies responsible for foreign or military affairs, each acting independently to meet the perceived needs of its parent organization. Congressional oversight of the intelligence activities of these organizations was minimal. Whatever oversight that did occur was undertaken by the committees of Congress responsible for authorizing or appropriating the budget for the department or agency with intelligence functions.[3]

The Post-World War II Years

Following the end of World War II, President Harry S. Truman sensed the need for a peacetime intelligence establishment. He was well aware of the intelligence failures that had lead to the successful Japanese surprise attack on Pearl Harbor and was dissatisfied with the haphazard nature of intelligence collection, with each department having its own information service that was frequently walled off from the others. He was concerned, as well, that there was no centralization of information for the benefit of the President. So Truman sought to create an intelligence organization that would provide for a greater degree of coordination and centralization of information, bring order and priority to the information he received, and operate effectively in peacetime and during conflicts.[4] In January 1946 he issued an executive directive establishing the National Intelligence Authority, the Central Intelligence Group under the direction of a Director of Central Intelligence, and an Intelligence Advisory Board.

The National Intelligence Authority, the forerunner of the National Security Council, was tasked with planning, developing, and coordinating the overall U.S. intelligence effort and was comprised of the Secretaries of Navy, State, and War, as well as the President's personal representative. The Central Intelligence Group, a small interdepartmental group, not an independent agency, was to assemble the intelligence available to the government as a whole and provide an objective assessment of the information.[5] The Central Intelligence Group retained many of the operational capabilities of the Office of Strategic Services, which had been disbanded following the end of the war, including the clandestine gathering of information.[6]

When Congress passed the National Security Act the following year, creating a postwar national security structure, it also had in mind the need for a peacetime centralized intelligence apparatus that would operate independent of the other departments and agencies of government. So as part of the National Security Act, Congress created the Central Intelligence Agency. The CIA, as successor to the Central Intelligence Group, was to be headed by a director who was to correlate, evaluate, and disseminate intelligence obtained by the intelligence elements of other departments and agencies. Thus, for all practical purposes, while other intelligence agencies retained their responsibilities for producing, analyzing, and disseminating intelligence related to their department's specific mission, the CIA became the focal point for national-level intelligence. Responsibility for overseeing the activities of the CIA was given to the committees of the Armed Services of both houses. Responsibility for approving CIA appropriations fell to the defense subcommittees of the House and Senate appropriations committees. For security reasons, the budget was classified and hidden in nondescript line items of the defense budget, and remains so today.[7] As for the remaining U.S. intelligence elements, oversight was largely limited to overseeing the budgetary needs of the departments with intelligence functions.

By the mid-1950s the CIA was acquiring new responsibilities. Shortly after the passage of the National Security Act of 1947, the CIA was given responsibility for covert actions[8] and with the coming of the Korean War was charged with the responsibility of providing its own independent analysis.[9] Similarly, the rest of the American intelligence apparatus was expanding dramatically to meet the needs of the Cold War. The Department of State had already acquired the Research and Analysis Branch of the former Office of Strategic Services in 1945, with the War Department (predecessor to the Department of the Army)[10] receiving remaining assets of the Office of Strategic Services.[11] The National Security Agency was created in 1952, National Reconnaissance Office in 1960, and the Defense Intelligence Agency in 1961.

Nevertheless, throughout this period, beyond seeing to intelligence agency appropriations, congressional involvement in U.S. foreign intelligence activities remained minimal. The Director of Central Intelligence and his representatives usually interacted directly with the chairmen and ranking minority members of the Armed Services or appropriations committees, who were, for the most part, strong supporters of intelligence and saw little need for or benefit from intrusive oversight by Congress.[12] Staff involvement also was limited to one or two senior members of each of these committees, who made certain that the needs of the Intelligence Community were adequately funded.[13] Formal hearings and testimony were rare. Intelligence subcommittees met only a few times each year and virtually all oversight was conducted behind closed doors. Thus, oversight was tightly circumscribed.[14] However, coming in the wake of the intelligence failures leading up to World War II and with the increasing challenges of the Cold War, it is not surprising that Congress was more concerned with funding and protecting the intelligence services than with questioning or restraining them. As a result, few in Congress had little more than a vague understanding of Intelligence Community activities.

Since the 1970s

By the mid-1970s the congressional laissez-faire attitude toward intelligence activities changed. U.S. intelligence agencies' abuses in the 1960s and 1970s, which included activities that seriously infringed upon the basic rights of Americans, covert activities against foreign leaders and governments, and involvement in assassination plots (see Chapter 7) caused an uproar. They also brought to an end the postwar period marked by congressional acquiescence. One of the first legislative efforts to reign in the U.S. intelligence agencies was the 1974

Hughes-Ryan amendment to the Foreign Assistance Act of 1961. Troubled by the findings that surfaced during the Senate Armed Service Committee hearing about U.S. covert activities in Cambodia, Laos, and North Vietnam during the Vietnam War and reports of other covert activities, Congress passed the Hughes-Ryan amendment, prohibiting the use of appropriated funds by or on behalf of the CIA for "operations in foreign countries, other than activities intended solely for obtaining necessary intelligence unless and until the President issued a *Finding* that each such operation is important to the national security of the United States." The amendment also required the President to report "in a timely fashion [widely understood to mean within 48 hours][15] a description and scope of such operation[s] to the appropriate committees of Congress." This was interpreted to mean the six congressional committees with intelligence oversight responsibilities—the Armed Services and Appropriations Committees of both Houses and the Senate Foreign Relations and House Foreign Affairs Committees.[16] The following year, Congress put teeth into its determination to reign in covert activities undertaken by U.S. intelligence agencies by passing, for the first time, legislation that terminated funding for covert activities in Angola.

Then came the Church and Pike Committee findings of serious, numerous, and widely spread intelligence agency abuses, after which both houses of Congress established new intelligence oversight structures (see Chapter 7). In May 1976 the Senate by a 72 to 22 majority passed Resolution 400, which established the Senate Select Committee on Intelligence. Among other things, the Resolution included the nonbinding statement that it was "the sense of the Senate" that intelligence agencies keep the Senate "fully and currently informed with respect to intelligence activities, including significant anticipated activities."[17] In July of the following year the House by a vote of 227 to 171 passed House Resolution 658 establishing the House Permanent Select Committee on Intelligence.

With the establishment of the House and Senate intelligence committees, Congress began to streamline its oversight activities as well as play a more active role in overseeing U.S. intelligence efforts (see Box).[18] To protect against unauthorized disclosure of classified materials, the committees worked with the CIA to establish informal ground rules governing the sharing of intelligence, thus permitting the intelligence committees to have access to an even greater variety of classified data and information.

Nevertheless, critical information concerning U.S. intelligence operations often was not made available to congressional oversight committees. The CIA-congressionally agreed ground rules governing the sharing of intelligence with Congress permitted the agency or the President or his advisors to limit access to information it deemed "sensitive." Moreover, to prove that the new oversight system could work, President Carter had issued Executive Order 12036. The executive order established restrictions on intelligence activities, including restrictions designed to protect individual privacy and civil liberties and a prohibition of assassination; directed intelligence officials to keep both congressional intelligence committees "fully and currently informed" of their intelligence activities,

Congress Steps In 1977–1978

- In 1977, the Senate intelligence committee, with the agreement of the Senate Armed Services committee, assumed responsibility for reviewing presidential nominations for Director and Deputy Director of Central Intelligence. The Senate committee also acquired the responsibility for assessing the ability of the U.S. Intelligence Community to verify arms control treaties, which required access to a huge volume of highly sensitive data.[19]
- In 1978, the intelligence committees of both houses of Congress produced their first bills authorizing appropriations for intelligence activities. Previously, appropriations for intelligence were incorporated in the Defense appropriations bills without systematic congressional scrutiny of intelligence activities.
- That same year, both the intelligence committees, in coordination with their respective Judiciary committees, developed legislation that led to the Foreign Intelligence Surveillance Act (FISA) of 1978. Now, for the first time, a court order from a special court established under the Act would be necessary before undertaking electronic surveillance for intelligence purposes within the United States.[20]

"including any significant anticipated activities"; and required intelligence agencies to provide congressional intelligence committees any information or document in their possession, custody, or control that the committees might request, as well report to both committees "in a timely fashion . . . intelligence activities that are illegal or improper and the corrective actions . . . taken or planned." However, the executive order bore the caveat that whatever was done had to be consistent with any procedures the President might establish, as well as consistent with authorities and duties conferred on the executive and legislative branches by the Constitution. Furthermore, implicit in the executive order was the right to withhold information based on the concept of "executive privilege"[21] Thus, rather large loopholes existed that afforded the President, as well as the intelligence agencies, the opportunity to limit information passed to the intelligence committees if they so wished, and they did.

As a result, in the wake of the Carter administration's failure to inform them of CIA activities relating to the rescue attempt during the Iranian hostage crisis of 1979–1980 and determined to strengthen further the oversight processes, Congress passed and the President signed the "Intelligence Oversight Act of 1980." Where the 1974 Hughes-Ryan amendment obliged the CIA to provide notice to Congress of its covert activities "in a timely fashion," the Intelligence Oversight Act of 1980 extended the reporting obligation to any agency conducting intelligence operations. The Act required the Director of Central Intelligence and heads of *all* [emphasis added] departments, agencies, and other U.S. entities involved in intelligence activities to

- furnish any information or material concerning intelligence activities in their possession that is requested by either of the intelligence committees, and
- keep the intelligence committees fully and currently informed of all intelligence activities, including any "significant anticipated intelligence" activities and report in "a timely fashion," "any illegal intelligence activity or significant intelligence failure and the corrective action that has been taken or is planned."

Should the executive branch departments or agencies fail to provide prior notice to the intelligence committees of intelligence operations in foreign countries, other than activities intended solely for obtaining necessary intelligence [i.e., covert actions], the Act required the President to "fully inform" "in a timely fashion" the committees of such activities and to provide a statement explaining the reasons for not giving prior notice.

In a concession to the executive branch, the Act limited the number of congressional committees receiving notice of covert actions from the previous six to just the two intelligence committees. Congress also recognized that under extraordinary circumstances affecting the vital interests of the United States, the President might find it essential to limit the number of those receiving prior notice. Under such circumstances, he could opt to limit notice to the chairman and ranking minority members of the intelligence committees, the Speaker and minority leader of the House of Representatives, and the majority and minority leaders of the Senate. This group became known as the "gang of eight."

By the time Ronald Reagan assumed office, relationships between executive branch intelligence agencies and the congressional oversight committees were reasonably well established.[22] In principle, the committees recognized no limit on their right to obtain information or documentation from the Intelligence Community. In practice, they recognized that they might be denied access to certain highly classified information, such as the identity of clandestine agents, or access might be limited to the committee chairman and ranking minority member and perhaps certain selected staff.[23] With such an accommodation in place, the sharing of classified information by intelligence agencies with Congress increased, including the sharing of such materials with nonoversight committees.[24] In return, congressional intelligence oversight committees, though carefully scrutinizing Intelligence Community budgets, were supportive of increases.

At the same time, congressional intelligence committees vigorously pursued their charter. Among other things, they investigated allegations of improper conduct on the part of Director of Central Intelligence William Casey, closely examined administration implementation of the 1978 Foreign Intelligence Surveillance Act to assure themselves and the public that their rights were being protected, and undertook extensive reviews of U.S. counterintelligence and security policies and practices following the Walker-Whitworth, Pelton, and Pollard espionage cases. They also became increasingly concerned over U.S. intelligence agencies' activities in Central America. Of serious concern were allegations that the CIA may have been involved in political violence in El Salvador and Guatemala and particularly the Agency's role in the civil war in Nicaragua.[25]

In Nicaragua, Congress was aware that President Reagan had authorized the CIA to provide assistance, including military assistance to an insurgent group known as the Contras. The Contras opposed rule of the pro-communist Sandinista government that had led the revolution against Nicaraguan dictator Anastasio Somoza and taken over control of the Nicaraguan government in 1979. Concerned that Nicaragua might become another Vietnam, congressional intelligence committees became involved in limiting covert assistance to the Contras. These restrictions, collectively known as the Boland amendments,[26] culminated in the passing of Public Law 98–215 in December 1982, which prohibited covert assistance to the Contras for the purpose of overthrowing the government of Nicaragua.

When Senate intelligence committee members learned in April 1984 that CIA operatives had covertly assisted the Contras in the mining of Nicaraguan harbors, many were notably upset. The mining of Nicaragua's harbors was a violation of international law. Moreover it had resulted in explosions that damaged ships from several foreign countries, including those of the Netherlands and Japan, both U.S. allies, as well as the Soviet Union. And, once again, the Senate committee had not been "fully and currently informed" of a major CIA covert operation.

In the wake of congressional investigations, an informal agreement known as the "Casey Accord" was reached in June 1984 with the executive branch promising to keep the oversight committees informed of significant changes or developments in ongoing covert operations.[27] To further strengthen intelligence oversight, the National Security Act of 1947 was amended, requiring Congress to specifically authorize and appropriate all monies to be spent on intelligence or intelligence-related activities. In addition, the Director of Central Intelligence had to give prior notice of any release of funds from the CIA Reserve Contingencies and any reprogramming or transfer of funds for purposes other than those for which they had been authorized and appropriated by Congress.[28]

Despite such arrangements, congressional intelligence committees were confronted with what many regarded as the most serious breach of oversight arrangements since the committees were created—the so-called Iran-Contra affair.[29] In October and November 1986, two closely linked covert operations were publicly exposed. The first involved the sale of arms to Iran. Hezbollah, a radical Islamic group based in Lebanon had taken a number of Americans hostage. Since Iran was a strong supporter and thought to be able to influence Hezbollah, Reagan administration officials thought that by selling arms to Iran, the Iranians might be able to gain the release of the hostages. However, such an action was in possible violation U.S. arms export controls and in contravention of U.S. policy.

The second covert activity involved providing the funds from the sale of arms to Iran to the Nicaraguan "Contra" rebels, which had been prohibited by the Boland amendments. Both activities were undertaken with CIA involvement and in neither case were congressional intelligence committees informed.[30] As a result, Senate and House intelligence committees immediately undertook intensive investigations of the events. On December 1, 1986, President Reagan also took action, with the creation of a Special Review Board, chaired by former Senator John Tower and known as the "Tower Commission." In early 1987, the Senate and House established select committees and agreed to undertake joint investigations.[31]

These investigations revealed that the Reagan administration had largely ignored the accountability structures that had been set in place since the Church and Pike committee reports. The President had not given prior approval to all covert actions that had been undertaken. Of those prior approvals given, not all had been in writing. Moreover, the President had approved a covert action and deliberately ordered the Director of Central Intelligence not to inform Congress.[32]

Once again, the executive branch recommitted itself to procedures that would permit effective congressional oversight. Following Director of Central Intelligence Casey's death in May 1987, the new Director Judge William Webster pledged to restore a cooperative relationship between the CIA and the oversight committees. In October, President Reagan signed National Security Decision Directive 286, prohibiting retroactive approval of special activities in foreign countries (i.e., covert actions). Moreover, in all but the "rarest circumstances" no such activity was to take place prior to the President having signed a written statement, or *Finding*, as it was called, that such activity is important to the national security of the United States.

However, since the President could revise or revoke any National Security Decision Directive without congressional consent, in the spring of 1988 the Senate, in an attempt to emphasize, once again, the need for the executive branch to comply with the law and previous agreements, overwhelmingly passed a bill requiring notice of covert activities within 48 hours. The House failed to act and the legislation never became law.

Nevertheless, during this period Congress made notable progress in its efforts to oversee the Intelligence Community. However, congressional oversight was primarily aimed at ensuring that intelligence agencies operated within the law and were adequately funded. They were not centrally focused on the quality of the intelligence effort nor, as was evident in the Iranian hostage crisis, in the mining of Nicaraguan harbors, and the Iran-Contra affair, were they ever 100 percent effective.

The Post-Cold War Period

By the end of 1991, the Soviet Union had been dissolved and a 69-year odyssey had come to an end. With it came a definitive end to a struggle between East and West that had consumed the energies of Western defense and intelligence specialists since the mid-1940s. Congressional intelligence committees were quick to recognize the need for change in U.S. intelligence efforts to adapt to the new environment. While continuing to review U.S. covert actions, monitor intelligence data to ensure compliance with arms control agreements, and improve U.S. counterintelligence efforts, congressional intelligence committees increasingly focused on such issues as drug trafficking and counternarcotics, economic intelligence, and the proliferation of chemical, biological, and nuclear weapons. They also directed the Intelligence Community to strengthen its collection and analysis capabilities in these areas[33] and examined events leading up to the Persian Gulf War of 1991, monitoring efforts to disarm Iraq prior to the conflict. More importantly, they continued to seek ways to improve their ability to oversee the U.S. intelligence apparatus.

Several months after taking Office in 1989, President H.W. Bush pledged to provide prior notice of covert actions. Should that not be possible, he would provide notice "within a few days." However, if notice were to be withheld for a longer period, he would rely on his authorities under the Constitution. These words, uncoded, meant that the President believed that, in certain circumstances, it was within his Constitutionally mandated prerogatives to withhold such information. Despite disagreements between the executive branch and Congress over wording,[34] an accommodation was reached and the following year the intelligence authorization bill for FY1991 was passed, which significantly revised the Intelligence Oversight Act of 1980.[35]

The bill reiterated all essential elements of the 1980 Oversight Act. However, for the first time, it placed an obligation on the President to keep the congressional intelligence committees fully and currently informed of all U.S. intelligence activities and significant anticipated intelligence activities, not just covert activities. Heretofore, only the Director of Central Intelligence and intelligence agency heads were legally required to do so. Additionally, it specifically defined "what was meant by "covert action" and reaffirmed the requirement, originally established by the 1974 Hughes–Ryan Amendment and amplified by Reagan's National Security Decision Directive 286, that the President provide written approval for covert actions in the form of a *Finding* that the action was necessary to support identifiable foreign policy objectives and important to the security of the United States. If events precluded written prior approval, a subsequent written approval had to be forthcoming within 48 hours. Once again, the legislation recognized that under extraordinary circumstances affecting vital interests the President might wish to limit the number of people made aware of the covert activity. Under such circumstances his written approval may be reported to the so-called congressional "Gang of Eight." Additionally, the new legislation prohibited the President from authorizing actions aimed at influencing U.S. political processes, public opinion, policies, or the media, as well as actions that were in violation of the Constitution or any statute of the U.S., unless the President determined such an action was necessary to support identifiable foreign policy objectives of the United States and was important to U.S. national security.[36]

In passing this bill, Congress again acknowledged that the President might exercise what he perceived as his prerogatives under the Constitution to withhold information for longer periods than specified in the legislation, but they expressed the view that the Constitution did not provide such authority to the President.[37]

In the fall of 1992 the intelligence oversight committees reached yet another significant agreement with the Bush administration. The agreement resulted in the passage of the Intelligence Organization Act of 1992,[38] which amended the National Security Act of 1947 and became the first successful attempt to enact organizational legislation for the U.S. Intelligence Community since 1947. Among other things the new law recognized the role of the Director of Central Intelligence as the principal intelligence advisor to the President, the statutory advisor to the National Security Council, head of the U.S. Intelligence Community, and head of the CIA. The Act gave the Director of Central Intelligence the responsibility for developing and presenting the National Foreign Intelligence Budget to the President and establishing Intelligence Community collection requirements and priorities. The Act also established in law the National Intelligence Council[39] within the office of the Director of Central Intelligence, composed of senior analysts from within the Intelligence Community and "substantive experts from the public and private sector." The Council was charged to assist the Director of Central Intelligence in carrying out his statutory responsibilities, to produce National Intelligence Estimates, and, when it considered it necessary, to include in those Estimates alternative views held by elements of the Intelligence Community.[40]

During the early part of the George H. W. Bush administration, the oversight committees also included a provision in the 1990 intelligence authorization bill that created an independent Inspector General at the CIA. The Inspector General was to be appointed by the President instead of the Director of Central Intelligence and under certain conditions to report directly to the oversight committees.[41]

However, while seeking to improve their oversight of the Intelligence Community and expand intelligence efforts beyond traditional Cold War-focused efforts, Congress sought to cut the intelligence budget. In the early 1990s, with budget deficits and the national debt reaching record levels, the Cold War over, and the United States with no peer military competitor in sight, the logical place to seek economies was in the area of national security. The defense budget began to decline in 1990. In the waning days of the Bush administration, Congress had already turned its eyes on intelligence budgets. After Bill Clinton was elected President, outgoing Senate intelligence committee chairman David Boren and his House counterpart Dave McCurdy cautioned against making hasty cuts in intelligence. Though Clinton heeded the warnings of Boren and McCurdy, submitting a budget that called for increased spending on intelligence, both the House and Senate intelligence committees voted to cut his request by $1.1 billion and $1.3 billion respectively. In addition, the House intelligence committee voted to repeal the National Security Education Act, of 1991 passed during the Bush years to provide funds to train the next generation of national security specialists in language and area studies.[42]

Nevertheless, congressional intelligence committees continued monitoring intelligence, focusing on such post-Cold War challenges as the proliferation of weapons of mass destruction, drugs, small wars and their aftermath, terrorism, and on such important issues as developments in Russia, the newly independent states of the former Soviet Union, central and eastern Europe, and China—including such issues as China's acquisition of U.S. nuclear weapons information. They also were closely involved in the investigation of the Ames Spy case. In the process of such efforts they reviewed a vast amount of material. For example, in 1995, approximately 5,000 copies of finished intelligence published by the Intelligence Community for general circulation were delivered to each intelligence committee of Congress, not including the daily current intelligence publications they receive (e.g., the *National Intelligence Daily*, now designated *The Senior Executive Intelligence Brief*, and the *Military Intelligence Daily*. For a listing of the publications generally received by Congress on a routine basis, as well as those not generally distributed to Congress see appendix C.) In addition, in 1996 both intelligence committees installed computer terminals linking them to the Intelligence Community network known as PolicyNet. This network provides the committees electronic access to most finished intelligence, and in some cases to intelligence reports that are not available in hard copy.[43]

The House intelligence committee also chartered a major staff study to examine Intelligence Community organizations, products, practices, relationships, and ways of doing business to determine if they were still completely applicable in the post-Cold War environment.[44]

Post-9/11 Oversight

Congressional oversight of the Intelligence Community during the presidency of George W. Bush has been dominated by investigations into intelligence failings prior to the 9/11 attacks and the Iraq war. In a major undertaking following the 9/11 attacks, Senate and House intelligence committees undertook a joint inquiry into the September 11, 2001, terrorist attacks on the World Trade Center and the Pentagon. Joint committee investigations covered a wide field of inquiry, ranging from terrorist activities leading up to the attacks and what U.S. intelligence understood of those activities to how the Intelligence Community managed the knowledge it had. On December 20, 2002, Joint Committee findings were presented in a 422-page document to their respective chambers. Among the findings identified by the Joint Committee were poor organization within the Intelligence Community, lack of collaboration and coordination, outdated technical systems, inadequately trained analysts, inconsistent strategic focus and quality of analyses, insufficient language specialists, and an inadequate development of human intelligence resources.

Both congressional intelligence committees became involved in legislative efforts that culminated in the Intelligence Reform and Terrorism Prevention Act of December 2004. The Act introduced a number of important Intelligence Community reforms, including the establishment of a Director of National Intelligence, the National Counterterrorism and National Counter Proliferation centers, and the Joint Intelligence Community Council, chaired by the Director of National Intelligence and whose members include the secretaries of Energy, Defense, Homeland Security, State, and Treasury and the Attorney General. It also directed the President to create an information sharing environment within the Intelligence Community, established an Information Sharing Council, mandated that the Director of National Intelligence, in consultation with the Secretary of Defense and the Director of the Central Intelligence Agency, develop procedures to improve coordination between their two entities, encouraged the development of human intelligence resources, and mandated improvements in professional intelligence, cross-disciplinary education and training, and language training.

Furthermore, congressional intelligence committees were involved in efforts that led to the U.S. Patriot Act,[45] which was passed very shortly after the 9/11 attacks, its subsequent refinement in 2006, and in investigations into the pre-Iraq war intelligence failings. In July 2004 the Senate intelligence committee published an extensive report detailing its findings on Intelligence Community judgments and misjudgments in the period leading up to the 2003 U.S. invasion of Iraq. Intelligence committees also played a role in congressional efforts that led to Foreign Intelligence Surveillance Act revisions (see Chapter 3) and such other issues as U.S. counterterrorism efforts, Iran and North Korea and the proliferation of weapons of mass destruction, and emerging global threats, as well as work on the intelligence authorization bills and the intelligence budget.

During this period, congressional intelligence committees became increasingly partisan, a trend that had begun in both the Senate and House during the Clinton administration. Unfortunately, it spread to the intelligence committees and reached a new level with the Iraq war, making harmony more difficult to achieve and maintain and with adverse impact on the committees' oversight functions.[46] L. Briit Snider, former counsel to the Church Committee, general counsel to the Senate intelligence committee (1987–1995, and former CIA inspector general (1998–2001) wrote:

> On the SSCI [Senate Select Committee on Intelligence] the divisive question arose of whether the committee would limit itself to looking either at the actions of the intelligence community (the preference of the Republican majority), or at how the prewar intelligence was used by the White House (the preference of the Democratic minority). After battling over this issue for *several months* [emphasis added], the majority had its way and limited the scope of the inquiry to the actions of the intelligence community.[47]

A memo prepared by the committee's Democratic staff in response to this majority vote to limit the inquiry fell into the hands of someone on the committee or committee staff (probably from the majority [Republican] party). The memo was leaked to the press, caused an uproar in the committee with mutual recriminations and a personal attack by the chairman on the vice chairman. As a result, the committee found it difficult to conduct its affairs and in an unprecedented step the Senate Majority leader suspended the committee's ongoing inquiry into pre-Iraqi war intelligence.[48] Though much of the previous rancor appears to have subsided, it has left a negative impression of the professionalism and quality of effort Americans can expect of intelligence oversight by Congress.

STRUCTURE AND FUNCTIONING OF OVERSIGHT COMMITTEES

Structure

Unlike other committees of the Senate and House, whose membership is decided by their respective party members through party committees established for that purpose, the Majority and Minority leaders name Senate intelligence committee members from their respective parties and at the beginning of each congress the Majority Leader names the committee chairman and the Minority Leader names the vice chairman. In the House, the Speaker of the House appoints each member of the House intelligence committee. However, the House Minority Leader, whose nominations are customarily accepted by the Speaker, nominates Minority party members.[49]

Also unlike other committees of Congress, when established, service on both intelligence committees was limited to no more than eight continuous years on the Senate committee and six on the House committee. However, in 2004, following the 9/11 Commission's recommendation, the Senate voted to remove intelligence committee term limitations. The House has retained, but modified tenure limits. Today a Member may not serve on the House intelligence committee for more than eight years in a 12-year period. There are, however, no limitations on tenure if a Member is appointed to serve as chairman or is the Ranking Minority Member.[50]

In a further dissimilarity with other committees, both intelligence committees have been structured to directly integrate the views of other committees of Congress with an interest in intelligence. The Senate committee includes two members each from the committees on Appropriation, Armed Services, Foreign Relations, and Judiciary, while the House committee only includes one member from each of those committees.

Similar to other committees of Congress, however, both Senate and House intelligence committee membership is distributed based on the political party's representation in the respective houses of Congress, with the chairperson selected from the majority party. The Senate intelligence committee, since inception, has followed a more bipartisan approach, distributing membership evenly between both parties, with the majority party given one more seat. Though the number of members has varied over time, today Senate intelligence committee has 15–8 Democrats and seven Republicans. The same size as it was when it was established in 1976. The chairperson is from the majority party, with the vice chairperson (who takes over in the absence of the chairman) from the minority party. The Majority and Minority leaders of the Senate, joined by two other Senators, serve as ex officio members of the committee, without a vote and can't be counted for purposes of determining a quorum.

House committee membership, however, is weighted in favor of the majority party with both chairperson and vice chairperson coming from the majority party. The House intelligence committee currently has twelve Democratic Party members and nine Republicans, though its size and composition has changed often in the past. The Speaker of the House and Minority Leader are ex officio committee members and as with the Senate intelligence committee they can neither vote nor be counted toward a quorum.

The House intelligence committee currently has four subcommittees: (1) Terrorism/HUMINT [human intelligence], Analysis, and Counterintelligence; (2) Technical and Tactical Intelligence; (3) Intelligence Community Management, and (4) Oversight and Investigations. The majority party chairs subcommittees, while a member of the minority party serves as vice chair. Currently the Senate intelligence committee is not organized into subcommittees.

Functioning

Most committees of Congress exercise some form of oversight over executive branch functions for which they are responsible. However, while oversight frequently has been a peripheral concern of such committees, oversight is the principal concern of the Senate and House intelligence committees. Their main tasks are:

- To make sure that appropriate departments and agencies of the United States provide informed and timely intelligence necessary for the executive and legislative branches to make sound decisions affecting the security and vital interests of the nations.
- To provide vigilant legislative oversight over the intelligence activities of the United States to assure that such activities are in conformity with the Constitution and the laws of the United States; and
- To authorize activities of the Intelligence Community and insure that the Community's budgets are sufficient to meet the tasks authorized by Congress and approved by the President.

In the execution of their oversight duties, both the Senate and House intelligence committees, in their respective chambers, have exclusive jurisdiction over the CIA, the Director of National Intelligence, and the National Intelligence Program, formerly called the National Foreign Intelligence Program. They share jurisdiction over the intelligence components of the remaining intelligence agencies with other committees (e.g., Appropriations, Armed Services, Foreign Relations/Affairs, Homeland Security, and Judiciary). Additionally, House intelligence committee jurisdiction extends beyond that of the Senate to include "tactical intelligence and intelligence-related activities of the Department of Defense," which covers tactical military intelligence. The House committee also has been given exclusive authority within the House to review and study the sources and methods of Intelligence Community entities.[51] In the Senate, the Armed Services Committee has jurisdiction over all aspects of defense intelligence. Each year the committees also prepare the intelligence authorization legislation and make recommendations on agency and department intelligence budgets and appropriations.[52]

To accomplish these tasks, the committees review classified materials, conduct hearings, receive briefings, undertake investigations, and write reports. Workload and time constraints (discussed below) force Members to rely on committee staff to accomplish much of the "leg work." The committees also have the authority to request documents, cross-question witnesses, issue subpoenas, and initiate contempt proceedings if an individual fails to provide documents or appear before a hearing. Regular meetings of the Senate intelligence committee are held every other Wednesday of each month, unless otherwise directed by the chairman. Correspondingly, the House committee meets on the first Wednesday of each month, unless otherwise directed by its chairman.

OBSTACLES TO OVERSIGHT

The Diffuse Nature of Congressional Oversight

Though the two congressional intelligence committees have exclusive jurisdiction over the CIA, the Director of National Intelligence, and the National Intelligence Program, intelligence agencies are frequently held accountable and called to testify or provide materials to a number of congressional committees. For example, in September 2007 Secretary of the Department of Homeland Security Michael Chertoff responded to a request by Congressmen Peter King, ranking minority member of the House Committee on Homeland Security, for information about the time and resources that the Department devotes to responding to congressional inquiries, preparing for and appearing at briefings and hearings, and writing and providing reports and other information.

In his response he noted that eighty-six committees and subcommittees assert some form of jurisdiction or oversight for the Department. As a result, he noted that from 2004 to mid-August 2007 the Department had participated in 696 congressional hearings, provided Congress nearly 8,000 briefings, and over 900 Department witnesses had furnished committees or subcommittees of Congress with oral and written testimony, estimated to cover some 4,475 to 10,740 pages. Moreover, just since February 2006, when the Department's Executive Secretariat began tracking congressional correspondence, Chertoff had responded to over 2,500 congressional letters or requests. This was in addition to the inquiries sent directly to other Department components or senior leaders. Chertoff further noted that often the information provided to committees or Members of Congress is redundant.[53]

There is little doubt that such a massive effort imposes a significant burden that takes time away from the department's principal task of providing for the security of the nation. It also can result in a diffusion of intelligence among a variety of committees that can obscure the broad picture necessary for truly effective oversight. Unfortunately an easy solution to this problem is not at hand. Since committees of Congress depend on information from the executive branch in exercising their responsibilities, a significant redefinition of functions, responsibilities, and span of jurisdiction of congressional committees undoubtedly will be required if this issue is to be resolved effectively. The fact that the 9/11 Commission Report released in July 2004 recommended that congressional oversight of the Department of Homeland Security be streamlined and yet nearly four years have passed and little has been done, a testimony of the complexity of the problem.

Secrecy

The most significant impediment to congressional oversight of the Intelligence Community is the high degree and pervasiveness of secrecy surrounding the intelligence processes.[54] Today, classified intelligence reports are routinely furnished only to the committees with national security responsibilities, with the bulk of the material going to the two intelligence committees. Other committees or members of Congress may request intelligence support, but are typically given a lower priority by the Intelligence Community.[55] However, Congress does not routinely receive copies of the CIA prepared President's Daily Brief, intelligence summaries prepared for the secretaries of State or Defense or the Chairman of the Joint Chiefs of Staff, "memo dissems" prepared by the CIA for senior White House officials, or "raw" intelligence—that is, unevaluated intelligence. Nevertheless, the Intelligence Community does try to accede to the needs of Congress.[56]

Protecting intelligence sources and methods, however, has long been a concern of the executive and legislative branches of government. The executive branch has a history of tight security controls over access to and the handling and disclosure of classified materials. Following the establishment of intelligence oversight committees in both houses of Congress, President Carter required the Director of Central Intelligence and heads of departments and agencies involved in intelligence activities to keep congressional intelligence committees fully and currently informed of such activities. However, such information as was provided was to be consistent with the requirement to protect sources and methods.[57]

Similarly, since their inception, both congressional intelligence committees have been concerned about the protection of classified material. Senate Resolution 400 (1976) and House Rule XLVIII (1977), which established the intelligence committees in the Senate and House respectively, set forth rules governing the handling of classified materials. These rules included, among other things, security clearances for staff access and nondisclosure oaths.[58] Other committees and members of Congress also must follow rules established in both chambers for the protection of classified materials.

Despite such precautions, classified information, on occasion, has been leaked. For example, in 1987 an editorial in the San Diego Union-Tribune contended that Senator Patrick Leahy (D-Vermont), while serving as the vice chairman of the Senate intelligence committee, disclosed classified information about U.S. intelligence capabilities in a 1985 television appearance, when he revealed that one of Egyptian President Hosni Mubarak's telephone conversations had been intercepted. The information that Leahy disclosed had been used by the United States in an operation that led to the capture of Arab terrorists who had hijacked the Italian cruise ship *Achille Lauro* and murdered an American citizen who was on board. According to one report, the leaked information cost the life of an Egyptian operative involved in the operation.[59] Along with David Durenberger (R-Minnesota) who was chairman of the Senate intelligence committee at the time, Leahy also was accused of leaking classified information in 1986 about a covert U.S. operation to overthrow the Libyan government of Moamar Gaddafi.[60]

More recently, on the morning of June 20, 2002, Senator Bob Graham, then chairman of the Senate intelligence committee, received a call from Vice President Dick Cheney. Cheney got right to the point. His morning paper reported that the National Security Agency had intercepted telephone calls on September 10, 2001 that apparently warned that al-Qaeda was about to launch a major attack against the United States, possibly the next day. The Arabic languages said "The match is about to begin" and "Tomorrow is zero hour." But the intercepts weren't translated until September 12, the day after the attacks on the World Trade Center and the Pentagon. Because someone had leaked highly classified information about the intercepts, Cheney warned Graham that the Bush administration was considering ending all cooperation with the joint inquiry by the Senate and House intelligence committees on the government's failure to predict and prevent the 9/11 attacks. Classified records would no longer be turned over to Congress and administration witnesses would not be available for interviews or testimony.[61] Federal investigators later concluded that Richard Shelby (R-Alabama), then a member of the Senate intelligence committee, was the source of the leak. Shelby denied having ever knowingly leaked classified information, was never charged by the Justice Department, and in late 2005 the Senate Ethics Committee dropped its investigation.[62]

In point of fact, however, most leaks of intelligence and other national security information come from the executive branch not Congress.[63] The noted journalist Daniel Schorr once pointed out, the leaking of classified information is not new to Washington. The air force "leaked" classified information about problems with army's missiles. At appropriations time the whole Pentagon leaked classified studies of Soviet military might. Henry Kissinger, while leaking classified information, condemned leaks.[64] Even presidents have been the source of leaks of classified information. For example, on April 14, 1969, a North Korean MIG fighter plane shot down an American EC-121 aircraft on an electronic intelligence-gathering mission over international airspace, well off the coast of North Korea. Four days later at a news conference President Nixon insisted that the North Koreans knew the U.S. aircraft was in international airspace stating:

> There is no uncertainty whatever as to where this plane was, because we know what their radar showed. We, incidentally know what the Russian radar showed. And all three radars [Russian, North Korean, and American] showed exactly the same thing.[65]

Though Soviet, Chinese, and North Korean radar systems were relatively unsophisticated by American standards, none of the countries were aware that the United States was reading their radars until Nixon revealed it. Shortly after Nixon's news conference all three countries changed every frequency and net structure all at once.[66]

In recent decades, the deliberate leaking of information has become an art form, used by members of the government to make their point with the public. The latest variant appears to be the "declassification" of information for political purposes, as was the reported case involving Dick Cheney's chief of staff Lewis "Scooter" Libby. Libby was indicted, tried, and convicted on charges resulting from a grand jury investigation into who leaked the identity of CIA operative Valerie Plame. During the court hearings Libby testified that the Vice President, allegedly with President Bush's approval, told him to pass classified information from the National Intelligence Estimate to Judith Miller, a *New York Times* reporter.[67] The information was intended to shore up the administration's claim that Iraq was seeking yellowcake, a uranium concentrate that could be used in the production of nuclear weapons, from the African country of Niger and to discredit Ambassador Joseph Wilson, Valerie Plame's husband, who had undertaken a mission on behalf of the CIA to investigate the claim and had concluded that the claim was false. Indeed, in a book, *What Happened: Inside the Bush White House and What's Wrong with Washington* to be released in May 2008, then White House press secretary Scott McClellan is reported to claim that the event went beyond the Vice President and Libby and included presidential advisor Karl Rove, the President's chief of staff Andrew Card, and "the President himself."[68]

Nevertheless, periodic leaks of information from Congress over the years have led to a continued tightening of the rules governing access and disclosure of classified information. For example, today both intelligence committees have established elaborate procedures governing access to and the handling and disclosure of classified information. Among those procedures:[69] office and meeting rooms must be secured, and classified materials must be stored in approved containers and its distribution carefully accounted for. Access to classified information by committee staff[70] is limited to those who have a need-to-know and an appropriate security clearance. Members, by virtue of their elected positions, do not need security clearances.

Strict rules also govern the disclosure of classified materials to individuals not on the intelligence committees. All members of the House, officers and employees, members of the Senate intelligence committee and the staffs of both intelligence committees must take a nondisclosure oath. Additionally, the House explicitly limits disclosure not only during a "person's tenure as a member of the [intelligence] Committee or Committee Staff," but also "at any time thereafter." Both committees, with some exceptions, also may deny access to classified materials in their possession to other members of their respective chambers who are not members of their committee.

On the other hand, the select intelligence committees of both chambers may disclose publicly any classified information in their possession if their respective committees determine that it is in the public interest to do so. Should the President object, the issue is remanded to the full Senate or House, as appropriate, which may, in turn, either approve, disapprove, or return the issue to the intelligence committee for further consideration.[71]

Finally, both chambers have established internal rules to punish those who violate the procedures established for protecting classified information. Punishment may include censure, removal from committee membership, or expulsion from the House, in the case of a Member, or removal from office or employment or punishment for contempt, in the case of an officer or employee.[72]

Such improved procedures for protecting classified information entrusted to Congress have led Intelligence Community officials to be less concerned about the unauthorized disclosure of intelligence they provide Congress, than about how the information will be used. As a result, while intelligence officials have become increasingly willing to share intelligence with congressional intelligence committees, they are careful about what they say and how they say it. Drawing on interviews with intelligence officials, L. Britt Snider noted:

> Intelligence officials worry more about what Congress will do with the intelligence it is given than they do about what policymakers do with it. While most intelligence officials acknowledge that Congress has a good track record where protection of classified information is concerned, they also recognize that they will have little control once the intelligence is imparted. One such official said, "Wittingly or not, this affects what analysts say on the Hill and how they say it. They are more guarded."[73]

The problem, as then Deputy Director of National Security Robert Gates noted twenty years ago, is that Congress has become better informed. "[M]any Senators and Representatives are often as well if not better informed about the CIA's information and assessments on a given subject than concerned policymakers." This puts them in a position to "criticize and challenge policy, to set one executive agency against another, and to expose disagreements within the administration."[74] Whether such actions are undertaken through leaks of information to influence the public debate or behind closed doors, it is generally an irritant to policymakers and the Intelligence Community alike and adds stress to their relationship with congressional oversight committees.

Such a situation also adds extraordinary stress to relationships between the CIA and policy agencies. Policymakers are often suspicious that the CIA has passed information to Congress in order to sabotage selected administration policies.[75] However, the CIA is not alone when it comes to intelligence leaks that can create stress between policymakers and the Intelligence Community. It is not above other departments or agencies within executive branch departments to leak intelligence that supports their point of view. Nevertheless, many in the executive branch, from the President on down, have oft publicly expressed their concerns about congressional leaks of classified information and frequently touted those concerns as a reason for their reluctance to release sensitive information to Congress.

Workload

Executive branch officials generally have defined areas of responsibility. Thus they are able to focus their daily efforts on an in-depth examination of the issues for which they are responsible. Members of Congress have no such luxury. While they may devote relatively more time to issues affecting the committees to which they are assigned, by virtue of their position as peoples' representatives in government, they not only must allocate a considerable amount of time to an understanding of issues across the gamut of public affairs, both national and international, but also must be attentive to a wide range of specific issues and interests of their constituents. A typical day in the life of a Senator or Representative might include subcommittee and committee meetings, House or Senate debates and floor votes, meetings with his or her staff, the party caucus, constituents, lobbyists, executive branch officials, visiting dignitaries, legislative strategy meetings, policy briefings, answering or returning constituent phone calls, and perhaps even a press interview or lunch at the White House. This is not to say that executive branch officials have fewer meetings or a less demanding day. Time is a precious commodity in both branches of government. However, the very busy days of executive branch officials are likely to be more focused. The broad nature of the responsibilities of members of Congress does not leave much time for an in-depth examination of specific issues. This is no less true for members of congressional intelligence committees. As former CIA Inspector General L. Britt Snider put it, Members "rarely have the time to keep abreast of day-to-day developments in intelligence reporting. Rather, the needs of most are episodic and reactive."[76]

Moreover, work on intelligence committees, because it often involves classified information that cannot be revealed to the public, does little to advance a member's standing with his or her constituents. As a result, absent a crisis or highly visible issue that involves intelligence, Members of Congress are likely to spend relatively more time addressing issues on the other committees and subcommittees to which they belong and attending to constituent affairs than on intelligence matters.

A survey conducted by the CIA Office of Congressional Affairs in 1988 found members of Congress "overwhelmingly disinterested" in intelligence in so far as the execution of their legislative duties was concerned. As one Senate Foreign Relations Committee staffer put it: ". . . most of what the committee needs to know can be obtained from *The New York Times* or CNN."[77] While it would be wrong to conclude from this that members of the intelligence committees are equally disinterested, it may be indicative of the relative balance of their daily priorities in the absence of public concern or a crisis.

Thus though congressional intelligence committees receive a large volume of hard copy and electronic intelligence from the Intelligence Community, neither the committee members nor their staffs apparently read these materials regularly. If Members are informed at all, it is usually because a staff member has read and adjudged the information worthy of the Member's attention. According to Snider,

> Most of the finished intelligence furnished to the two oversight committees is, in fact, read by no one, and only occasionally does that which is read prompt a followup. Both members and staff say they are too busy to keep up with the voluminous amount of reporting that comes in each day. As one staffer conceded, "I cannot, in good conscience, recommend to my member that it is worth his time to come in here and read this stuff. Frankly, it is not even worth my time.[78]

Congressional Self-restraint

Prior to the 1970s, Congress was mostly content to allow intelligence agencies to operate without any form of vigorous oversight. Concerned over Cold War developments, Congress was fearful that they would be unable to protect classified material entrusted to them. And certain that America's security depended on robust intelligence efforts, Congress focused their efforts on seeing to it that money was available for intelligence purposes. Indeed, Massachusetts Senator Leverett Saltonstall, who had chaired the Senate Armed Services Committee and its CIA subcommittee from 1953 to 1955 said:

> [I]t is not a question of reluctance on the part of CIA officials to speak to us. Instead, it is a question of our reluctance, if you will, to seek information and knowledge on subjects which I personally, as a Member of Congress and as a citizen would rather not have.[79]

Echoing a similar view, Saltonstall's successor Senator Richard Russell in a letter to the Chairman of the Senate Rules Committee wrote:

> It is difficult for me to foresee that increased staff scrutiny of CIA operations would result in either substantial savings or a significant increase in available intelligence information.[80]

Though congressional interest in intelligence changed dramatically since the revelations of the Church and Pike Committees, there may still be an element of self-restraint present today. Call it the Blind Eye Syndrome. Where additional knowledge may prove inconvenient to the politics at hand, where further investigation may result in an embarrassment to the administration, where a closer examination may raise questions about the validity of administration policies, there may well be a preference for restraint among some members of the intelligence committees.

Intelligence Taken At Face Value

Often policymakers complain that congressional intelligence committees uncritically accept intelligence analyses presented to them by the Intelligence Community. They contend that members of Congress are often unaware of the context within which the intelligence must be understood, nor do they take time to understand the context. In his interviews with members of Congress and congressional staffs, L. Brit Snider noted:

> Most of the members and staff interviewed . . . acknowledged the need to obtain appropriate "context" in order to evaluate the intelligence they receive, and they conceded that at times this does not happen. Some, noted, however, that the fault often lies with policymakers who refuse to appear at intelligence briefings to provide "the policy side" of an issue.[81]

Also, intelligence oversight committees are sometimes faulted for failure to probe the judgments provided by intelligence agencies in their briefings or reports. According to Snider, as one member put it:

> Many members take what the Intelligence Community says as gospel, when in fact they should look on it as an educated opinion. . . . The real problem is, members do not spend enough time probing what they hear from the Intelligence Community. If they spent more time analyzing what they were hearing, they would know more what needs to be fleshed out in order to make their own judgments.[82]

Unfortunately, too often intelligence oversight committees spend more time on reviewing agencies' budgets and annual programs and reviewing current intelligence than they do probing the judgments made by Intelligence Community analysts or the quality of the information upon which such judgments are based. Though the latter might, on occasion, run headlong into concerns about revealing sources and methods, it need not. For example one does not need to know the name or code names of sources or have direct access to raw signals, communications or imagery intelligence. However, knowing that the information was based on a single type or source of intelligence, or perhaps several sources all with similar political objectives would be helpful to committee understanding and perhaps more importantly force the Intelligence Community and its policymaker consumers to face the quality of information and analysis head-on. One can only speculate on what the outcome might have been had this been the case in the run-up to the Iraqi war, where leading judgments on Iraqi mobile biological facilities were principally derived from information provided by one person, or judgments on growing Iraqi chemical capabilities were mainly the result of a reliance on one form of intelligence, or where much of the case for Iraqi nuclear capabilities was based on information provided by Ahmed Chalabi and Iraqi National Congress members eager to see Saddam Hussein removed from power. Though such information was made available to members of Congress in the form of a 92-page National Intelligence Estimate, few ever read it. According to one report, no more than six senators and a handful of representatives read beyond the five-page executive summary.[83] As one senior intelligence committee member put it to me during an interview, "I don't think most members [of Congress], including myself, doubted the conclusions [of the Intelligence Estimate] that Saddam Hussein had weapons of mass destruction. . . . I believed he had weapons of mass destruction. I didn't feel the need to challenge that conclusion."[84]

Politics

Politics, by its very nature, encourages the development and exposition of opposing views, and the more so under democratic governance than under any other form of government. Indeed, a great strength of democracy is the diversity of views that is given impetus by the very freedoms and liberties democracy bestows. The freedom to express diverse views gives rise to a persistent challenging of conventional wisdoms—a challenging upon which all human creativity and concomitant human advancement depends. America's republican form of democracy, coupling a multiplicity of freedoms with manifold checks and balances, provides fertile soil for the competition of views. Where competing views are grounded in an interest in advancing "the permanent and aggregate interests of the community," they must be applauded for they will ultimately provide for the general advancement of society.

Yet there is a darker side. Opposing views find their roots in the differing interests, opinions, passions, and faculties of mankind. When passion rules reason, when limited faculties cloud perspective, or when self, minority, or even majority interests rule over the common good, politics can intrude on good governance—the very concern expressed by James Madison in Federalist Paper #10, when he wrote of the danger of a party or group within governments that is often contentious and self-seeking, which he called a political "faction."[85] It is this aspect of democratic governance that often results in untoward frictions among those who govern, paralyzes efforts to achieve sound policy, and undermines public confidence in government.

Neither Congress nor the executive branch is immune from the "factious spirit" identified by Madison. Too often, members of Congress use intelligence as a political football, to criticize, for partisan or personal reasons, policies of the executive branch or the President himself. On the other hand, Congress has a Constitutional responsibility, among other things, to provide for the common defense and general welfare of the United States. To insure that Congress could carry out those responsibilities, the framers of the Constitution imbued Congress with powers designed to preclude the exercise of arbitrary rule by the executive branch. Thus, in exercising its responsibilities, Congress not only has the right but the duty to examine carefully policies advanced by the executive branch to insure that they are indeed providing for the general welfare and common defense of the United States.

The executive branch is aware that information provided Congress could be used to challenge its preferred policies. Given its vast bureaucracy, its access to a monumental amount of material, and its everyday engagement on issues, the executive branch, rightfully or wrongfully, is self-assured of the correctness of its policies, It also recognizes that it depends on Congress to authorize and appropriate funds needed to support those policies. Thus, rather than engage Congress in a dialogue on policy options, too often in order to avoid challenges, the executive branch is tempted to try to shape the views of Congress by limiting the information available to congressional committees or Members. The masters of doublespeak do this by first publicly declaring its total willingness to cooperate, followed then either by refusing to provide documents requested, delaying their delivery, excising significant content, claiming executive privilege, or refusing to testify. The executive branch also recognizes that Congress, as the arm of the people, is likely to be responsive to the popular concerns. Thus, to dampen remaining congressional impulses to pursue matters further, the executive branch may attempt to manipulate the media through a selective release of information, particularly when an important policy issues is at stake.

While Congress holds less sway over the media, it does have tools at its disposal to command information from the executive branch. Unfortunately, the use of these tools is often politically circumscribed. On this, former Congressman Mickey Edwards noted at a conference held at American University in 2006:

> (T)here have been a lot of hearings conducted. Nothing comes of them—no follow-up. . . . What happens when the executive branch refuses to answer questions posed by members of Congress? Nothing happens. . . . The Congress cannot allow members of the executive branch to just tell them to get lost . . . . There has to be a price paid. The Congress has subpoena power.[86]

The problem is though Congress has both subpoena power and the power to declare a member of the executive branch in "contempt" of Congress for failure to comply with congressional requests to provide testimony or documents and other materials, members of the minority party cannot easily employ these tools. For example, only the chairman, or vice chairman or Member designated by the chairman of the Senate intelligence committee can issues subpoenas.[87] The House intelligence committee subpoenas can be issued by the chairman of the full committee, in consultation, but only consultation with the Ranking Minority Member, or by vote of the committee.[88] To take the further step and declare a person in contempt, both committees require a majority decision of committee members to forward the request to their respective houses, which in turn requires a majority decision in those chambers. Such procedures make the use of Congress' subpoena or contempt powers difficult. This is particularly true for minority members when faction rather than the public good predominates within the majority party and where the chamber concerned is in the hands of the party that occupies the White House.

While genuine debate is essential, party politics should play no role in intelligence oversight. Once again the words of Mickey Edwards are instructive. He argued that demanding that the executive branch comply with legitimate congressional requests for information in the execution of its oversight function is not just "an obligation of the party that opposes the policies of the President in power. It is the obligation of every congressman." Members are not sitting in Congress as a representative of their party or as a representative of the President of the United States. They are in Congress with "certain constitutional obligations." "It is not the opposition party that is supposed to hold the President in check, it is the opposing institution." Edwards went on to note:

> I think what's happened is that too many members of Congress have allowed their party interests . . . [to dominate], believing that if the president were to have political difficulties it would hurt the party and hurt them and so forth. They have allowed their political and party interests and, quote, "loyalty to the president," . . . to trump their institutional obligations . . . .[89]

CONCLUSIONS

Clearly congressional oversight of the Intelligence Community has come a long way since the 1970s. Today, the congressional intelligence committees and other committees with intelligence responsibilities have much greater access to materials, receive regular briefings, and find intelligence agencies very receptive to committee needs. Concerns that classified materials given to Congress may be leaked have largely become a nonproblem from a national security perspective, certainly no more of a problem than leaks that periodically occur from within the executive branch.

Yet, some problems persist and continue to limit the effectiveness of intelligence oversight. First, the workload of members of both Congress and their staffs is enormous and is no less for those serving on committees with intelligence oversight responsibilities. Perhaps this could be mitigated somewhat if the oversight processes were more streamlined. In some cases, the number of committees to which Intelligence Community components must report is extensive leading the 9/11 Commission to recommend that Congress create a single, principal point of contact of oversight and review for the Department of Homeland Security.

Second, though Congress has clearly moved beyond the era of restraint from investigations into the activities of the Intelligence Community, some measure of self-restraint creeps in as a result of partisan politics. Sometimes such self-restraint may not even breach the consciousness of Members. Yet, its effect is to limit the reach of Congress in the exercise of its oversight responsibilities.

Third, the darker side of politics, frequently engaged in by either the executive or the legislative branch or both, too often has marginalized intelligence oversight. Too often, despite public pronouncements to cooperate, delays, refusals to provide materials, the barring of testimony, or the excising of significant content characterize executive branch responses to congressional requests pursuant to their oversight responsibilities. And, too often members of Congress find it convenient to use information furnished by intelligence agencies as a political football in their clashes with the executive branch or with each other in Congress. Such activities undermine effective oversight, the security of the nation, and the general welfare of its peoples.

Finally, perhaps the most insidious and most pernicious challenge to effective oversight is the too-oft willingness to take intelligence at face value. While on the surface, congressional intelligence committees have spent a significant amount of time diligently working on Intelligence Community authorizations, examining their budgets, investigating accusations of Intelligence Community wrongdoing, and challenging the executive on intelligence efforts that might be contrary to the law, evidence suggests they spend relatively little time examining the quality of the intelligence product. This was nowhere more evident in recent years than in the period leading up to the 2003 Iraq War. One must give credit to Congress for demanding that the Intelligence Community produce a National Intelligence Estimate on the situation in Iraq. However, having requested the Estimate, had members of the intelligence committees read beyond the executive summary they would have found ample evidence that the facile conclusions were, at best, supported by extremely weak intelligence. They also would have better understood exceptions taken to the overall conclusions by many, including intelligence officials from the departments of State and Energy and perhaps come to realize that the entire executive branch case for going to war based on Iraq's possession of weapons of mass destruction was built on a house of cards.

The failure of Congress to probe the quality of the intelligence, in many cases to take time to read the National Intelligence Estimate or even, in some cases, to read the executive summary may have been driven by workload, by politics, or by deference to the executive branch in the area of foreign affairs and security. Whatever the excuse in any individual case may have been, it has led to an appalling loss of lives, heavily taxed the American economy, polarized the nation, caused severe damage to America's reputation abroad, and perhaps even undermined rather than strengthened American security. It is clear that for Congress as a whole and specifically for the congressional committees charged with intelligence oversight, there has been an abdication of responsibility.

Concluding Comments

Good intelligence is an essential ingredient to the development of effective foreign and national security policies. As such knowledge is power. However, the road to be traveled from the identification of information needed to its collection, analysis, and dissemination is complex and littered with obstacles. Indeed the challenges are so great that it is unrealistic to believe that intelligence failures can ever be completely eliminated. A nation's knowledge of the world will always be imperfect. Nevertheless, the number of failures can be reduced and their severity limited by improvements in organization, technology, and training. However, even with such improvements, the effectiveness of the intelligence apparatus will be limited if policymakers permit its use to be clouded by their own personal biases and policy preferences.

Unfortunately, democracies for all their checks and balances, too often see those checks and balances fail, particularly during times of crisis. In the United States this phenomenon has become more visible as Congress has increasingly abdicated its responsibility in the area of foreign and security policy in favor of presidential authority and where members of the media have increasingly become scribes for the Oval office, abdicating their responsibilities as journalists. History is replete with examples where great states have fallen prey to arrogance and certainty, ignoring the rules of good common sense.

Appendix A: The Intelligence Cycle[1]

The Intelligence Cycle is the process of developing raw information into finished intelligence for policymakers to use in decision making and action. There are five steps that constitute the Intelligence Cycle.

PLANNING AND DIRECTION

Planning and direction involves the management of the entire effort, from identifying the need for data to delivering an intelligence product to a consumer. It is the beginning and the end of the cycle—the beginning because it involves drawing up specific collection requirements and the end because finished intelligence, which supports policy decisions, generates new requirements.

The whole process depends on guidance from public officials. Policymakers—the President, his aides, the National Security Council, and other major departments and agencies of government—initiate requests for intelligence.

COLLECTION

Collection is the gathering of the raw information needed to produce finished intelligence. There are many sources of information, including open sources such as foreign broadcasts, newspapers, periodicals, and books. Open source reporting is integral to CIA's analytical capabilities. There are also secret sources of information. CIA operations officers collect such information from agents abroad and from defectors who provide information obtainable in no other way.

Finally, technical collection—electronics and satellite photography—plays an indispensable role in modern intelligence, such as monitoring arms control agreements and providing direct support to military forces.

PROCESSING

Processing involves converting the vast amount of information collected into a form usable by analysts. This is done through a variety of methods including decryption, language translations, and data reduction.

ALL-SOURCE ANALYSIS AND PRODUCTION

All-Source Analysis and Production is the conversion of basic information into finished intelligence. It includes integrating, evaluating, and analyzing all available data—which is often fragmented and even contradictory—and preparing intelligence products. Analysts, who are subject-matter specialists, consider the information's reliability, validity, and relevance. They integrate data into a coherent whole, put the evaluated information in context, and produce finished intelligence that includes assessments of events and judgments about the implications of the information for the United States.

The CIA, Department of State Intelligence and Research, and DIA are responsible for all-source analysis.

DISSEMINATION

The last step, which logically feeds into the first, is the distribution of the finished intelligence to the consumers, the same policymakers whose needs initiated the intelligence requirements. Finished intelligence is provided daily to the President and key national security advisers. The policymakers, the recipients of finished intelligence, then make decisions based on the information, and these decisions may lead to the levying of more requirements, thus triggering the Intelligence Cycle.

Appendix B: The U.S. Intelligence Community

INDEPENDENT COMPONENT

Central Intelligence Agency (CIA) collects intelligence, principally through human means, and provides comprehensive, all-source analysis related to national security topics for national policymakers, defense planners, law enforcement officials, and the military services. CIA also conducts counterintelligence overseas and undertakes special activities at the direction of the President.

DEPARTMENT OF DEFENSE COMPONENTS

Defense Intelligence Agency (DIA) provides comprehensive, all-source, foreign, military intelligence for the military services, defense and national security policymakers, and defense planners.

National Security Agency (NSA) collects and processes foreign Signals Intelligence information for members of the policymaking and military communities and protects critical U.S. information systems from compromise. It has collection sites around the world.

National Geospatial-Intelligence Agency (NGA) provides geospatial intelligence, including maps and charts and sophisticated data bases—necessary for targeting in an era dependent upon precision-guided weapons.

National Reconnaissance Office (NRO) designs, builds, operates, and maintains the nation's reconnaissance satellites.

Army, Navy, Air Force, and Marine Corps intelligence organizations collect and process intelligence relevant to their particular service needs.

NON-DEFENSE DEPARTMENTAL COMPONENTS

Department of State/Bureau of Intelligence and Research (INR) supports U.S. foreign and national security policies by providing all-source analysis of global developments to the State Department and contributes its unique perspectives to the Intelligence Community's National Intelligence Estimates. INR's primary mission is to harness intelligence to serve U.S. diplomacy.

Department of Homeland fuses law enforcement and intelligence information relating to terrorist threats to the homeland. The ***Information Analysis and Infrastructure Protection Directorate*** monitors, assesses, and coordinates indications and warnings of threats to the U.S. homeland; gathers and integrates terrorist-related information; assesses and addresses the vulnerabilities of the nation's critical infrastructures: and along with the FBI ensures that state and local law enforcement officials receive information on terrorist threats from national-level intelligence agencies.

Department of Homeland Security/U.S. Coast Guard Intelligence assesses and provides information related to threats to U.S. economic and security interests in any maritime region, including international waters and America's coasts, ports, and inland waterways.

Department of Justice/Federal Bureau of Investigation (FBI) is responsible for intelligence issues related to counterespionage, terrorism and counterintelligence inside the United States, and data about international criminal cases. Because of its law enforcement mission, the FBI is not, in its entirety, part of the Intelligence Community.

Department of Justice/Drug Enforcement Administration (DEA) is responsible for enforcing U.S.-controlled substance laws and regulations.

Department of Energy (DOE)/Office of Intelligence (IN) analyzes foreign nuclear weapons programs, as well as nuclear nonproliferation, and energy-security-related intelligence issues. It also has a robust counterintelligence capability.

Department of Treasury/Office of Terrorism and Financial Intelligence (INF) collects and processes information that bears on U.S. fiscal and monetary policy and threats to U.S. financial institutions.

Note: In addition to the sixteen organizations listed above, the Intelligence Community also includes two important *national centers* operating under the jurisdiction of the Director of National Intelligence: the National Counterterrorism Center (NCTC), and the National Counterproliferation Center (NCPC). The

NCTC, established in August 2004, is the primary U.S. Government organization for integrating and analyzing all intelligence pertaining to terrorism and counterterrorism. Its precursor organization was the Terrorist Threat Integration Center established in 2003. NCPC was established in December 2005 to enhance coordination, planning, and information sharing within the Intelligence Community in support of U.S. efforts to stem proliferation of weapons of mass destruction and related systems. Personnel from organizations across the Intelligence Community staff these organizations.

Appendix C: Congressional Access to IC Materials[1]

Congress Generally Has Routine Access to Most "Finished Intelligence"

Congress generally has access to most finished intelligence products that are published for general circulation within the executive branch. Finished intelligence is a product in which one or more analysts have taken, evaluated, interpreted, integrated and placed into context raw intelligence.

Congress Also Has Access to Intelligence Information through Briefings

Although Congress receives numerous written intelligence products, it receives the preponderance of its intelligence information through briefings, which generally are initiated at the request of congressional committees, individual members, or staff.

Such briefings can include a discussion of more sensitive information pertaining to intelligence sources and methods, particularly when the briefings involve the congressional intelligence committees. But even then, if the intelligence analyst determines that such information is particularly sensitive, he may choose to brief only the chairmen and ranking members of the two intelligence committees, or in lieu of the committee leadership, the committees' majority and minority staff directors. Or, based upon the executive branch's perspective that it is not legally obligated to provide Congress access to all intelligence, the analyst could choose not to share the sensitive information with anyone in Congress.

CLASSIFIED INTELLIGENCE PRODUCTS WHICH GENERALLY ARE ROUTINELY SHARED WITH CONGRESS

National Intelligence Community (NIC) Products

- *National Intelligence Estimates (NIEs)* express the coordinated judgments of the Intelligence Community, and thus represent the most authoritative assessment of the DNI with respect to a particular national security issue. NIEs are considered to be "estimative" intelligence products, in that they present what intelligence analysts estimate (not predict) may be the course of future events. Coordination of NIEs involves not only trying to resolve any interagency differences, but also assigning confidence levels to the key judgments and rigorously evaluating the sourcing for them. Each NIE is reviewed and approved for dissemination by the National Intelligence Board (NIB), which is comprised of the DNI and other senior leaders within the Intelligence Community.
- *Intelligence Community Assessments (ICAs)* are research papers 20–30 pages or more in length that provide a detailed data logic trail on key national security issues. They differ from NIEs in that they are less "estimative." National Intelligence Officers are expected to coordinate ICAs with other Community analysts, noting any disagreements in analytic judgments. Thus, ICAs are Community-coordinated, and are disseminated only after the approval of the NIC chairman.
- *Intelligence Community Briefs (ICBs)* are six-page, quick turnaround estimative analytical intelligence products that focus on particular issues. Before ICBs are disseminated to intelligence consumers, National Intelligence Officers overseeing their drafting and coordination are expected either to resolve any analytic disagreements or note any such continuing disagreement between Intelligence Community analysts. Thus this product is considered to be "Community-coordinated."
- *Sense of Community Memos* are one-page memoranda that evaluate current or day-to-day events. They are Community-coordinated and approved for dissemination by the NIC chairman.
- *Conference Reports* are memoranda-for-the-record of conferences that the NIC sponsors on various topics. In addition to Intelligence Community personnel, participants can include experts from outside the Community.

CIA Directorate of Intelligence Products

- *The Senior Executive Intelligence Brief (SEIB)*, known for decades as the *National Intelligence Daily* and viewed by the CIA as one of its flagship products, is a daily publication containing six to eight relatively short articles or briefs covering an array of topics. The SEIB's format and content, although generally similar to that of the President's Daily Brief, usually contains less information in order to protect intelligence sources and methods. It is disseminated to several hundred senior executive branch policymakers and to the congressional oversight committees, and although prepared by the CIA, the SEIB is produced in coordination with other Intelligence Community producers. It is viewed as a current intelligence product in that it focuses on the events of the past day or two, or on issues expected to arise over the next few days.

- *Serial Fliers (SFs)* are short and concise memorandum-style products, generally a few pages in length, on a discrete topic of current relevance. SFs generally do not contain summaries, but may contain graphics or maps.
- *Intelligence Assessments (IAs)* are the primary vehicle for in-depth research, and can focus on larger analytic questions or provide great detail on a more narrow, but complex issue. IAs generally are from 5 to 25 pages or more in length; they always contain a "Key Findings" or "Summary" section and often include graphics, maps and other supporting material.
- *Strategic Perspective Series (SPSs)*, like IAs, are based on extensive research, but are focused on a key strategic issue—frequently at the direction of the Directorate of Intelligence leadership. SPS papers often cut across analytic disciplines or regions. Examples include Muslims in the EU: Reshaping Islam and Transforming Europe, and China's Global Strategic Ambitions. SPSs use an IA format, but carry the SPS moniker. SPS papers include a "Key Findings" or "Summary" section and may include graphics, maps, and other supporting material.
- *Research Projects/Papers (RPs)* are the primary vehicle used to explore new analytic research areas and to develop the Directorate of Intelligence's corporate knowledge of a given issue. A research project may culminate in a SF, IA or SPS—or, depending upon the results, may be disseminated only within the Intelligence Directorate and Intelligence Community, serving as a "capital-building" research paper.
- *Leadership Profiles (LPs)* are biographic assessments of foreign leaders, generally 1-2 pages in length. They often are tailored for a particular meeting or event. Whenever possible, LPs contain a photo of the leader being assessed.
- *Situation Reports* are short reports that comment on current, fast-breaking events. Up to two or three situation reports can be issued daily, if warranted.

Department of Defense Products

- *Military Intelligence Digest (MID)* is produced by the Defense Intelligence Agency and is seen as a military-oriented counterpart to the SEIB. It is viewed as a current intelligence product in that it focuses on the events of the past day or two, or on issues expected to arise over the next few days. The MID can include analysis of topic covered in the SEIB, but it also includes articles of particular interest to the defense department, and can provide a different analytic perspective. It is principally prepared for the use of defense department policymakers, but is circulated elsewhere in the executive branch and provided to the congressional intelligence committees.

CLASSIFIED INTELLIGENCE PRODUCTS WHICH GENERALLY ARE NOT ROUTINELY SHARED WITH CONGRESS

The President's Daily Brief (PDB) is a written intelligence product that is briefed daily to the President orally by a small cadre of senior Intelligence Community analysts. As previously mentioned, it consists of six to eight relatively short articles or briefs covering a broad array of topics and is viewed as a current intelligence product, in that it focuses on the events of the past day or two, or on issues expected to arise over the next few days. The PDB is viewed as highly sensitive, in part, because it can contain sensitive intelligence source and operational information. Thus its dissemination is limited to the President and a small number of presidentially designated senior administration policymakers.

Presidential Daily Brief Memoranda are products containing responses to questions posed by the President and any of the small number of designated senior policymakers who receive the PDB. After briefing the handful of designated policymakers, members of the analytic briefing team return to CIA each morning, and task Intelligence Community personnel to provide answers to the various inquiries posed during each briefing session.

Senior Executive Memoranda are tailored analytic products that also can be produced in response to policymaker questions arising from PDB briefings.

National Terrorism Brief (NTB) is prepared by the National Counterterrorism Center, is appended to the daily PDB, and is briefed to the President by the DNI.

The Director's Daily Report is prepared by the Federal Bureau of Investigation (FBI) and is used by the FBI Director to verbally brief the President.

Red Cell analyses are products that are speculative in nature and sometimes take a position at odds with the conventional wisdom.

Raw intelligence is unevaluated intelligence.

TDs (Telephonic Disseminations) are raw intelligence reports disseminated by the CIA's Directorate of Operations. TDs are slightly finished intelligence, in that they contain some commentary as to the credibility of the source providing the intelligence.

Chief of Station (COS) Reports are reports prepared by the CIA's chief representative in a particular country and contain the COS's views of the current situation. The COS can share his reports with the resident ambassador for comment, but is under no obligation to incorporate any comments by the ambassador into his final report.

Notes

PREFACE

1. Francis Fukuyama, "The End of History?" *The National Interest* (Summer 1989): 18.

2. The U.S. Intelligence Community is a confederation of executive branch agencies and organizations that gather, analyze, and disseminate information and undertake other intelligence activities deemed necessary for the conduct of foreign relations and the protection of the security of the United States. See Appendix B.

3. "Testimony of R. James Woolsey," U.S. House of Representatives, Committee on National Security, February 12, 1998.

4. For a discussion of the events leading to this intelligence failure see Jeffrey T. Richelson, *A Century of Spies: Intelligence in the Twentieth Century* (New York: Oxford University Press, 1997), 111–115.

5. Major General Chaim Herzog, *The War of Atonement* (Boston: Little, Brown and Company, 1975), 283.

6. Robert M. Clark, *Intelligence Analysis: A Target Centric Approach* (Washington, D.C.: CQ Press, 2004), 2–3.

7. For example, accurate and timely intelligence about Soviet strategic and tactical nuclear capabilities contributed greatly to our understanding the nature of the threat Soviet nuclear forces posed and how those threats might be mitigated through well-designed defensive capabilities and arms control agreements.

8. Such successes include the thwarting of an attack against New York landmarks in 1993, the disruption of a Manila-based plot to assassinate the Pope and blow up twelve American airliners over the Pacific in 1994–1995, identification and prevention of a planned 1998 attack at the U.S. Embassy in Albania, and the derailing of some fifteen plots against American targets as we approached the Millennium celebrations. See *Testimony of Samuel*

L. Berger *Before the National Commission on Terrorist Attacks Upon the United States* (March 24, 2004), 2.

9. Mark M. Lowenthal, *Intelligence: From Secrets to Policy*, (Washington, D.C.: CQ Press, 2003), 6.

10. The morality and ethics of intelligence gathering has frequently been the subject of debate. Martin Luther, whose letters had been opened by the Duke of Saxony, is reported to have said that "a thief is a thief, whether he is a money thief or a letter thief." See David Kahn, "Back when Spies Played by the Rules," *New York Times*, January 13, 2006. In 1929 U.S. Secretary of State Henry Stimson shut down the State Department's cryptanalytic office saying "Gentlemen don't read each other's mail." As Mark Lowenthal, former deputy assistant secretary of state for intelligence, has noted, some people regard Intelligence Community activities such as spying, eavesdropping, and covert action "as antithetical to what they believe the United States should be as a nation and as a model for other nations." Lowenthal, *Intelligence: From Secrets to Policy*, 1. For a more thorough discussion see Ibid., Chapter 13. Also see Abram N. Shulsky and Gary J. Schmitt, *Silent Warfare: Understanding the World of Intelligence* (Dulles, Virginia: Potomac Books, Inc, 2002), 167–168.

11. Jennifer Sims notes that even Britain, America's closest ally in the twentieth century, has used secret intelligence and special access to sway U.S. government decision making—particularly before both world wars. Jennifer E. Sims, "Understanding Friends and Enemies: The Context for American Intelligence Reform," in Jennifer E. Sims and Burton Gerber, *Transforming U.S. Intelligence* (Washington, D.C.: Georgetown University Press, 2005), 24.

12. Thus, intelligence is not just about gathering information from foreign enemies. It also includes gathering information on potential threats to the security and well-being of a nation from grave domestic threats like sabotage and terrorism.

13. Shulsky and Schmitt, *Silent Warfare*, 1.

14. Sims, "Understanding Friends and Enemies," 16.

15. *The Commission on the Intelligence Capabilities of the United States Regarding Weapons of Mass Destruction. Report to the President of the United States March 31, 2005* (Washington D.C.: Commission on Intelligence Capabilities, 2005), 666. Also known as the Silberman-Robb Report, hereafter it will be referred to as the "*President's Commission on WMD*." Perhaps the best means to detect and counteract foreign intelligence activity is by penetrating the hostile intelligence service by human or technical means. During the Cold War the Soviet Union was particularly successful at gaining access to western intelligence services. As a result, countless spies for Western countries were compromised and many lost their lives. See Shulsky and Schmitt, *Silent Warfare*, 109–110.

16. For a more detailed discussion of this kind of support for foreign political organizations, including political groups that employ violent means in an effort to seek change, see Shulsky and Schmitt, *Silent Warfare*, 86–90.

17. "Covert Action in Chile 1963–1973," *Staff Report of the Select Committee To Study Governmental Operations With Respect to Intelligence Activities* (94th Congress 1st Session, U.S. Senate, December 18, 1975): 148.

18. Covert action includes a vast array of political, economic, propaganda, and paramilitary activities. For example, any list of U.S. post–World War II covert activities would likely include such undertakings as attempts to influence the outcome of elections in Western European countries during the early cold war, efforts to overthrow the duly constituted governments of Mohammed Mossadegh in Iran in 1953, Jacobo Arbenz in Guatemala in 1954, Juan Bosch in the Dominican Republic in 1965, and Norodom Sihanouk in Cambodia in 1970, the 1963 attempt to assassinate Fidel Castro in Cuba, and

the 1965 propaganda campaign to overthrow the Sukarno government in Indonesia, See David Isenberg, "The Pitfalls of U.S. Covert Operations," *Cato Policy Analysis No. 118* (April 7, 1989) at www.cato.org/pubs/pas/PA118.HTM. To this one might add, inter alia, the Iran-Contra affair of the mid-1980s and perhaps alleged recent U.S. efforts in support of the ouster of President Hugo Chavez of Venezuela.

19. "Extraordinary rendition" or "rendition" is a CIA term used to describe the practice of sending suspected terrorists and their supporters to other countries for imprisonment and interrogation. Critics of this practice contend that the United States renders suspects to other countries to circumvent U.S. laws that prohibit torture and require due process.

20. Admiral Stansfield Turner, *Burn Before Reading* (New York: Hyperion, 2005), 42–43.

21. Ibid., 43. Cited from Arthur B. Darling, *The Central Intelligence Agency: An Instrument of Government to 1950* (New York: Da Capo Press, 1956), 58.

INTRODUCTION

1. Later, the Defense Intelligence Agency, under the Department of Defense, which was also established by the National Security Act of 1947, became the principal organization for collecting, analyzing, and disseminating military intelligence.

2. See for example, Executive orders 12036, 12139, 12537, 12334, and especially 12333.

3. In December 2004 Congress passed the most extensive reorganization of the Intelligence Community since the National Security Act of 1947. Among other reforms mandated by the Intelligence Reform and Terrorism Prevention Act of 2004 (hereafter referred to as P.L.(Public Law) 108–458), the newly established Director of National Intelligence possesses statutory authorities to establish priorities for budgets, for directing collection across the spectrum of human and technical intelligence capabilities, and for the preparation of the Intelligence Community's analytical products.

4. The Intelligence Community likes to characterize itself as a "federation." However, it has acted more like a confederation of loosely knit elements lacking clearly defined leadership. It remains to be seen whether current reforms will substantially alter the nature of the Intelligence community.

5. Some of the information gathered and processed by the Intelligence Community is what is generally called "open source" and thus is available to the general public. However, much of the information is held in secret by governments or organizations.

6. *President's Commission on WMD*, 666.

7. Ibid.

PART I

1. Jeffrey T. Richelson, *The U.S. Intelligence Community* (4th Edition). Boulder: Westview Press, 1999, 16.

2. *President's Commission on WMD*, 10.

CHAPTER 1

1. The quote is on the Eagle and Fledgling statue that stands outside of the Mitchell Hall at the U.S. Air Force Academy. The statue was given to the Academy by personnel from Air Training Command in 1958.

2. For example, CIA covert operatives in Afghanistan provided a wealth of valuable information prior to and during post-9/11 operations in that country; from identifying individuals and tribes willing to cooperate with the United States, to information about specific targets that markedly hastened American successes on the battlefield once the war began. For a fascinating discussion of Human Intelligence efforts in Afghanistan see Henry A. Crumpton, "Intelligence and War: Afghanistan, 2001–2002" in Sims and Gerber, *Transforming U.S. Intelligence*, 162–178.

3. The National Geospatial-Intelligence Agency, the successor to the National Imagery and Mapping Agency, was established in 1996 to combine several separate agencies involved in imagery processing and dissemination.

4. Shortly after the end of the Cold War, former director of the CIA Admiral Stansfield Turner demonstrated his faith in America's technical know-how when he wrote that given the money "Washington can construct a system that will detect any significant activity on the surface of the earth, day or night, under clouds or jungle cover and with such frequency as to make deliberate evasion difficult . . ." Stansfield Turner, "Intelligence for a New World Order," *Foreign Affairs* 70, no. 4 (Fall 1991): 151.

5. *President's Commission on WMD*, 665.

6. For a further look at such "fused" intelligence operations see Crumpton, "Intelligence and War: Afghanistan, 2001–2002," 162–178.

7. Up until the intelligence reform of 2004 the task of establishing requirements and priorities to govern collection of national intelligence fell to the Director of Central Intelligence.

8. As a result of recent intelligence failures, the requirements process has been undergoing substantial changes. However, for an example of how this process functioned prior to 9/11 and failures associated with the run-up to the 2003 war in Iraq in terms of both formal and informal requests generated by analysts see *President's Commission on WMD*, 415–417. The Joint House/Senate 9/11 report also noted that in spring 2001, National Security Agency shifted its emphasis from "analyzing what was collected" to a dissecting of its targets' communication practices in order to determine "what to collect." At the National Security Agency this procedure is commonly referred to as "hunting" rather than gathering. See "*Report of the Joint Inquiry into the Terrorist Attacks of September 11, 2001—by the House Permanent Select Committee on Intelligence and the Senate Select Committee on Intelligence*" (Hereafter cited as the *HPSCI-SSCI Report*), S. Rept. No. 107-351 107th Congress, 2nd Session H. Rept 107-792, 400, December 2002. Note: page numbers cited for this report are those that appeared on the original, non-redacted, Top Secret report. Those numbers appear in light grey in the redacted report.

9. Established October 1, 2007, by the Director of National Intelligence, the Center provides the Director a means of integrating all U.S. collection assets and activities and focusing their efforts on current and emerging threats. The Center remains a work in progress. However, it has helped to ensure a more rapid response of intelligence assets to developing problems, whereas the National Intelligence Collection Board has generally had a broader and more general and long-term focus.

10. First established in 1993 by Director of Central Intelligence Directive 3/26, the National Intelligence Collection Board assists the Director of National Intelligence in managing the overall intelligence collection requirements process and is tasked to ensure coordination among the major collection efforts and evaluate the performance of collection efforts in satisfying the needs of intelligence consumers. Among its members are the Directors of the National Security Agency, Defense Intelligence Agency, Department of

State Assistant Secretary for Intelligence and Research, and National Reconnaissance Office.

11. The National Intelligence Council reports to the Director of National Intelligence. The Council is the Intelligence Community's center for mid- and long-term strategic thinking. Among its tasks, it is responsible for producing intelligence estimates of current and future threats and for articulating substantive priorities to guide intelligence collection, evaluation, and procurement.

12. In response to recent intelligence failures, functional and country-specific Mission Managers have been established. Among their tasks are setting collection priorities and determining the state of collection against their assigned missions,

13. Issue Coordinators were the National Intelligence Officers from the National Intelligence Council, the Center chiefs (e.g., Weapons Intelligence and Non-Proliferation Center, National Counterterrorism Center, etc.), and key officials from the Defense Intelligence Agency and the Joint Chiefs of Staff. In the wake of intelligence failures associated with the 9/11 attacks, the intelligence system is in the process of reform. As a part of the reform effort, Issue Coordinators have been replaced by "Mission Managers," presumably with broader authority and responsibilities.

14. *HPSCI-SSCI Report*, 42.

15. See "IC21: The Intelligence Community in the 21st Century." Staff Study, Permanent Select Committee on Intelligence, House of Representative, 104th Congress, April 9, 1996, Sec III at www.access.gpo.gov/congress/house/intel/ic21/. Hereafter cited as IC 21. Also see "Remarks by Admiral William O. Studeman, Acting Director of Central Intelligence at Marquette University." April 20, 1995, at www.cia.gov/cia/public_affairs/speeches/1995/, and *PDD-35 Intelligence Requirements* at www.fas.org/irp/offdocs/pdd35.htm

16. James Monnier Simon Jr., "Managing Domestic, Military, and Foreign Policy Requirements: Correcting Frankenstein's Blunder" in Sims and Gerber, *Transforming U.S. Intelligence*, 152.

17. More than 2000 years ago Sun Tzu wrote: ". . . what is of supreme importance in war is to attack the enemy's strategy." This concept is as true in peacetime as during times of warfare. Writing about 1200 years later Tu Mu noted: "He who excels at resolving difficulties does so before they arise. He who excels in conquering his enemies triumphs before threats materialize." See *Sun Tzu: The Art of War.* Translated and with Introduction by Samuel B. Griffith, (London: Oxford University Press, 1971), 77.

18. See for example, Ernest R. May, "The Twenty-first Century Challenge for U.S. Intelligence" in Sims and Gerber, *Transforming U.S. Intelligence*, 4–5. May notes: "The decade and a half following the end of the cold war thus put before the U.S. intelligence community a whole range of issues different from those of the cold war era. They called for collection on and analysis of governments, most of which had not been important cold war targets. They called also for collection and analysis of non-governmental organization, particularly in the Muslim world," 5.

19. Robert M. Gates, "The CIA and American Foreign Policy," *Foreign Affairs* 66 (Winter 1987/88), 226.

20. General Shinseki warned that the coalition would need "something on the order of several hundred thousand" military forces during the post-war phase of operations in Iraq. Yet it would seem for short-term political-military purposes—perhaps to insure congressional support, perhaps to get operations underway before the weather got too hot, the administration chose to ignore his warning.

21. Turner, *Burn Before Reading*, 109–110.

22. Rhodri Jeffreys-Jones, *The CIA and American Democracy*, 2nd ed. (New Haven, CT: Yale University Press, 1998), 148. Quoted in Turner, *Burn Before Reading*, 110.

23. Ibid.

24. The function of the National Security Council is to advise the President with respect to the integration of domestic, foreign, and military policies relating to national security. Arguably, as a nonstatutory member of the Council, the Director of National Intelligence is the best placed member of the Council to provide the type of information that such an integration would require, including information necessary to build a domestic constituency for policies. The revised definition of "national intelligence" provided by P.L 108-458, Section 1012 amending the National Security Act of 1947 appears to further sanction such activity by explicitly including within the definition "information gathered within . . . the United States."

25. See *IC 21*, Sec III at www.access.gpo.gov/congress/house/intel/ic21/

26. In his highly insightful examination of U.S. strategy during the Vietnam War, Harry Summers provides an insight into the mentality that may well have led to our failure in Vietnam. In his opening to the introduction he quotes a conversation he had with one of his North Vietnamese counterparts to the Four Party Joint Military Team in April 1975. "You know you never defeated us on the battlefield," said Colonel Summers. The North Vietnamese Colonel replied: "That may be so, but it is also irrelevant." Harry Summers, *On Strategy: the Vietnam War in Context* (Carlisle, PA: US Army War College, Strategic Studies Institute, 1981), 1.

27. Max G. Manwaring, ed., *Uncomfortable Wars: Toward a New Paradigm of Low Intensity Conflict* (Boulder, Colorado: Westview Press, 1991). Also see John T. Fishel and Max G. Manwaring, *Uncomfortable Wars Revisited* (University of Oklahoma Press: Norman, OK, 2006).

28. Simon Jr., "Correcting Frankenstein's Blunder," 154.

29. Ibid.

30. Christopher Andrew, *For the President's Eyes Only: Secret Intelligence and the American Presidency from Washington to Bush* (New York: HarperCollins Publishers, 1995), 439.

31. Turner, *Burn Before Reading*, 180.

32. Andrew, *For the President's Eyes Only*, 440. Also see Gary Sick, *All Fall down: America's Fateful Encounter with Iran* (London: Tauris, 1985), 30.

33. Yellowcake is a widely available uranium concentrate used in the preparation of fuel for nuclear reactors and weapons. It is the first step toward enriched uranium.

34. *National Security Act of 1947*, Section 3 (6) as amended.

35. Ibid.

36. The tension between these two entities, of course, is not new. It dates to the formative days of American intelligence efforts, when Franklin Delano Roosevelt selected William "Wild Bill" Donovan to be the "Coordinator of Information," in an effort to "coordinate the intelligence efforts of the FBI, Army, Navy, and the Department of State. His appointment immediately led to attacks by the military services against the concept of a centralized intelligence effort that have persisted through the decades and are alive and well today. See Turner, *Burn Before Reading*, 15.

37. Admiral Stansfield Turner notes that President Carter signed an executive order giving him "more authority over the Intelligence Community than any former DCI [Director of Central Intelligence] had had" and "more authority than any subsequent DCI has had." Turner, *Burn Before Reading*, 159.

38. *HPSCI-SSCI Report*, 46.
39. Ibid., 45.
40. Ibid., 45.
41. Turner, *Burn Before Reading*, 252.
42. P.L. 108-458, December 17, 2004, Sec. 102A (c) (1) (A) and (B).
43. Ibid., Sec. 102A (c) (5) (B).
44. Ibid., Sec. 102A (c) (5) (A).
45. Ibid., Sec. 102A (c) (3) (A). In 2005, the Department of Defense combined the Joint Military Intelligence Program and the Tactical Intelligence Program and Related Activities into the Military Intelligence Program.
46. Ibid., Sec, 102A (d) (1) (B).
47. Ibid., Sec. 102A (f) (1) (B) (ii).
48. For another view of the complexities confronting those who seek to strengthen the authority of the Director of National Intelligence, the limitations and risks of the Intelligence Reform Act efforts to do so, and an alternative approach see Turner, *Burn Before Reading*, 252–269.
49. John McLaughlin, "The Intelligence Challenge," *Washington Post*, January 7, 2007.
50. According to one former CIA official—"For both the CIA's NCS [National Clandestine Service] and the pentagon to be conducting uncoordinated spy operations in the same geographic area would be a disaster." Moreover he further contends: ". . . the NCS, in order to maximize and protect it operations, needs to be in charge of liaisons with foreign intelligence services and responsible for overseas counterintelligence and counterterrorism." Haviland Smith, "CIA, R.I.P Now What?" *Baltimore Sun*, May 16, 2006.
51. Jennifer E. Sims, "Understanding Ourselves" in Sims and Gerber, *Transforming U.S. Intelligence*, 42.
52. For a further discussion of the requirements and priorities problem see Mark M. Lowenthal, *Intelligence: From Secrets to* Policy (Washington: D.C.: CQ Press, 2003), 43–44.
53. The latter has often been a problem where a nondefense agency has attempted to influence the collection priorities of platforms operationally controlled by the Department of Defense.
54. *HPSCI-SSCI Report*, 52–53.
55. Ibid., 53.
56. Ibid.
57. See, for example, Ibid., 52.
58. See *IC 21*, Sec III.
59. Ibid.
60. This problem was highlighted over a decade ago in a House Permanent Select Committee on Intelligence staff study. See Ibid.
61. *HPSCI-SSCI Report*, 42–43. Also see *The 9/11 Commission Report: Final Report of the National Commission on Terrorist Attacks Upon the United States* (Authorized Edition) (New York: W.W. Norton, n.d.) 357. Hereafter referred to as the *9/11 Commission*.
62. *President's Commission on WMD*, 358.
63. See *9/11 Commission*, 400.
64. *President's Commission on WMD*, 358.
65. *500 Day Plan: Integration and Collaboration*, Director of National Intelligence, October 10, 2007.

66. *HPSCI-SSCI Report*, 80.

67. Lowenthal, *Intelligence: From Secrets to Policy*, 45.

68. See 9/11 Commission, 400.

69. Simon Jr., "Correcting Frankenstein's Blunder," 151.

70. See Lowenthal, *Intelligence: From Secrets to Policy*, 46.

71. See "Mission Management," *Intelligence Community Directive Number 900*, December 21, 2006.

72. For greater detail see "Management, Integration, and Oversight of Intelligence Collection and Covert Activity," *Intelligence Directive Number 300*, October 3, 2006.

CHAPTER 2

1. Richelson, *The U.S. Intelligence Community*, 257. The shift away from human intelligence in favor of technical intelligence can trace its roots to William Colby. When Colby took over as Director of Central Intelligence in 1973 he sought a leaner directorate of operations, "more dependent on technical intelligence collection, and freer of what he took to be the melodramatics of espionage." Thomas Powers, "Inside the Department of Dirty Tricks," *The Atlantic Online* at www.theatlantic.com/doc/197908/cia-dirty-tricks/6.

2. Ibid. Also see Shulsky and Schmitt, *Silent Warfare*, 35–36.

3. See Ibid., 79.

4. *Panama: The Résumé of Manuel Noriega, the Most Famous Graduate of the School of the Americas*, www-personal.umich.edu/~lormand/poli/soa/panama.htm

5. Turner, *Burn Before Reading*, 225.

6. *HPSCI-SSCI Report*, 279.

7. Within the CIA opinions are divided on the impact of the Deutch guidelines. See Ibid., 92–92.

8. Ibid., 279.

9. Ibid., 92–93.

10. Ibid., 409.

11. Those who "volunteer" information to U.S. intelligence agencies frequently need to be carefully scrutinized. See Ibid., 409. Some "volunteers" could well be members of foreign intelligence services or agents of radical Islamic or other groups, whose task is to disrupt U.S. intelligence collection efforts by providing false or deceptive information or by serving as counterintelligence agents.

12. Ibid., 76.

13. Ibid., 76.

14. Ibid., 75.

15. Ibid., xvii.

16. Ibid., 75.

17. Ibid., 75.

18. Ibid., 403.

19. Tim Weiner, "C.I.A. Study Details Failures; Scouring of System is Urged," New York Times, June 3, 1998.

20. President's Commission on WMD, 12.

21. See for example, *HPSCI-SSCI Report*, 402.

22. For a very informative discussion of denial and deception see Donald C. Daniel, "Denial and Deception" in Sims and Burton, *Transforming U.S. Intelligence*,134–146. Also

see Shulsky and Schmitt, *Silent Warfare*, 116–126 and Joseph W. Caddell, *Deception 101—Primer on Deception* (Carlisle, PA: Strategic Studies Institute, U.S. Army War College, December 2004.

23. While there were, of course, a number of defectors to the West during the Cold War, not many were of senior rank. Among the more notable defections were KGB (the Soviet Union's principal security and intelligence agency) intelligence officer Peter Deryabin, who defected in Austria in 1953; Soviet secret police (MVD) colonel Vladimir M. Petrov and his wife Evdokia Petrova, also an MVD official, who defected in 1954 while serving in Australia; the controversial KGB agent Anatoli Golitsyn, who defected in 1961 and provided information on Kim Philby, Donald Maclean, and Guy Burgess; senior KGB official Oleg Lyalin, who defected in 1971 while in Britain, providing the British with information that led to the expulsion of over 100 suspected Soviet spies. The highest level Soviet official to defect to the United States was Arkady Shevchenko. Skevchenko had served as an advisor to Foreign Minister Andrei Gromyko. In 1973 he was appointed Under Secretary General of the United Nations. In 1975 he decided to defect to the United States, but was persuaded by the CIA to remain at his post and provide the United States with information on Soviet intentions and plans. Suspicious that he had been discovered, he defected to the United States in 1978. For his story see Arkady N. Shevchenko, *Breaking with Moscow* (New York: Ballentine Books, 1985).

24. For eighteen months prior to his arrest by the KGB in 1962 and execution for espionage and treason the following year, Oleg Penkovsky provided invaluable information to the United States. However, Penkovsky, a colonel with the Soviet military intelligence (GRU) and highly "trusted" and a "key member" of the GRU, was self-recruited. For a detailed account of his efforts see Oleg Penkovsky, *The Penkovsky Papers* (London: Collin Fontana Books, 1965).

25. John Lewis Gaddis, *We Now Know: Rethinking Cold War History* (Oxford: Clarendon Press, 1997), 244.

26. Shulsky and Schmitt, *Silent Warfare*, 19. Stanfield Turner notes that when he was DCI the CIA had nearly succeeded in inserting an agent into a Middle Eastern Terrorist group. However, the last rite of passage was that the agent had to assassinate a particular government official in order to prove his *bona fides*, which Turner was not willing to permit. Turner, *Burn Before Reading*, 267.

27. *HPSCI-SSCI Report*, 405.

28. Ibid., 97.

29. Ibid., 405

30. Ibid., 98.

31. Ibid., 96.

32. Ibid., 405.

33. Ibid., 99.

34. *President's Commission on WMD*, 15.

35. Ibid., 163.

36. For example, after the Gulf War, to prevent United Nations weapons inspectors from discovering weapons of mass destruction that were still hidden, Saddam Hussein ordered their destruction in July 1991. According to information now available from the Iraqi Survey Group, that decision was probably only shared with a handful of senior Iraqi officials. Ibid., 156.

37. See Ibid., 154–155.

38. Indeed, the President's Commission on WMD, in one of its major findings, concluded "Iraq's denial and deception efforts successfully hampered U.S. intelligence collection. Ibid., 167.

39. Ibid., 154–155.

40. *HPSCI-SSCI Report*, 405.

41. Donald C. F. Daniel, "Denial and Deception" in Sims and Gerber, *Transforming U.S. Intelligence*, 143.

42. See Shulsky and Schmitt, *Silent Warfare*, 121–122. For additional information see Leo Marks, *Between Silk and Cyanide: A Codemaker's War, 1941–1945* (New York: The Free Press, 2000).

43. Gregory F. Treverton, *Reshaping National Intelligence for an Age of Information* (Cambridge: Cambridge University Press, 2003), 18.

44. See for example Leon Festinger, *A Theory of Cognitive Dissonance* (Stanford, CA: Stanford University Press, 1957).

45. See James S. Atherton, *Learning and Teaching: Assimilation and Accommodation*, [On-line] UK: 2005 at www.learningandteaching.info/learning/assimacc.htm

46. The Intelligence Community has often been criticized for lack of imagination in its analysis of events. However, lack of imagination in identifying requirements for collection can be equally or even more damaging to the intelligence processes.

47. Gaddis, *We Now Know*, 239.

48. All inspectors were withdrawn in December 1998 following an autumn of much Iraqi obstruction of inspection efforts and in anticipation of U.S. and British bombing in support of Operation Desert Fox. Iraq refused to readmit inspectors until the sanctions had been lifted. Inspections did not recommence until November 2002. For details of this period see Hans Blix, *Disarming Iraq* (New York: Pantheon Books, 2004).

49. See Ibid., 230, and 211–212 and Ambassador Joseph Wilson, *The Politics of Truth* (New York: Carroll & Graf Publishers, 2004), 1–29. Particularly 2.

50. Jack Fairweather and Anton La Guardia, "Chalabi Stands By Faulty Intelligence That Toppled Saddam's Regime," *London Daily Telegraph*, February 19, 2004. Also see Seymour M. Hersh, "Selective Intelligence," *The New Yorker*, Monday May 5, 2003.

51. For an informative treatment of the counterespionage problem see Shulsky and Schmitt, *Silent Warfare*, 108–114.

52. Harold P. Ford, "The Primary Purpose of National Estimating," 74: http://www.au.af.mil/au/awc/awcgate/nic/purpose_of_estimating.pdf.

53. *HPSCI-SSCI Report*, 287–288.

54. Clark, *Intelligence Analysis*, 72.

55. *HPSCI-SSCI Report*, 285.

56. Even the FBI greatly expanded its presence overseas and its efforts to work with foreign governments against terrorism. *HPSCI-SSCI Report*, 285.

57. Ibid., 404.

58. As a part of these efforts, in some parts of the world, the United States helped pay for and train the intelligence services of other nations. See Ibid., 286.

59. This section draws on Ibid., 288–290.

60. *President's Commission on WMD*, 186.

61. *HPSCI-SSCI Report*, 289.

62. Ibid.

63. James R. Gosler, "The Digital Dimension" in Sims and Gerber, *Transforming U.S. Intelligence*, 102. For an account of some of the innovative uses of technology employed by

the Soviet Union see Victor Sheymov, *Tower of Secrets: A Real Life Spy Thriller* (Annapolis, MD: Naval Institute Press, 1993).

64. For example see Angela Charlton, "Attack on Moscow Embassy Foiled," (March 28, 1999) at www.moscowmarines.ambassadors-in-blue.net/news.htm—confirmed by Victor Sheymov, *Tower of Secrets*, 150.

65. See John Diamond, "To Catch a Spy," *Chicago Tribune*, December 9, 1999 online at www.fas.org/irp/news/1999/12/991210-rus-spy.htm

66. Sheymov notes that "most restaurants frequented by foreigners had sufficient "*literniye*" or "marked" tables . . . permanently equipped with listening devices. . . . " Sheymov, *Tower of Secrets*, 295.

67. For a fascinating account of undersea espionage see Sherry Sontag and Christopher Drew with Annette Lawrence Drew, *Blind Man's Bluff: The Untold Story of American Submarine Espionage* (New York: Harper Paperbacks, 1998), particularly the account of America's tapping of the cable that ran from the Soviet Pacific Fleet Headquarters in Vladivostok under the Sea of Okhotsk to its missile submarine base at Petropavlovsk, 221–257.

68. Indeed, by the end of the Cold War technological advances made it possible, as war with Iraq approached following Iraq's August 1990 invasion of Kuwait, for the U.S. Intelligence Community to assemble actual pictures of the enemy facing the U.S. forces. See Ernest R. May, "The Twenty-first Century Challenge for U.S. Intelligence," 5–6.

69. David Laque, "Chinese see military dependence on computers as weakness," *International Herald Tribune*, August 29, 2007.

70. "The Invasion of the Chinese Cyberspies," *Time* (September 5, 2005): 35–36.

71. See for example May, "The Twenty-first Century Challenge for U.S. Intelligence," 3.

72. Information gained through the deciphering of messages sent by Enigma was called "Ultra." For a brief but fascinating account of Polish and British efforts to break the Enigma codes see Colonel John Hughes-Wilson, *Military Intelligence Blunders* (New York: Carroll & Graf Publishers, 1999), 20–24.

73. Navajo code talkers took part in every assault the U.S. Marines conducted in the Pacific from 1942 to 1945. Serving in all six Marine divisions in the theater, Marine Raider battalions and Marine parachute units, they transmitted messages by telephone and radio in their native language. Navajo, an unwritten language of extreme complexity, is spoken only on the Navajo lands of the American Southwest. Its syntax, tonal qualities, and dialects, make it unintelligible to anyone without extensive exposure and training. According to one estimate there were less than 30 non-Navajos, none of them Japanese that could understand the language at the outbreak of World War II. See www.history.navy.mil/faqs/faq61-2.htm.

74. "The Evolution of the U.S. Intelligence Community—An Historical Overview" at www.access.gpo.gov/intelligence/int/int022.html, 5–6.

75. See "Stealth Technology." Wikipedia: http://en.wikipedia.org/wiki/Stealth_technology.

76. *President's Commission on WMD*, 17.

77. Ibid., 16.

78. Terrorist themselves have become more aware of the vulnerabilities they are exposed to through use of the Internet and communications technologies, and increasingly seek ways to limit their vulnerabilities. See for example, Yuki Noguchi and Sara Kehaulani Goo, "Terrorists' Web Chatter Shows Concern About Internet Privacy Groups Advise Members on Anonymity, Avoiding Intercepts," *Washington Post* (April 13, 2006): A14.

79. Lt. Gen. Michael V. Hayden, USAF, "Address to Kennedy Political Union of American University," (February 17, 2000) 2. Cited in A. Denis Clift, "Intelligence in the Internet Era" available at www.cia.gov/csi/studies/vol47no3/article06.html.

80. See Thomas Homer-Dixon, *Foreign Policy* (January/February 2002). Also see May, "The Twenty-first Century Challenge for U.S. Intelligence," 7–8. Also see James R. Gosler, "The Digital Dimension," 101. Gosler notes that today's terrorist organizations are assisted by globally available, affordable, sophisticated Internet technologies that permit them to communicate and coordinate activities at nominal cost. "Terrorists benefit from the ability to hide their communications within billions of other transactions. From the terrorist's perspective, this is a weak signal in a high-noise environment, providing him both cost-effective and high-impact operations."

81. Homer-Dixon, *Foreign Policy* (January/February 2002).

82. Ibid.

83. *HPSCI-SSCI Report*, 387.

84. Daniel, "Denial and Deception," 143.

85. *9/11 Commission*, 88.

86. The so-called "Gingrich supplement" did add to the intelligence budget in FY1999, as did two smaller supplements later. See Ibid., 93.

87. Ibid.

88. While supplemental appropriations are usually needed and welcomed, by definition they are frequently a stopgap measure, supposedly granted in reaction to unforeseen events. They are not meant to pay for additional personnel or for structural upgrades in future years. Thus, they contribute little to efforts to develop comprehensive longer-term intelligence plans and operations. See *HPSCI-SSCI Report*, 51–52.

89. As he was leaving office in 2004, James Pavitt, former CIA deputy director for operations, highlighted the consequences of this lack of resources on Human Intelligence activities: "budgets were not big enough and policy attention not forceful enough" in the 1990s, which led at that time to a 30 percent decline in funding for the CIA's Human Intelligence programs in his directorate and to personnel reductions of 20 percent. Douglas Jehl, "Answering Call to Duty at the CIA," *New York Times* (May 11, 2004): A20. Cited by Burton Gerber, "Managing HUMINT: The Need for a New Approach" in Sims and Gerber, *Transforming U.S. Intelligence*, 180.

90. *HPSCI-SSCI Report*, 250.

91. Counterterrorism spending at least doubled in most Intelligence Community agencies. During the Clinton administration federal governments spending on counterterrorism more than doubled from $5 billion in FY1996 to over $11 billion in FY2000. The FBI's counterterrorism staff budget increased by 250 percent and their counterterrorism budget increased by nearly 350 percent, with similar increases in the CIA's counterterrorism budget. However, one is cautioned to keep such percentage increases in budget in proper perspective. These budget increases did result in an increase in the personnel allocated to counterterrorism. Nevertheless the numbers generally remained small. See HPSCI-SSCI Report, xvi and 48.

92. Ibid., 47 and 250.

93. Jehl, "Answering Call to Duty at the CIA,"A20. Cited by Gerber, "Managing HUMINT: The Need for a New Approach" in Sims and Gerber, *Transforming U.S. Intelligence*, 180.

94. Gosler, "The Digital Dimension," 104.

95. See Gosler, "The Digital Dimension," 104–105. Also see Ken Thompson, "Reflections on Trusting Trust," *Communication of the Association for Computer Machinery* (August 27, 1984): 761–763. Cited by Gosler, "The Digital Dimension," 105.

96. Michael Wynne, acting undersecretary of defense for acquisition, technology, and logistics, "Memorandum for the Chairman, Defense Science Board, Terms of Reference," Defense Science Board task force on high performance microchip supply, December 18, 2003. Cited in Gosler, "The Digital Dimension," 105.

97. Gosler, "The Digital Dimension," 110.

98. Ibid., 106.

99. *HPSCI-SSCI Report*, 250.

100. Ibid., 46.

101. "Playing Defense," *U.S. News and World Report*, November 13, 2006, 47.

CHAPTER 3

1. The Office of Strategic Services was established by President Franklin D. Roosevelt in June 1942 to collect and analyze strategic information required by the Joint Chiefs of Staff and to conduct special operations not assigned to other agencies.

2. Quoted in Turner, *Burn Before Reading*, 40.

3. Ibid., 51

4. Ibid., 60.

5. Ibid., 141–142.

6. Ibid., 132.

7. From Richard Helms and William Hood, *A Look over My Shoulder: A Life in the Central Intelligence Agency*, 1st ed.(New York: Knopf, 1979, 395–396 quoted in Turner, *Burn Before Reading*, 124.

8. Ray S. Cline, *The CIA Under Reagan, Bush ad Casey: the Evolution of the Agency from Roosevelt to Reagan* (Washington: D.C.: Acropolis Books, 1981), 240. Quoted in Turner, *Burn Before Reading*, 124–125.

9. Turner, *Burn Before Reading*, 76, 115, 196.

10. Analysis comes in many forms and at many levels. For example, a photointerpreter working for the military will undertake an analysis of photos taken, say of an adversary's military forces deployed in a specific area, and provide such information as the nature and size of the force, the type of equipment it has available to it, whether it has the latest tanks or artillery pieces, etc., and in some cases the precise real-time location of specific types of equipment. It was just this kind of analysis that permitted the United States to determine that the Soviet Union had deployed ballistic missiles to Cuba in 1962. This was current intelligence of a strategic nature. On the other hand, all-source analysts may be called upon to analyze the capabilities of al-Qaeda to develop and deploy a radiological weapon for use against the United States. This would involve a strategic estimate of al-Qaeda capabilities.

11. See Central Intelligence Agency, *A Consumer's Guide to Intelligence, n.d.3.*

12. Lowenthal, "Intelligence Analysis" in Sims, *Transforming U.S. Intelligence*, 221.

13. For a further discussion of this issue see Ibid., 223.

14. Russ Travers, "The Coming Intelligence Failure," *Studies in Intelligence* 1–1 (1997), 4.

15. Sherman Kent, "Estimates and Influence," *Studies in Intelligence*, 12–13 (Summer 1968): 11.

16. While a National Intelligence Estimate was produced, it was prepared at the behest of Congress not the President.

17. Intelink, which is patterned after the Internet, began test bed operations in 1994. Today it provides a means for the exchange of intelligence among intelligence providers and users.

18. A. Denis Clift, "From Semaphore to Predator: Intelligence in the Internet Era," *Studies in Intelligence*, 43-3 (2003), 5.

19. *HPSCI-SSCI Report*, 42–43.

20. Ibid., 45.

21. *HPSCI-SSCI Report*, 46.

22. Lowenthal, "Intelligence Analysis," 224.

23. Ibid.

24. Travers, "The Coming Intelligence Failure," 2.

25. Ibid., 3.

26. For example see, *HPSCI-SSCI Report*, 94.

27. Adapted from Lowenthal, *Intelligence: From Secrets to Policy*, 89.

28. See *HPSCI-SSCI Report*, 64–65.

29. *President's Commission on WMD*, 5.

30. Douglas MacEachin, "Analysis and Estimates," in Sims, *Transforming U.S. Intelligence*, 117.

31. Lowenthal, "Intelligence Analysis" in Sims, *Transforming U.S. Intelligence*, 229.

32. *HPSCI-SSCI Report*, 69.

33. Ibid., 358.

34. Lowenthal, "Intelligence Analysis," 230–231.

35. Quoted in Lowenthal, "Intelligence Analysis," 231.

36. *HPSCI-SSCI Report*, 357.

37. Ibid., 69.

38. Ibid, 62.

39. For an account of shortcomings in the U.S. collection efforts prior to the Japanese attack, see Richelson, *A Century of Spies*, 115–123.

40. Ford, "The Primary Purpose," 72.

41. *HPSCI-SSCI Report*, 83.

42. *9/11 Commission Report*, 353.

43. *President's Commission on WMD*, 177.

44. For example, Director of Central Intelligence George Tenet and former FBI Director Louis Freeh testified before the joint House-Senate intelligence committees that collaboration and information sharing in the Intelligence Community had markedly improved in recent years. Nevertheless, the committees found that "the agencies still act too often and at too many levels as a loose collection of entities. *HPSCI-SSCI Report*, 82. Also see *President's Commission on WMD*, 14.

45. See *Executive Order 12958*, April 17, 1995, amended March 25, 2003.

46. Lowenthal, *Intelligence: From Secrets to Policy*, 58.

47. *9/11 Commission Report*, 91–92.

48. *HPSCI-SSCI Report*, 380.

49. Ibid., 381.

50. See Ibid., 373–375.

51. Odom, *Fixing Intelligence*, 153.

52. Ibid.

53. *HPSCI-SSCI Report*, 87.

54. *President's Commission on WMD*, 86 and House of Commons, "Review of Intelligence on Weapons of Mass Destruction," *Report of a Committee of Privy Counsellors*, July 14, 2004, par. 406, p. 101.

55. *HPSCI-SSCI Report*, 59.

56. Ibid., 59–60.

57. Ibid., 341.

58. Ibid., 61.

59. Ibid.

60. Ibid., 59.

61. Ibid.

62. Ibid., 62.

63. Ibid., 381–382.

64. Ibid., 383.

65. Ibid. For greater detail see 50 U.S.C., Chapter 36, Foreign Intelligence Surveillance Act.

66. For greater detail see *HPSCI-SSCI Report*, 384–388.

67. Ibid., 13–15 & 87.

68. "U.S. persons" is the collective designation for American citizens, permanent resident aliens, unincorporated associations substantially composed of U.S. citizens or permanent resident aliens, or corporations not directed and controlled by a foreign government or governments that are incorporated in the United States.

69. Public Law 108–458, SEC 102A(f)(1)(A).

70. Ibid., SEC 102A(l).

71. Ibid., SEC 102A(h).

72. See Public Law 99-433.

73. U.S. Government Accountability Office, *Information Sharing: Report to Congressional Requesters*, GAO-06-385, 4.

74. Ibid., 5.

75. Ibid., 5–6.

76. Richard A. Best, *Sharing Law Enforcement and Intelligence Information: The Congressional Role*, A Congressional Research Service Report to Congress, February 13, 2007, CRS-11.

77. See Public Law 107-56. Also see Best, *Sharing Law Enforcement and Intelligence Information*, CRS-12.

CHAPTER 4

1. According to Robert M. Clark the basic problem confronting the analyst is determining the reliability of the evidence and that weighing evidence involves three steps: "evaluating the source, evaluating the communications channel through which the information is arrived, and evaluating the evidence itself." Clark, *Intelligence Analysis*, 101.

2. Geosynchronous satellites remain stationary or near-stationary over a point on the earth. Thus they can constantly monitor activity in the area below. A satellite in nongeosynchronous orbit does not remain stationary. Rather it continues to circle the earth, passing over its intended target at specifically identifiable times, which oftentimes afford opponents the opportunity to conceal what they don't wish to be revealed.

3. Robert M. Clark notes that the effect of entropy on the communications channel can result in the transformation of "an intelligence assertion that "X is a possibility" very often, over time and through diverse communication channels, [to] "X may be true," then "X probably is the case," and eventually "X is a fact." Clark, *Intelligence Analysis*, 109.

4. Adapted from Sherman Kent, "A Crucial Estimate Relived," *Studies in Intelligence* 36-5 (Spring 1964): 112–113.

5. Clark, *Intelligence Analysis*, 63.

6. *President's Commission on WMD*, 128.

7. Ibid., 129.

8. Clark, *Intelligence Analysis*, 63.

9. HPSCI-SSCI Report, 373–374.

10. Ibid., 374.

11. *President's Commission on WMD*, 57.

12. Ibid., 83, 112–113, 139.

13. Ibid., 83.

14. HPSCI-SSCI Report, 7–8.

15. Andrew, *For the President's Eyes Only*, 342.

16. Ibid.

17. See James J. Wirtz, *The Tet Offensive: Intelligence Failure in War* (Ithaca, N.Y.: Cornell University Press, 1991), 172–176, 274, cited in Andrew, *For the President's Eyes Only*, 342. Also see *History of Vietnam: Tet Offensive* at www.vwam.com/vets/tet/tet.html.

18. *President's Commission on WMD*, 116.

19. NIC, National Intelligence Estimate, *Iraq's Continuing Programs for Weapons of Mass Destruction* (NIE 2002-16HC) (October 2002), 9 and 28, hereafter referred to as *NIE 2002* quoted in *President's Commission on WMD*, 115. This conclusion was not without caveats. The NIE cautioned that the Intelligence Community had "little specific information on Iraq's CW stockpile," and had almost no information on size, composition, or location of Iraq's CW stockpile." Ibid., 122. However, it is doubtful that such caveats were included in the executive summary. It is equally doubtful that senior decision makers in the executive branch or members of the congressional select committees on intelligence read beyond the executive summary.

20. There was apparently some very limited confirming evidence from "small streams of human (none of which was considered highly reliable) and signals intelligence." See Ibid., 115, 120–121.

21. Ibid., 120.

22. *NIE 2002*, 5 and 35 quoted in Ibid., 83.

23. *President's Commission on WMD*, 84.

24. At the time of the National Intelligence Estimate, reporting from three other sources provided one report each on Iraq's mobile BW facilities. All three sources later proved to be problematical. One source was judged to be a fabricator by both a foreign intelligence liaison service and the CIA's Directorate of Operations well before the 2003 War. Ibid., 87–88.

25. Senior German officials revealed the German role in an interview with the Los Angeles Times. See Bob Drogin and John Goetz, "Source that led to Iraq war lied," *The Atlanta Journal Constitution*, November 20, 2005.

26. American intelligence officials knew this information before Secretary of State Colin Powell's address to the United Nations on February 5, 2003. Indeed, as early as March

2001, the Germans were expressing their doubts about him. So were the British by April 2002. The record is unclear whether this information ever reached then Deputy Director of Central Intelligence McLaughlin, nor does McLaughlin recall any recommendation that the draft of Secretary Powell's address be altered as a result of this information. See Ibid and *President's Commission on WMD*, 104. For a more detailed commentary on the "Curveball" story see Bob Drogin, *Curveball: Spies, Lies, and the Con Man Who Caused A War* (New York: Random House, Inc., 2007).

27. Ibid., 86.

28. CIA, DCI Nonproliferation Center, *New Evidence of Iraqi Biological Warfare Program* (SIR 2000-003X) (December 14, 2000) quoted in Ibid., 86–87.

29. *President's Commission on WMD*, 92, 110–111.

30. Andrew, *For the President's Eyes Only*, 391.

31. Ibid.

32. Gosler, "The Digital Dimension," 107.

33. Ibid.

34. Weiner, "C.I.A. Study Details Failures."

35. *9/11 Commission Report*, 141.

36. Ibid., 255–260. Also see *Bin Laden Determined to Strike US*, declassified and approved for release, April 10, 2004, at www.gwu.edu/~nsarchiv/NSAEBB/NSAEBB116/index.htm.

37. *9/11 Commission Report*, 259.

38. *HPSCI-SSCI Report*, 341.

39. Ibid., 347.

40. Ibid., 345.

41. See Clark, *Intelligence Analysis*, 121–122; Daniel, "Denial and Deception," 134.

42. For example, see Caddell, *Deception 101*, 6–8. Caddell also notes that camouflage can have an active form that entails the artificial creation of an image or impression. For example, creating dummy pieces of military equipment to convey to an opponent a false impression of the disposition of your military forces.

43. Operation Fortitude, or properly named Fortitude South, was actually part of a much broader plan of deception code-named Operation Bodyguard. Bodyguard included: Operation Fortitude North, a fictitious invasion of Norway; Fortitude South, a fictitious invasion on the coast opposite Dover in the Pas de Calais; Operation Zeppelin, code name for the Allied feint through the Balkans, and seven other subsidiary operations.

44. See Andrew, *For the President's Eyes Only*, 140–142; Anthony C. Brown, *Bodyguard of Lies* (New York: Harper and Row, 1975; Michael Howard, *British Intelligence in the Second World War*, Vol. 5, *Strategic Deception* (London: HMSO, 1990); Donald C. Daniel and Katherine l. Herbig, *Strategic Military Deception* (New York; Pergamon Press, 1982); Thaddeus Holt, *The Deceivers: Allied Military Deception in the Second World War* (New York: Scribner, 2004; and Major Jon S. Wendell, "Strategic Deception Behind the Normandy Invasion" at www.globalsecurity.org/military/library/report/1997/wendell.htm.

45. Douglas MacEachin, "Analysis and Estimates: Professional Practices in Intelligence Production," in Sims and Gerber, 117.

46. *President's Commission on WMD*, 151.

47. Kent, "A Crucial Estimate Relived," 114.

48. President Franklin Delano Roosevelt's opening comment in his address to Congress on December 8.

49. Roberta Wohlstetter, *Pearl Harbor: Warning and Decision* (Stanford, CA: Stanford University Press, 1962).

50. See Andrew, *For the President's Eyes Only*, 119.

51. Hughes-Wilson, *Military Blunders*, 62–62.

52. Ibid., 104, 107, and 121.

53. Richelson. *A Century of Spies*, 122.

54. Ford, "The Primary Purpose of National Estimating," 74.

55. A.R. Northridge, "Pearl Harbor: Estimating Then and Now," *Studies in Intelligence* 9:4 (1965): 69–70.

56. Andrew, *For the President's Eyes Only*, 121–122.

57. John Dower, "War Without Mercy: Race and Power in the Pacific War (New York: Pantheon Books, 1986), 105, cited in Andrew, *For the President's Eyes Only*, 122.

58. Michael Totten's *Middle East Journal*, April 5, 2007, at www.michaeltotten.com/archive.

59. Abraham Rabinovich, *The Yom Kippur War: The Epic Encounter that Transformed the Middle East* (New York: Schocken Books, 2004), 34.

60. Major Michael C. Jordan, "The 1973 Arab-Israel War: Arab Policies, Strategies, and Campaigns" at www.globalsecurity.org/military/library/report/1997/Jordan.htm.

61. Southern Command included the southern part of Israel (i.e., Negev region), as well as the Sinai Peninsula.

62. Major General Chaim Herzog, *The War of Atonement: The Inside Story of the Yom Kippur War* (Boston: Little, Brown and Company, 1975), 283.

63. Anwar el-Sadat, *In Search of Identity* (New York: Harper & Row, 1977), 215, cited in Ibid.

64. Ibid.

65. For details see Sadat, *In Search of Identity*, 219–221.

66. For a more detailed account of events leading to the outbreak of hostilities, see *The Yom Kippur War* (Garden City, New York: Doubleday & Company, Inc., 1974), 46–113.

67. Elizabeth Monroe and A.H. Farrar-Hockley, A.H., "The Arab-Israel War, October 1973: Background and Events," *Adelphi Papers No. 111*(1975):18.

68. *Yom Kippur War*, 106.

69. Rabinovich, *Yom Kippur War*, 44.

70. Clark, *Intelligence Analysis*, 2.

71. Rabinovich, *Yom Kippur War*, 8.

72. Shulsky and Schmitt, *Silent Warfare*, 67.

73. Jordan, "The 1973 Arab-Israel War."

74. Henry Kissinger, *Years of Upheaval* (Boston: Little, Brown, 1982), 465, cited in MacEachin, "Analysis and Estimates," 129.

75. Andrew, *For the President's Eyes Only*, 392.

76. Rabinovich, *Yom Kippur War*, 56.

77. *President's Commission on WMD*, cover letter to the President.

78. Ibid., 3.

79. Bob Woodward, "CIA Aiding Iraq in Gulf War; Target Data from U.S. Satellites Supplied for Nearly 2 Years," *Washington Post*, December 15, 1986.

80. U.S. Senate Committee on Banking, Housing, and Urban Affairs Committee, "Second Staff Report on U.S. Chemical and Biological Warfare-Related Dual-Use Exports to Iraq at www.gulfwarvets.com/arison/banking.htm, and "The Possible Impact on the Health Consequences of the War," May 25, 1994 at www.gulfwarvets.com/arison/banking.htm.

81. See United Nations Resolution 687, April 3, 1991.

82. Hans Blix, *Disarming Iraq* (New York: Pantheon Books, 2004), 24–25.

83. *President's Commission on WMD*, 56.

84. Blix, *Disarming Iraq*, 29–30.

85. See Ibid., 30 and *President's Commission on WMD*, 85 and 90.

86. The International Atomic Energy Agency had only limited difficulty carrying out inspections between 1992 and 1998, UNSCOM (the United Nations Special Commission on Iraq) found it increasingly difficult to conduct inspections.

87. See Blix, *Disarming Iraq*, 28–34.

88. Ibid., 35.

89. UNSCOM Chairman Butler's Report to the UN Secretary General, dated December 15, 2002, at www.fas.org/news/un/iraq/s/butla216.htm.

90. Blix, *Disarming Iraq*, 35.

91. *President's Commission on WMD*, 121. Also see U.S. Senate, "Report of the Select Committee on Intelligence on the Intelligence Community's Prewar Intelligence Assessment on Iraq," July 9, 2004, 143–144 (hereafter listed as SSCI).

92. *President's Commission on WMD*, 57–58.

93. Ibid., 79.

94. Peter Eisen and Knut Royce, *The Italian Letter* (New York: Rodale, 2007), 4. Also see *President's Commission on WMD*, 79–80.

95. Blix, *Disarming Iraq*, 29.

96. Ibid., 28.

97. Ibid., 90–91.

98. See Ibid., 84–85.

99. *President's Commission on WMD*, 58.

100. Ambassador Joseph Wilson, *Politics of Truth* (New York: Carroll & Graf, 2004), 2.

101. *President's Commission on WMD*, 81. Also see *SSCI*, 36–42.

102. *President's Commission on WMD*, 54.

103. Ibid., 56.

104. Ibid., 174.

105. Ibid., 175.

106. Richard Betts, "Analysis, War, and Decision: Why Intelligence Failures Are Inevitable," in Loch L. Johnson and James J. Wirtz, *Strategic Intelligence: Windows Into a Secret World* (Los Angeles: Roxbury Publishing Company, 2004), 102.

107. Ibid., 102–103.

108. *President's Commission on WMD*, 56.

109. Ibid., 91.

110. Ibid., 68–69.

111. Ibid., 79.

112. MacEachin, "Analysis and Estimates," 119.

113. HPSCI-SSCI, 62–63.

114. Ibid., 64.

115. Ibid., 337.

116. Robert M. Gates, "Guarding Against Politicization," remarks by the Director of Central Intelligence made on March 16, 1992 in the CIA auditorium, 1 at www.cia.gov/csi/kent_csi/docs/v36i1a01p_0001.htm.

117. Ibid.

118. Lowenthal, "*Intelligence: From Secrets to Policy*," 105.

119. Gates, "The CIA and American Foreign Policy," 221.

120. Ibid.

121. See Andrew, *For the President's Eyes Only*, 534.

122. For example, see Paul F. Horvitz, "Ex-Aide Calls CIA Under Casey and Gates Corrupt and Slanted," *International Herald Tribune*, October 2, 1991.

123. Turner, *Burn Before Reading*, 190.

124. Treverton, *Reshaping National Intelligence*, 198.

125. Turner, *Burn Before Reading*, 117.

126. Ibid., 128.

127. Ibid., 165.

128. *President's Commission on WMD*, 196–197.

129. Richard A. Clark noted that Vice President Cheney made several trips to CIA Headquarters. During most of the visits he "focused on Iraq and left midlevel managers and analysts wondering whether the seasoned Vice President was right about the Iraqi threat" and "perhaps they should adjust their own analysis." Richard A. Clark, *Against All Enemies: Inside America's War on Terror* (New York: Free Press, 2004) 227–228.

130. MacEachin, "Analysis and Estimates," 129.

131. Lowenthal, "Intelligence Analysis," 235.

132. Ibid.

133. Jack Davis, "Combatting Mindset," *Studies in Intelligence* 38-5 (1992) at www.odci.gov/csi/kent_csi/docs/v35i4a03p_0001.htm.

134. U.S. Congress, Senate, "The National Intelligence Estimates A-B Team Episode Concerning Soviet Strategic Capability and Objectives," *Report of the Senate Select Committee on Intelligence, Subcommittee on Collection, Production, and Quality February 16, 1978* (Washington, D.C.: US Government Printing Office, 1978), 2–3.

135. Ibid., 5–6.

136. Ibid., 4.

137. Gates, "Guarding Against Politicization."

138. Paul R. Pillar, "Intelligence, Policy, and the War in Iraq," *Foreign Affairs* 85–2 (2006): 16.

CHAPTER 5

1. U.S. Department of Justice, Federal Bureau of Investigation, *Report to the National Commission on Terrorist Attacks upon the United States: The FBI's Counterterrorism Program Since September 2001*, April 14, 2004, 66. Also see Office of the Inspector General, *The Federal Bureau of Investigation's Effort to Improve the Sharing of Intelligence and Other Information*, Report No. 04-10, December 2003 at www.usdoj.gov/oig/reports/FBI/a0410/findings3.htm

2. Lowenthall, *From Secrets to Policy*, 48.

3. Gates, "The CIA and American Foreign Policy," 218.

4. *National Security Council Directive No. 1*. Truman Library, Papers of Harry S. Truman, President's Secretary's Files, Subject File, Current Policies of the Government of the United States of America Relating to the National Security. Top Secret (subsequently declassified).

5. Ford, "The Primary Purpose," 69–70. Richelson, *A Century of Spies*, 119. Also see "Science Question of the Week." Goddard Space Flight Center, 2001 at www.gsfc.nasa.gov/scienceques2001/20011207.htm and "East Wind, Rain," *Time*, November 12, 1945 at www.time.com/time/magazine/article/0,9171,792491,00.html.

6. Ibid., 72–73.
7. Ibid.
8. Ibid., 70.
9. Sims, *Transforming U.S. Intelligence*, 42.
10. *HPSCI-SSCI Report*, 85.
11. Ibid., 86.
12. Ibid., 89.
13. Ibid., 92
14. Quoted in Turner, *Burn Before Reading*, 199 from an interview with Admiral Bobby Ray Inman, April 1, 2004.
15. *Against All Enemies*, 2004), 230–231. Also see *9/11 Commission*, 201.
16. *President's Commission on WMD*, 14, 52–53.
17. Ibid., 14.
18. Ibid., 188.
19. For additional information on the Team A and B approach see Chapter 4.
20. "The National Intelligence Estimates A-B Team Episode," 3.
21. Ibid.
22. Gates, "The CIA and American Foreign Policy," 221.
23. Ibid., 222.
24. Ibid., 223–224.
25. Ibid., 224.
26. *President's Commission on WMD*, 644–645.
27. Ibid., 13.
28. Ibid., 52.
29. Ibid., 59. Only the Department State Bureau of Intelligence and Research dissented from this view.
30. CIA and DIA analysts found the acquisition of aluminum tubes provided "compelling evidence" of reconstitution. The Department of Energy while concurring in the assessment that Iraq was reconstituting its nuclear programs, did not concur with the finding that the aluminum tubes could be used in centrifuges designed to produce nuclear weapons grade materials. Ibid., 59.
31. Ibid., 77.
32. Ibid.
33. Ibid., 84–86.
34. Ibid., 13.
35. Ibid., 120.
36. David E. Lilienthal, *Journals II: The Atomic Energy Years* (New York: Harper & Row, 1964), 376. Quoted in Turner, *Burn Before Reading*, 53–54.

CHAPTER 6

1. Gates, "The CIA and American Foreign Policy," 225–226.
2. Turner, *Burn Before Reading*, 69–70.
3. Ibid., 89–93.
4. Andrews, *For the President's Eyes Only*, 272.
5. Turner, *Burn Before Reading*, 106 and 124–126.
6. Andrews, *For the President's Eyes Only*, 353.
7. Turner, *Burn Before Reading*, 142.
8. Ibid., 165.

9. Ibid., 196–198.
10. Ibid., 209.
11. Ibid., 225–226.
12. Ibid., 243–244.
13. "Yugoslavia Transformed," *National Intelligence Estimate* 15–90, October 18, 1990 at www.dni.gov/nic/foia_yugoslavia_chrono.html. Also see "Evolution in Europe; Yugoslavia Seen Breaking Up Soon," *The New York Times*, November 28, 1990 and Treverton, *Reshaping National Intelligence*, 177
14. Treverton, *Reshaping National Intelligence*, 177.
15. Ibid.
16. See Ibid., 178.
17. Cheryl Y. Marcum, Lauren R. Sager Weinstein, Susan D. Hosek, Harry J. Thie, *Department of Defense Political Appointments: Positions and Processes* (Santa Monica, CA: Rand Monograph Report, 2001), xi–xii at http://rand.org/pubs/monograph_reports/MR1253
18. Paul C. Light, "Our Tottering Confirmation Process," *Public Interest* (Spring 2002). 11. Wendy Cloud, "Federal Family Advocate Resigns" at www.citizenlink.org/content/A000004308.cfm
19. Light, "Our Tottering Confirmation Process," 11.
20. Gates, "The CIA and American Foreign Policy," 226.
21. See "The National Intelligence Estimates A-B Team Episode," Also see Robert Kennedy, "The Changing Strategic Balance and US Defense Planning," in Robert Kennedy and John Weinstein, eds., *The Defense of the West: Strategic and European Security Issues Reappraised* (Boulder, Colorado: Westview Press, 1984), 5–37.
22. For example see Richard Pipes, "The Soviet Strategy for Nuclear Victory," *Commentary*, July 1977.
23. George Perkovich, *India's Nuclear Bomb: The Impact on Global Proliferation* Berkeley, CA: University of California Press, 1999), 34.
24. Jeffrey T. Richelson, *Spying on the Bomb* (New York: W.W. Norton & Company, 2006), 220.
25. Ibid., 226.
26. Ibid., 221. On India's reaction to the Chinese nuclear test, also see Perkovich, *India's Nuclear Bomb*, 66–85.
27. Outside estimates were as low as 4 to 6 kilotons. See "Nuclear Weapons" at www.fas.org/nuke/guide/india/nuke/index.html.
28. Raj Chengappa, *Weapons of Peace: The Secret Story of India's Quest to Be a Nuclear Power* (New Delhi: HarperCollins India, 2000), 221 quoted in Richelson, *Spying on the Bomb*, 427.
29. See Chengappa, *Weapons of Peace*, 246–247, 256–257 noted in Richelson, *Spying on the Bomb*, 427–428.
30. Because of its extreme positions, the Party had remained on the fringes of Indian politics for most of its existence. Even when it was called upon to form a minority government in 1996, other parties were not willing to join in a coalition with it and the government fell in thirteen days. "BJP Flexing Muscles, But How Far Will It Go?" *Intelligence Report*, CIA, Office of Near Eastern, South Asian, and African Analysis, May 29, 1998, 5 (Formerly Secret, declassified).
31. Treverton, *Reshaping National Intelligence*, 4.
32. Weiner, "CIA Study Details Failures," A1, A8.
33. Ibid.

34. See Richelson, *A Century of Spies*, 111–113. For additional reading see Colonel John Hughes-Wilson, *Military Intelligence Blunders* (New York: Carroll and Graf, 1999) and Barton Whaley, *Codeword Barbarossa* (Cambridge, MA: MIT Press, 1973).

35. Richelson, *A Century of Spies*, 114.

36. See David E. Murphy, *What Stalin Knew: The Enigma of Barbarossa* (New Haven, CT: Yale University Press, 2005), 258 cited in a review by Donald P. Steury by the same name in *Studies in Intelligence* 50:1 (2005): 2.

37. Richelson, *A Century of Spies*, 115.

38. Clark, *Intelligence Analysis*, 1.

39. For an excellent account of the fall of Singapore see Alan Warren, *Britain's Greatest Defeat: Singapore, 1942* (New York and London: Hambledon Continuum, 2002).

40. Hughes-Wilson, *Military Intelligence Blunders*, 102.

41. Warren, *Britain's Greatest Defeat*, 21.

42. See Hughes-Wilson, *Military Intelligence Blunders*, 102–120; Warren, *Britain's Greatest Defeat*, chapter *5; and* "The Fall of Singapore" at www.historylearningsite.co.uk/fall_of_singapore.htm.

43. Hughes-Wilson, *Military Intelligence Blunders*, 10.

44. Ibid.

45. "US – Dominican Republic (1959–2005)." Cooperative Research History Commons at www.cooperativeresearch.org/timeline.jsp?timeline=dominican_republic. Excerpted from William Blum, *Killing Hope:* U. S. Military and CIA Interventions Since World War (Monroe, ME: Common Courage Press, 1995).

46. Though few in Washington considered Bosch a communist, many considered him to be an inept politician and administrator, who had lost touch with his country's predicament. Typical of such views were those of then Undersecretary of State George Ball, who saw Bosch as "unrealistic, arrogant, and erratic. I thought him incapable of running even a small social club, much less a country in turmoil. He did not seem to me a Communist... but merely a muddle-headed, anti-American pedant committed to unattainable social reforms. George W. Ball, *The Past Has Another Pattern: Memoirs* (New York: W. W. Norton, 1982), 327 quoted in Lawrence A. Yates, "Powerpack: U.S. Intervention in the Dominican Republic, 1965–1966," *Leavenworth Papers*, Number 15, July 1988 at www.cgsc.army.mil/carl/resources/csi/yates/yates.asp.

47. See Yates, "Powerpack: U.S. Intervention" for an interesting discussion surrounding these events.

48. Lyndon B. Johnson, *The Vantage Point* (London: Weidenfeld and Nicolson, 1972), 180–196 quoted in Andrews, *For the President's Eyes*, 325.

49. See Andrews, *For the President's Eyes*, 325.

50. Ibid.

51. Kirsten Lundberg, "The SS-9 Controversy: Intelligence as a Political Football," Case Study C16-89-884.0, Kennedy School of Government, Harvard University, Cambridge, MA, 1989, 2.

52. Ibid., 1.

53. Foster had been impressed by Air Force Systems Command analysis of fall 1968 tests of the new version of the SS-9 and its Foreign Technologies Division conclusion, derived from analysis of telemetry, that the new version of the SS-9 could have a primitive system capable of releasing multiple independently targeted warheads. Lundberg, "The SS-9 Controversy," 7.

54. Ibid., 10.

55. Ibid., 9.

56. Andrews, *For the President's Eyes*, 356. Quoted from Seymour M. Hersh, *Kissinger: The Price of Power* (New York: Simon and Schuster, 1982), 159.

57. Andrews, *For the President's Eyes*, 356.

58. Also see "Combating Proliferation of Weapons of Mass Destruction," Report of the Commission to Assess the Organization of the Federal Government to Combat the Proliferation of Weapons of Mass Destruction, July 14, 1999, 2–3.

59. Testimony of Gary Milhollin Before the Senate Committee on Foreign Relations, June 11, 1998, 2 at www.wisconsinproject.org/pubs/testimonies/1998/6-11.html

60. The Missile Technology Control Regime is an informal and voluntary partnership between thirty-four countries to prevent the proliferation of missile technology. The People's Republic of China is not a member of the Regime but agreed to abide by the original 1987 Guidelines and the Equipment, Software and Technology Annex.

61. "Clinton battles China syndrome," BBC News, July 3, 1998.

62. Testimony of Gary Milhollin, 4.

63. Ibid.

64. "Clinton Administrations Response to the Threat Posed by Proliferation." Testimony by Curt Weldon, Chair, Subcommittee on Military Research and Development before the Military Procurement Subcommittee and Military Research and Development Committee, House National Security Committee, June 20, 1996 reported by Global Security at www.globalsecurity.org/wmd/library/congress/1996_h/h960620b.htm.

65. Chidanand Rajghatta, "US Doublespeak in China Deals Bared," www.indianexpress.com/res/web/ple/ie/daily/19980613/16450854.html

66. "Sen. Helms Targets China Export Waivers," CNN, All Politics, at www.cnn.com/ALLPOLITICS/1998/06/11/helms/.

67. "Senator Thompson Revises China Proliferation Act," Washington File, U.S. Department of State International Information Programs, July 26, 2000 at www.nti.org/e_research/official_docs/dos/72600.DOS.pdf

68. See John Gershman, "Clinton Administration Continues to Stumble with China," Foreign Policy in Focus (2000), 2 at http;//fpif.org/papers/china/stumbling_body.html. Also see Robert Walpole, "Foreign Missile Developments and the Ballistic Missile Threat to the United States Through 2015," paper prepared under the auspices of the National Intelligence Council, September 1999 and "China and Weapons of Mass Destruction: Implications for the United States," conference papers, November 5, 1999 at www.fas.org/irp/nic/china_wmd.html.

69. "President Bush Outlines Iraqi Threat." Remarks by the President on Iraq, Cincinnati Museum Center – Cincinnati Union Terminal, Cincinnati, Ohio, October 7, 2002 at www.whitehouse.gov/news/releases/2002/10/20021007-8.html

70. Seymour Hersh, *Chain of Command: The Road From 9/11 to Abu Ghraib* (New York: HarperCollins, 2005), 230. Quoted in F. Ugboaja Ohaegbulam, *A Culture of Deference: Congress, the President, and the Course of the U.S.-Led Invasion and Occupation of Iraq* (New York: Peter Lang, 2007), 140–141.

71. "Vice President Speaks at VFW 103rd National Convention." Remarks by the Vice President to the Veterans of Foreign Wars 103rd National Convention, August 26, 2002 at www.whitehouse.gov/news/releases/2002/08/20020826.html

72. "Interview With Condoleezza Rice; Pataki Talks About 9-11; Graham, Shelby Discuss War on Television," Transcript: CNN Late Edition with Wolf Blitzer, September 8, 2002 at http://transcripts.cnn.com/TRANSCRIPTS/0209/08/le.00.html

73. "Transcript: David Kay at Senate Hearing," January 28, 2004 at www.cnn.com/2004/US/01/28/kay.transcript/

74. *President's Commission on WMD*, 85.

75. Ibid., 56.

76. Based on revelations of then Secretary of Treasury Paul O'Neill in Ron Suskind, *The Price of Loyalty; George W. Bush, the White House, and the Education of Paul O'Neill* (New York: Simon & Schuster, 2004), 80.

77. Jim Lobe, "What is a Neoconservative Anyway? *Asia Times* online at www.atimes.com/atimes/Front_Page/EH13Aa01.html. Also see Robert Kennedy, "Neocon policy a source of insecurity," *The Atlanta Journal Constitution*, July 19, 2004 and Ohaegbulam, *A Culture of Deference*, 120–121.

78. For example, see Letter to President Clinton, January 26, 1998 signed by eighteen individuals including prominent neoconservatives Donald Rumsfeld, Paul Wolfowitz, Richard Perle, Elliot Abrams, William Kristol, John Bolton, Zalmay Khalilzad, Francis Fukuyama, Robert Kagan, and Peter Rodman. Also see "Speaking of Iraq," *Washington Times*, January 27, 1998; William Kristol and Robert Kagan, "Bombing Iraq Isn't Enough," *The New York Times*, January 30, 1998; Stephen Solarz and Paul Wolfowitz, "Letter to the Editor," *Foreign Affairs*, 78(2) (March–April 1999); and Gary Schmitt, "State of Terror: War by Any Other Name," *Weekly Standard*, November 20, 2000.

79. Suskind, *The Price of Loyalty*, 70–72.

80. Ibid., 75.

81. Ibid.

82. Ibid., 96.

83. Ibid., 184.

84. Ibid., 186.

85. Ibid., 186–188.

86. Ibid., 204.

87. "President Bush Delivers Graduation Speech at West Point," at www.whitehouse.gov/news/releases/2002/06/20020601-3.html

88. Walter Pincus, "British Intelligence Warned of Iraq War." *Washington Post*, May 13, 2005.

89. For example, see Mark Eagan, "Bush Defends Iraq Policy Amid Dissent at Home," *Reuters*, August 16, 2002.

90. David E. Sanger, "The World: First Among Evils? The Debate Over Attacking Iraq Heats Up," *The New York Times*, September 1, 2002.

91. Suskind, *The Price of Loyalty*, 279.

92. "Vice President Speaks at VFW National Convention," August 26, 2002.

93. "President Delivers 'State of the Union.'" January 28, 2003 at www.whitehouse.gov/news/releases/2003/01/20030128-19.html

94. "President George Bush Discusses Iraq in National Press Conference," March 6, 2003 at www.whitehouse.gov/news/releases/2003/03/print/20030306-8.html

95. "President Says Saddam Hussein Must Leave Iraq Within 48 Hours," Remarks by the President in Address to the Nation, March 17, 2003, The White House at www.whitehouse.gov/news/releases/2003/03/20030317-7.html.

96. David Cloud and Mark Mazzetti, "Prewar Intelligence Unit at Pentagon Is Criticized," *The New York Times*, February 9, 2007.

97. Blix, *Disarming Iraq*, 29.

98. Wolf Blitzer, "Did the Bush Administration exaggerate the threat from Iraq?" CNN.com/inside politics, July 8, 2003 at www.cnn.com/2003/ALLPOLITICS/07/08/wbr.iraq.claims/

99. Wilson, *The Politics of Truth*, 325.

100. Blix, *Disarming Iraq*, 211.

101. Ibid., 177–178.

102. Ibid., 10–11.

103. G. M. Gilbert, *Nuremburg Diary* (New York: Farrar, Straus, 1947), 278.

CHAPTER 7

1. See Andrews, *For the President's Eyes Only*, 11.

2. Ibid., 1.

3. "The Evolution of the U.S. Intelligence Community—An Historical Overview" at www.access.gpo.gov/intelligence/int/int022.html, 2.

4. Ibid., 2–3.

5. From its founding in 1908 the Bureau grew from thirty-four agents primarily focused on banking issues to 300 agents with an expanded charter that included internal security. Ibid., 3.

6. See Andrews, *For the President's Eyes Only*, 13.

7. Public Law 253, 80th Congress, passed July 26, 1947, Sec. 101 and 102. Hereafter referred to as the National Security Act of 1947.

8. See National Security Act of 1947 (Amended). SEC 102.

9. Ibid., SEC 103 (c) (3) and (d) (2).

10. See CIA, *Factbook on Intelligence* at ftp.fas.org/irp/cia/product/fact97/index.html and National Security Act of 1947 (Amended).

11. For example see, "Organization of the National Security Council System," signed by the President, February 13, 2001.

12. See "National Security Council Staff Reorganization," Memorandum for the President, et al., signed by Stephen J. Hadley, March 28, 2005, Tab A.

13. See National Security Staff at www.clinton4.nara.gov/WH/EOP/NSC/html/NSC_Staff.html.

14. See "Evolution of the U.S. Intelligence Community," 8–9.

15. See President's Foreign Intelligence Advisory Board at SourceWatch www.sourcewatch.org/index.php?title=President%27s_Foreign_inteliigence_Advisory_Board. Much of the information at Source Watch is cited from the Miller Center of Public Affairs Web site.

16. Ibid.

17. Ibid.

18. See Executive Order 12331—President's Foreign Intelligence Advisory Board, October 20, 1981.

19. *SourceWatch*.

20. For example, the Board has included such individuals as physical chemist and signals intelligence expert at AT&T Bell Laboratories William O. Baker (3 times), soldier, diplomat, and Chairman of the Joint Chiefs of Staff General Maxwell Taylor, editor,

playwright, politician, journalist, and diplomat Clara Boothe Luce (2 times), businessman, politician, statesman, art collector, philanthropist, and later Vice President Nelson Rockefeller, Lawyer and Watergate Special Prosecutor Leon Jaworski, billionaire businessman Ross Perot, Chief Executive Officer of Continental Airlines Robert F. Six, astronaut and Chairman of the Board of Eastern Airlines Frank Borman, National Security Advisor and Secretary of State Henry Kissinger, distinguished physicist and arms control specialist Sidney Drell, Deputy Director of the National Security Agency Ann Z. Caracristi, international lawyer, peace activist Rita E. Hauser, president of the National Bureau of Economic Research Martin S. Feldstein, and former commander of the U.S. Strategic Command and president and Chief Executive Officer of the Institute of Nuclear Power Operations Admiral James O. Ellis.

21. Ibid.

22. See for example, John M. Williams, Ph.D., "Reports of the Presidents' Foreign Intelligence Advisory Board: An Introductory Overview, *Kennedy Assassination Chronicles*, 7:4 at the Mary Ferrell Foundation Web site at www.maryferrell.org/mffweb/archive/viewer/showDoc.do?absPageId=223374; "White House Statement on the President's Meeting With the Foreign Intelligence Advisory Board," July 14, 1987, at www.reagan.utexas.edu/archives/speeches/1987/071487b.htm; and SourceWatch.

23. Excerpt from Robert O'Harrow, *No Place to Hide* (New York: Free Press, 2005), Chapter 1. featured on ABC News on the Web, June 13, 2007, at www.abcnews.go.com/GMA/Books/story?id=424002&page=1

24. Ibid.

25. "Inside the Department of Dirty Tricks," *The Atlantic Online*, 4.

26. Ibid., 4–5.

27. Among other things, though in March 1975 President Ford gave the Commission the task of examining allegations of assassination plots against Trujillo, Diem, and Castro, the report contained nothing about the assassination of foreign leaders. "Leaving Murky Murders to the Senate," *Time* at www.time.com/time/printout/0,8816,917516,00.html.

28. The Committee was formed on February 19, 1975 and initially chaired by Congressman Lucien Nedzi. However, concerned that as chairman of the House Armed Services Intelligence Subcommittee, one of the four committees briefed by Colby, Nedzi had read the entire Family Jewels report and had done nothing about it, Nedzi's colleagues found him to be an inappropriate pick for chairman. A new committee was then formed under Pike. See *CIA: The Pike Report* (Nottingham: Spokesman Books, 1977), 11–12. "Inside the Department of Dirty Tricks," 5; "Leaving Murky Murders to the Senate," 2; and Gerald K. Haines, "Looking for the Rogue Elephant: The Pike Committee Investigations and the CIA" at www.bss.sfsu.edu/fischer/IR%20360/Readings/pike.htm. For a detailed account of the work of the Nedzi, Pike, and Church committees see Frank J. Smist, Jr., *Congress Oversees the United States Intelligence Community, 1947–1994* (Knoxville, TN: University of Tennessee Press, 2nd Ed., 1994), 135–213.

29. See Haines, "Looking for the Rogue Elephant," 2.

30. Ibid., 6.

31. See "Pike Committee" at http://en.wikipedia.org/wiki/Pike_Committee

32. Haines, "Looking for the Rogue Elephant," 6.

33. See Executive Order 13301, May 14, 2003.

34. The word "Constitution" was added by Executive Order 12334, December 4, 1981.

35. Dan Eggen, "FBI Papers Indicate Intelligence Violations," *Washington Post*, October 24, 2005.

36. *Legislative Oversight of Intelligence Activities: The U.S. Experience*, a report prepared by the Senate Select Committee on Intelligence, United States Senate, 103 Congress, 2nd Session, October 1994, 13.

37. Neither President Ford's executive order nor the Inspector General Act passed by Congress in 1978 required that departments establish a separate IG to oversee only intelligence efforts.

38. See "Mission and History: Assistant Secretary of Defense (Intelligence Oversight)" at www.pentagon.mil/atsdio/mission.html. Also see Department of Defense Directive Number 5148.11, May 21, 2004.

39. See Department of Energy Orders DOE 5670.1A, January 15, 1992 and Delegation Order No. 0204-146, effective January 21, 1993.

40. A U.S. person is generally defined by federal law and executive order as a U.S. citizen, an alien lawfully admitted for permanent residence, an unincorporated association substantially composed of U.S. citizens or permanent resident aliens, or, with few exceptions, a corporation incorporated in the United States. See 8 U.S.C. 1324b(a)(3), 8 U.S.C. 1101(a)(20), and DOD Directive 5240.1-R, Appendix A, para. 27.

CHAPTER 8

1. See Justice Louis Brandeis' separate dissenting view in Meyers v. United States, 1926.

2. Lowenthal, *Intelligence: From Secrets to Policy*, 156.

3. *Legislative Oversight of Intelligence*, 2.

4. Many of Truman's concerns mirrored those of President Franklin D. Roosevelt. In July 1941, with war ongoing in Europe and Asia and the prospects of American involvement growing with each day, Roosevelt needed a source of good intelligence. Concerned that "his intelligence sources consisted of uncoordinated agencies, each going its own way to meet the perceived needs of its parent organization and not necessarily cooperating with others," Roosevelt created the Office of the Coordinator of Information (COI) with William "Wild Bill" Donovan as head. Following the U.S. entry into the war, COI was redesignated the Office of Strategic Services and placed under the Joint Chiefs of Staff. See Turner, *Burn Before Reading*, 11–13. Among its wartime tasks, the OSS conducted a wide range of intelligence and counterintelligence activities, including recruiting spies, collecting and analyzing strategic information for Joint Chiefs of Staff, and arming, training, and supplying resistance movements.

5. *Legislative Oversight of Intelligence*, 3.

6. For details on the issues and politics surrounding the dissolution of the OSS see Michael Warner, "The Creation of the Central Intelligence Group," *Studies in Intelligence* 39:5 (1996): 111–120. Also see Turner, *Burn Before Reading*, 37–41 and *Legislative Oversight of Intelligence*, 3.

7. See *Legislative Oversight of Intelligence*, 2–3.

8. "National Security Council Intelligence Directive No. 5," dated December 12, 1947. National Archives and Records Administration, RG 59, Records of the Department of State, Records of the Executive Secretariat, NSC Files: Lot 66 D 95, NSCIDs.

9. *Legislative Oversight of Intelligence*, 3.

10. The U.S. Department of War became part of the National Military Establishment (NME) with the passage of the National Security Act of 1947. NME was renamed the Department of Defense in 1949. The War Department was renamed the Department of the Army.

11. Warner, "The Creation of the Central Intelligence Group," 113.

12. L. Britt Snider, "Congress as a User of Intelligence: Sharing Secrets with Lawmakers," at www.cia.gov/library/center-for-the-study-of-intelligence/csi-publications/csi-studies/studies/spring98/Congress.html.

13. *Legislative Oversight of Intelligence*, 3.

14. For a more detailed discussion of Senate and House approaches to oversight see Smist, *Congress Oversees the United States Intelligence Community*, 4–9.

15. Kathryn S. Olmsted, *Challenging the Secret Government: The Post-Watergate Investigation of the CIA and FBI* (Chapel Hill, NC: University of North Carolina Press, 1996), 44.

16. See *Foreign Assistance Act of 1974*, Public Law No. 93-559. 88 stat, 1804.

17. Senate Resolution 400, 94th Congress (1976), Sec. 11(a).

18. Though significant majorities in both houses voted to establish the intelligence committees, debate on their establishment was fraught with disagreements over such issues as jurisdiction, committee size, membership selection and length of terms, partisan composition, ability to disclose classified material, and leadership structure. See Frederick M. Kaiser, "Congress and the Intelligence Community: Taking the Road Less Traveled," in *The Postreform Congress*, ed. Roger H. Davidson (New York: St. Martin's, 1991), 279.

19. Snider, "Congress as a User."

20. *Legislative Oversight of Intelligence*, 20–21.

21. Executive privilege is a right of the President or by one of the executive departments to withhold information from the legislative and judicial branches of the U.S. government. Executive privilege, a right not explicitly granted by the U.S. Constitution, is derived from the separation of powers doctrine. Since the time of President George Washington, presidents had argued that the need for complete candor and objectivity from advisers within the executive branch calls for confidentiality on oral and written communications. Thus, the efficiency and effectiveness of the executive branch may require the President and other senior policymakers to preserve that confidentiality by withholding information from other branches of government. This concept was reaffirmed by the U.S. Supreme Court in *U.S. v. Nixon*, 1974, but not without qualification. While there is a presumption of "privilege" once declared, the limits of "Executive Privilege" have yet to be fully tested in the courts.

22. Snider, *Congressional Oversight of Intelligence*, 7.

23. Ibid., 7–8.

24. Snider, "Congress as a User."

25. *Legislative Oversight of Intelligence*, 21–22.

26. The Boland amendments were named after Congressmen Edward Boland, Chairman of the House Permanent Select Committee on Intelligence.

27. *Legislative Oversight of Intelligence*, 22.

28. Smist, *Congress Oversees*, 257.

29. *Legislative Oversight of Intelligence*, 22.

30. For an extensive discussion of these events see *Final Report of the Independent Counsel for Iran/Contra Matters: Volume1, Investigations and Prosecutions*, Washington: D.C., August 4, 1993.

31. Smist, *Congress Oversees*, 259.

32. *The Tower Commission* (New York: Random House, 1987), 78. Noted in Ibid., 263.

33. See Ibid., 279–280 and 289.

34. See Lock K. Johnson, "Monitoring America's Secret Foreign Policy: Congress and the Intelligence Agencies After the Cold War," *Extensions* at www.ou.edu/special/albertctr/extensions/spring2001/Johnson.html

35. *Legislative Oversight of Intelligence*, 24.

36. *Title V, National Security Act of 1947* (1991), Section 501-3. Also see Alfred Cumming, "Statutory Procedures Under Which Congress Is To Be Informed of U.S. Intelligence Activities, Including Covert Actions," *Congressional Research Service Memorandum*, January 18, 2006, footnote 2.

37. *Legislative Oversight of Intelligence*, 25.

38. Enacted as part of the Intelligence Authorization Act of 1993.

39. The NIC, which had been established by executive authority under DCI Turner, now had the sanction of law.

40. See *Legislative Oversight of Intelligence*, 25–26 and 54.

41. *Legislative Oversight of Intelligence*, 24.

42. See Smist, *Congress Oversees*, 308–311.

43. Snider, "Congress as a User."

44. This committee was pursued in parallel with the Aspin-Brown Commission established by Clinton to determine the poor quality of intelligence that the White House received during the 1993 humanitarian intervention in Somalia that led up to the deaths of seventeen marines. For additional discussion of the Aspin-Brown Commission see Johnson, "Monitoring America's Secret Foreign Policy."

45. Public Law 107-56, the "Uniting and Strengthening America by Providing Appropriate Tools Required to Intercept and Obstruct Terrorism Act of 2001," signed into law October 26, 2001.

46. L. Britt Snider, "Congressional Oversight of Intelligence after September 11" in Sims and Gerber, *Transforming US Intelligence*, 242–246.

47. Ibid., 242–243.

48. See Ibid., 243 for greater detail.

49. *Legislative Oversight of Intelligence*, 7.

50. See 110th Congress House Rules Manual, Rule X.

51. Frederick M. Kaiser, "Congressional Oversight of Intelligence: Current Structure and Alternatives," CRS Report to Congress RL 32525, updated February 15, 2007, 3.

52. For a discussion of relationships between the various committees with oversight responsibilities see Lowenthal, *Intelligence: From Secrets to Policy*, 35.

53. Michael Chertoff, Secretary, Department of Homeland Security, letter to the Honorable Peter King, September 4, 2007.

54. Kaiser, "Congressional Oversight," 21.

55. While the intelligence committees receive a wide range of classified information, other committees with national security responsibilities generally only receive copies of the National Intelligence Daily (NID) and the Military Intelligence Digest (MID). They have to request copies of other finished intelligence from lists that are regularly provided by the CIA and DIA. Other committees regularly receive either classified information or the lists of classified publications. Snider, "Congress as a User."

56. Ibid.
57. Executive Order 12036, Sec 3–4.
58. For example see Senate Res. 400, Sec. 6–8 and House Rule XLVIII (1977), Para. 5–7.
59. Carl Limbacher, "Bush Right to Tighten Loose Lips—Remember 'Leaky Lefty'," *Newsmax.com*, October 10, 2001.
60. "Purposeful Leaks—Congressional Leaks to Press," *National Review*, September 11, 1987.
61. Murray Waas, "Cheney's Call," *National Journal*, February 15, 2007.
62. Allan Lengel and Dana Priest, "Investigators Concluded Shelby Leaked Message: Justice Dept. Declined to Prosecute Case," *Washington Post*, August 5, 2004 and Reuters, "Ethics Committee Clears Senator in Sept. 11 Leak Investigation," *The New York Times*, November 14, 2005.
63. Lowenthal, *Intelligence: From Secrets to Policy*, 163.
64. Daniel Schorr, *Clearing the Air* (Boston: Houghton Mifflin Company, 1977), 179–180.
65. Andrews, *For the President's Eyes Only*, 356–357.
66. Ibid., 357.
67. "Bush 'approved intelligence leak'," *BBC News: International Version*, April 7, 2006 at www.news.bbc.co.uk/2/hi/americas/4885100.stm
68. Matt Apuzzo, "Bush, Cheney, accused of deceit in Plame scandal," *Atlanta Journal Constitution*, November 21, 2007.
69. See *Rules of Procedure for the Select Committee on Intelligence United Sates Senate*, amended March 1, 2007, Rules 9–10 and *Rules of Procedure for the Permanent Select Committee on Intelligence, United Sates House of Representatives, 110th Congress* (January 18, 2007), para. 11–14.
70. Staff has been defined to include others engaged by contract or otherwise to perform a service for the committee.
71. *Rules of Procedure, SSCI*, Rule 9.7 and Senate Res. 400, Sec. 8.
72. 110th Congress House Rules Manual, Rule X.
73. Snider, "Congress as a User."
74. Gates, "The CIA and American Foreign Policy," 224.
75. Ibid, 224–225.
76. Snider, "Congress as User."
77. Ibid.
78. Ibid.
79. See John Ranelagh, *The Rise and Decline of the* CIA (New York: Simon and Schuster, 1986), quoted in Snider, *Congressional Oversight of Intelligence*, 2.
80. Snider, *Congressional Oversight of Intelligence*, 2.
81. Snider, "Congress as User."
82. Ibid.
83. Dana Priest, "Congressional Oversight of Intelligence Criticized," *Washington Post*, April 27, 2004.
84. Anonymous interview with a member of the Senate Select Committee on Intelligence, March 2005.
85. James M. Madison, "The Federalist No.10: The Utility of the Union as a Safeguard Against Domestic Faction and Insurrection," *Daily Advertiser*, November 22, 1787.

86. Transcript of Panel 1: What is Good Congressional Oversight? Congressional Oversight Conference, Center for Congressional and Presidential Studies, School of Public Affairs, American University, August 22, 2006, at www.spa.american.edu/ccps/events.php?ID=401

87. *Rules of Procedure for the Select Committee on Intelligence United States Senate*, 110th Congress, 1st Session, March 2007, Rule 7.

88. *Rules of Procedure for the Permanent Select Committee on Intelligence United States House of Representatives*, 110th Congress, January 18, 2007, para. 10(a).

89. Ibid.

APPENDIX A

1. Quoted from the CIA "The Intelligence Cycle," *Factbook on Intelligence* at www.cia.gov/

APPENDIX C

1. Adapted from "Congress as a Consumer of Intelligence," a Memorandum to Senator Dianne Feinstein from Alfred Cumming, Specialist in Intelligence and National Security, Congressional Research Service, December 14, 2005 at http://feinstein.senate.gov/crs-intel.htm#N_1_

Index

About the Author

ROBERT KENNEDY is Professor at the Sam Nunn School of International Affairs, Georgia Institute of Technology, Atlanta, Georgia, and he previously served as Director of the joint German-American George C. Marshall European Center for Security Studies in Germany. In nearly 35 years of government service, he also has served as Civilian Deputy Commandant, NATO Defense College in Rome; Dwight D. Eisenhower Professor of National Security Studies and research analyst at the U.S. Army War College; and as Foreign Affairs Officer, U.S. Arms Control and Disarmament Agency.

70309744R00154

Made in the USA
Columbia, SC
21 August 2019